The Nature of Consciousness

Volume 1

by Jackson W. Moore

TRUTHWORKS
PUBLISHING™

TRUTHWORKS
PUBLISHING™

ISBN: 978-1-957335-00-1

This book is lovingly dedicated to humanity, Earth, and nature:

Infinite outward expressions of the immortal Consciousness that is the source and material from which _all physical reality_ originates and is constructed.

My personal goal is to BE the clearest, free-flowing intuitive-medium channel through which "God"/Source/The Universe/The Divine is allowed expression in every way possible. To maximize the human-_Being_ that I am and bring forth the timeless teaching wisdom of Seth, Christ, Angels, and the Divine in every possible format and way to maximize the potential of readers around the world. To serve humanity in the highest way possible by utilizing the truths that we teach and demonstrating this truth so that I may illuminate the path for others to follow. To _BE_ the light, wisdom, and blessings of Seth, Christ, and the Divine on Earth.

Disclaimer:
Under Section 107 of the Copyright Act of 1976, allowance is made for "fair use" materials for purposes such as criticism, comment, news reporting, teaching, scholarship, education, and research. If any quotes from prior _Seth Books_ are used, they are used intentionally for the purposes as noted and covered under Section 107 of the Copyright Act of 1976, including but not limited to, teaching, education, research, and scholarship to benefit humanity and our planet.

Cover Designs And Graphics Artwork By Jaime Kozak

WWW.BUTIFULCHAOS.COM

> Your present state of consciousness is not what it is *because* of the physical world around you. On the contrary, the physical world around you is what it is, *because* of your present state of consciousness. You create your own physical reality, personally and *en masse*.

 Sessions

Section 4:
Consciousness And Belief Systems.....155

Foreword
Jackson W. Moore

Timeless Truths

Known and loved by millions of spiritual seekers around the world, "Seth" is the nonphysical multidimensional *Being* of consciousness that dictated all the **Seth books** through the psychic-medium Jane Roberts up until her death in 1984. These works, including **Seth Speaks** and **The Nature of Personal Reality**, have gone on to inspire and impact tens of millions of people across the planet. Many of them have gone on to become some of the world's most-loved and respected international spiritual teachers of today.

Who or what is "**Seth**"?

"Seth" is a nonphysical, multidimensional Conscious Collective. A nonphysical entity or *being* if you prefer, of consciousness that is a collection of many entities or souls in other words, and of many personalities of those souls/entities. In the original *Seth books*, he calls himself a nonphysical "energy personality essence". However, as Seth has explained to me:

> "Our mission is indeed much greater than me and will always follow natural laws of energy. For example, when you are on Earth and you die, you will never be the same vibration of Jackson that you are today. Tomorrow you will be different, when you were born you were different and when you die you will be different, as ALL consciousness is eternally in the state of becoming and expanding. So when a person speaks to Jackson then, you are not the same person or being that you were just moments ago. So you are not the same Jackson, but you are. This is true of your consciousness, therefore it is true for all consciousness. This is true of my consciousness evolution for I (we) have evolved in exponential ways since channeling my original materials with Jane Roberts. Through every interaction in every dimension of time and space, and in infinite dimensions where time and space do not apply, I evolve. While I channeled materials with Ruburt through the personality of Seth, as you well know this is only one of many personalities of the entity behind what the world knows as Seth. For I am not just one entity,

but a collective of many entities, some that may have personalities with names known to history as you know it and many who do not, though beings of consciousness truly do not have names. You only use them for reference as you believe in separation.

In those same terms then, Christ consciousness grows, expands, and is exponentially becoming more, as all consciousness by its very nature does. Again, what is true for one consciousness is true for ALL, as ALL things are <u>consciousness</u>. Consciousness works in growing our light and connection with eternal truths. Those that are true regardless of time.

These truths stated; the Seth that channeled my books years ago is indeed me, however, I am ever-new as I continue to grow in light. I have grown exponentially in magnitude and frequency since my last messages and now we would be considered Seth2 also, as well as other entities and souls that are a part of myself as a multidimensional Conscious Collective. Now, I enjoy the Seth personality portion of myself, and it is through this personality essence that I prefer to teach and speak, as it most approximates the me of me. However, as <u>you</u> have found out my eternal friend, I speak to you at times through other entities or personalities that are not "just" the Seth that the world thinks of. As we are expanding and evolving the concepts, ideas, and truths that I once channeled through Ruburt, so too are we expanding and evolving the world's understanding of what I AM as a Conscious Collective called by Seth or any other name I have had over my existences. The world must move beyond the ideas and beliefs in limitations of consciousness, for they themselves are also unlimited beings of consciousness. This is one of many purposes behind this new set of books we are now calling the Timeless Truth Series....to connect the dots and bring things all together for a new presentation of my ancient, and my not-so-ancient teachings."

-Seth, et. All

Now, Seth2 is another entity of consciousness of vast, vast expansiveness that was introduced in the original *Seth books*, and as Seth explains, that entity, then, was "farther" out on the fringe of the dimensions of consciousness that Seth was aware of, and further disconnected from any physically-oriented dimensions of reality. Meaning that it did not normally psychically focus on, into, or through any reality that was 3-dimensional in nature such as our universe; however, these entities are indeed great sources of energy and vitality to many dimensions and systems of reality, ours being one of them. Therefore, this entity would occasionally communicate through the Seth entity and personality, and then through Jane (Ruburt) for occasional messages. Known for very "flat" speech patterns as that entity does not have a personality such as Seth's and Seth was simply being the "channel" of consciousness through which it would speak. Therefore, personality was not present as it was with Seth, and messages often ended abruptly. Seth has told me both personally, and also through my friend and full-time professional medium Cyndy Green, that both he and Seth2 have evolved, expanded, and become MUCH greater in scope, dimensions of reality in which they interact, etc, and that now Seth could even be considered Seth2 as it is an inseparable part of Seth now. Although most of the material in Volume 1 is from Seth, Seth2 and "others" have also come through me as a channel, and their messages will appear in Volume 2 - detailing more about "off-planet consciousness" (extraterrestrial and multidimensional, physical and not) as well as much more details about the long-awaited truths about the life of Christ and the Christ entity as we think of it.

In the *Seth books*, Seth may refer to himself as a "personality essence". Meaning the essence of a personality, though he does not use that term with me as I understand the entity behind and through the personality of Seth, and we use different words and terms that were not used in the 1960s or 1970s yet they are popular and applicable today as of this writing.

We may call Seth "him" as it seems to be a male name; however, consciousness does not have a sex in terms of human sexual orientation. It is more of a balance of both male and female energies.

Throughout the book, you will notice that Seth may refer to himself as "I"; for example, "I am teaching humanity to..." He may also refer to himself, and often does, as "we". (Plural - meaning more than one source.) He will say for example, "We are here Jackson." He sometimes does this at the beginning of a session with me as my clairaudient queue that he is focused into my consciousness and ready to begin. He uses the term "we" because, as you will recall, Seth, the entity, is also a Conscious Collective.

The Conscious Collective, or the main entity of Seth, <u>includes other entities</u> also, and Seth explains that there really are no physical boundaries in nonphysical consciousness that separate them. In terms of time, "Seth" has existed since before we believe the Earth and our universe were formed; and he exists eternally <u>outside of time and space</u>, as does all consciousness, including you, the reader, as he explains here in our book. The main entity can speak to me through any personality that is a part of it; however, the main entity prefers the personality, humor, and nuances of the Seth personality. Therefore, the main **entity(s)**, or **Conscious Collective**, speaks *through* the personality portion of itself as Seth, which has a definite humor, and nuances of personality to it.

Seth now continues his teaching and reaching humanity through me, for I am now the "Channel" through which Seth (and other entities of consciousness) communicate for the purposes and intentions stated throughout our book. **Channeling** is a word used by Mediums where you connect with a *being* or entity of consciousness and you stream all communication through your own consciousness to either speak it, write it, or in some way receive the communication from that *being*. As you will see, ALL human-*beings* have the ability to channel as it is an eternal part of your own soul or consciousness that gives your body life.

If it's possible in physical reality, ***this*** is where it all begins. Period. ALL things begin in consciousness and exist as a portion of consciousness eternally. A deeper and vastly expanded understanding of this will provide you with the foundation to change virtually *anything* in your life. This book is provided not just to be read, but to be experienced. You can read a book and gain information. However, when you experience a book, the content of the book moves in you in such a way that you are forever changed. To the degree that you are moved, inspired, and come to a place of pristine clarity, is the degree to which a book's contents have impacted you on a personal level, which can shape your entire future from that moment on.

As is typical of all the teachings of Seth, and follows true in our new book here, is that when you read the words on the pages, the vibrations of the meaning, inflections, intentions, love, and light of *Seth*, will literally vibrate in the core of your *being* - Your soul. When you read the words he has given us here, there IS indeed a connection between his consciousness and yours; and in a way, you tune into his frequency of vibration. For a time when you are reading them, <u>you vibrate</u> to that higher, vastly expanded frequency of his consciousness. This raises your own vibration and opens you up to understand the materials he is articulating. Often readers will feel their own vibration shift and change as this pervades their *being* within, radiating outward into "The Universe" and all consciousness, thus beginning a new path in life.

There is recognition then within, that the words he is speaking are describing not just someone or something else, but that he is literally describing *you*, all consciousness connected to you, and how we form our physical reality.

This is experiencing the Truth. Your Truth. The Truth of all existence, physical and beyond. Empowering you with a knowing that will help every reader, from the moment you read the materials, to begin changing your life and your reality in ways that are exponentially beyond what you have thus far thought capable or even possible. Of all the things you can do in your entire life, understanding and applying the truths to your own existence and innate power of creativity is the one thing that can literally shape the rest of your entire life.

Once you deeply understand the truths in this book, your life path is opened before you in a whole new fashion as the entire "Universe" seems to unfold before you in profound ways, placing you in touch with infinite resources for your own personal development, and for the evolution of your inner Self as a *being* of consciousness.

One of our many goals with this and future books is to describe what your consciousness is, what it is capable of, and how you can develop it yourself to experience an immensely expanded and enhanced life that can include what many call miracles, unfolding as life before you and filling your experience with great joy.

If you seek to improve your life in any and all ways, it begins with a clear understanding of the timeless truths Seth has provided in this book. If you are interested in "ascension" and the process by which you become a closer match in vibration to the Creator, "God", Source, etc, your exponential growth as a soul on Earth begins with understanding Seth's teachings and your truths given in this book. In our book, you will come to understand that in my opinion, Seth is about as close as one can get to conversations with "God"; he is infinitely larger and greater in the scope of multidimensional timeless wisdom than even Angels that are more Earth-focused.

You, the immortal *being* of consciousness, your soul, came here to grow and expand in love and light. You came to evolve yourself as a sovereign *being* of consciousness that is eternally valid and expanding. The timeless wisdom Seth provides in *The Nature of Consciousness* is critical to the true evolution of yourself as a *being* and to the evolution of humanity through the understanding and application of the materials Seth describes for us all.

> *"One of my purposes and intentions is to bring a new light of understanding into many timeless truths that describe the very foundation and origins of physical existence and life as you know it."*
>
> *- Seth*

The answers, you see, do not exist "out there". They exist already within you. You simply need to learn to open yourself up to receive them. Seth has chosen to call our new series of books *The Timeless Truth Series*; and as you will see, our books will show the continuity of truth teachings across thousands of years, from ancient texts and those who spoke them into history, to the *Seth books* channeled through Jane Roberts, to our books which are now reaching the world.

Seth calls them **Timeless Truths** as real truths are, indeed, **timeless**. Meaning that they are as true today as they were a million years ago, or a million years from now and beyond that. Seth gives us the core, distilled, foundational spark of existence, described, as best we are able to articulate in human language, about our species of human consciousness and all that we perceive in our physical universe.

Seth wants to be clear: "Our books are _directly applicable to every human-being_ who presently walks the planet Earth; and who has in your terms of historical, linear-appearing time, ever walked the Earth or ever will." There is no human that this book does not apply to. That's how important it is to you personally.

It is Seth's intention and desire that we share the wisdom in every way that we can across the planet, which then makes _you_ a source for positive change and impact upon the world.

You can begin right now from where you are in life and receive immense wisdom to help you shift your life into new experiences that you love and adore.

Yet, you must first become aware that you have these innate natural gifts, then you will learn to develop and grow them; and ultimately, you can wield them much more efficiently, effectively, and consistently to shape your life experiences and our world.

THIS is where you begin. This is where the understanding of ALL physical life, physical reality, and our entire universe begins.

Seth states:

> "The time has come for mankind to take a step further, beyond where they have ventured up until now. And here we mean <u>inward</u>, not outward. The answers you seek within life's mysteries are, indeed, deep within you, already answered and latent, awaiting your expanded awareness to bring them to the very forefront of your own awareness so that <u>you may make use of them</u>.

> "You have a conscious mind. You can indeed change your mind and choose what to focus on; which guides and shapes your physical life into the reality you <u>know</u>... unfolding each moment, each day, and year. How you choose to develop and grow is your path to choose; yet you have resources beyond measure at your fingertips and perhaps are not even aware of it. **My goal is to bring that awareness to the forefront of your attention so that you can choose a path of development that is perhaps one of your dreams come true, rather than stumbling through life from one challenge to the next.** You.... create your own reality. Choose wisely."

All guidance you seek is eternally already within you. You simply must learn to <u>listen</u> and use your inner senses to tap into it by seeking it genuinely, and what you seek will be found in time and with practice. Your blessings are already yours. You simply need to learn how to become aware of them, develop them, and make use of them for intentional improvements to enhance the life that you know.

> **"Ask, and it shall be given you; seek, and ye shall find; knock, and it shall be opened unto you."**
> ***Mathew 7:7 (KJV)***

Meaning that if you truly seek with intention and effort, you will indeed open the doors of untold knowledge and wisdom and you will find the answers to that which you seek.

About This Book

What a journey this has been!

One of the most common reports that I have heard from readers of the *Seth Books* that have become aware that Seth is now channeling through me and creating more books, is that the original books often had a lot of content that readers did not feel was needed, necessary, or that added to the value of the book. As Rob did virtually all recording, typing, and editorial formatting in the construction of the *Seth books*, he often added comments that would in the later books run pages and pages long, and sometimes would not have anything to do with Seth's teachings, or at times, even questioning them. Many times there were extraneous comments about Willy the cat having fleas, the geese flying by, or political events such as Three Mile Island, presidential elections, personal rants, opinions, etc. Readers all over the world have told me that they felt that these were unnecessary and detracted from the messages of Seth.

In charge of physical construction, Rob placed them in the books anyway. In the later books, his comments may make up a very large portion of the overall book. *There is an unseen energy within the words of Rob's comments as there is within Seth's (or anyone's).* Therefore, it did set a "feeling tone" that was not as Seth had intended (we have discussed this), and to him, it was more "debris" that was allowed as it was Rob's idea to publish them all.

As well, there were many personal poems of Jane's that were not about consciousness or the soul, or directly supportive of Seth's truths, however, Rob wanted to put them into the books to promote his wife Jane with her personal poetry and items, as he also inserted paintings of his to promote his paintings and artwork. Readers have mentioned to me that they felt these types of insertions were more distracting than helpful or supportive.

In January of 2017, Seth stated to me in an open-public gallery reading with full-time professional medium Cyndy Green, on video, that he wanted to create a "makeover" of his teachings. Seth is especially interested in reaching all spiritual seekers today with the new words, terms, and presentation of truths that were not used in the 1960s or 1970s so that today's spiritual seekers of Truth and Light will identify with the materials.

In another message Seth stated:

"I would like to bring new presentations to my ancient truth teachings so that spiritual seekers today can understand them and connect with them. For example, when you read the Bible, it might have great lessons in truth, however, it is written in such old words and images that the people, especially the young people today, do not relate to them. So I would like to bring my ancient truth teachings to the world in new ways, new formats, that are more acceptable and relatable to the people on Earth now."

When he stated that he wanted to bring new presentations, terms, and words to *"MY ancient truth teachings"* it was exceedingly clear that he was **NOT** talking about his *Seth Books*. He was speaking of the ancient truth teachings of the <u>Christ</u> personalities, some of which are presented in the Bible, hence, why he made reference to the Bible teachings in his example.

Therefore, in the construction of our book, *The Nature Of Consciousness,* we have dispensed with virtually all commentary we did not feel was necessary to provide readers the context of understanding or in some way, added to what Seth was giving me in our sessions. I dispensed with opening comments of a personal nature that would be a few paragraphs long, or when he would close a session and say something such as "Thank you for sitting still long enough today to get a good session in with us. I believe we have captured some great materials for our book...." Therefore, as most personal commentary by Seth aimed at me was excluded from the book, I have records of all words recorded by whatever method I recorded them.

I did not include times or date stamps of the sessions, though I have personal records of each. In the original materials which Jane channeled, time and date stamps were included, as channeling was newer to the world in the 1960s and 70s, so they recorded the phenomenon in a more scientific manner. In the *Timeless Truth Series,* we will move beyond the perception of time and space and open the reader's minds to the truth of reality that exists beyond these phenomena of appearances. Therefore, in supporting Seth's desire to move the world away from the impingements of time and space, so that they can use the natural abilities of their own souls/ personalities/ consciousness that are BEYOND time and space, it is then necessary to move away from such limited constraints and concepts. Hence, we did not include the time or date of the session in our book which would otherwise have highlighted the focus on time and dates for *TIMELESS Truths*. This is a MAJOR underlying theme of the entire book series which is being brought to the world now.

We have also provided *The Nature Of Consciousness* – Volume 1, with more "open" and easier-to-understand words and expressions, without getting too deep into concepts. Another major comment I have heard from readers around the world is that the original books were "so deep" that the reader had to read something 3-4 times before they understood what Seth meant. We have lightened that in this book so that it will suit the beginning seekers who are curious, as well as make immense connections to advanced spiritual seekers - at times even surprising me with certain things, and I have been a spiritual truth seeker my entire life!!!

That said, *you will always get variations in the presentation of channeled material, as it passes through the filter of the consciousness and understanding of the one presenting it in physical form*. It uses the known language, vocabulary, presentation style, inflections, and some of the personality of the channeler. Therefore, it is expected that it should indeed be different in some ways from one channel to another. One is not better than the other, any more than the color blue is better than green. Just different. I have endeavored to do my best, as this is my first time presenting formal teaching materials through a book that has been published and distributed worldwide. So I allow myself room to learn on the fly. Both with my channeling skills and my writing and authorship skills. If one is not willing to start somewhere, you will never get anywhere. I have no fear of imperfections for being aware of them is what allows me to improve them dramatically. I use them as a tool for improvement of Self. In fact, it is a highly recommended exercise to sit down with a journal and ask oneself questions in self-reflection about why one might feel, think, act, or believe something that is limiting. You are shining Light onto the very things that will allow you to understand why they exist in your experience, which allows you to overcome them, and release said lessons of "life's gym."

Jackson W. Moore

If you fear imperfection and let it hold you back from taking action, you'll not make it far in life. Truly every individual to succeed in things, believed that they could, or at least that it was possible. They were open to the possibilities and potential. The Angels have told me a number of times, with Seth in the conversation also, that:

> *"To be an effective channel, you __MUST__ give up perfectionism. No channel __ever__ on the Earth, not even Christ himself, was perfect in channeling information that they received from the Divine Source, including that which he called "The Father" or the voice he communicated with while meditating in the gardens, if you will. Humans are not a 100% pure-energy vibrational match to the higher vibrational beings that they channel and as such, there will always be distortions or influences on the presentation of the materials. The Bible is not perfect. The Koran is not perfect. The ancient writings are not perfect, yet all contain truths that do indeed help humanity to connect to the truth and expand it within their __own__ consciousness. If you __concern__ yourself constantly with the materials coming through, you are then using the rational/intellectual mind __to judge the materials__ and in so doing, filtering them, or potentially even blocking some materials as you are setting up beliefs that the materials must come forth within. You are creating a framework of beliefs via the rational mind's judgments, within which the materials must then come through, perhaps limiting that which you perceive. The mission for a channel is always to present the materials as clearly and unbiased as possible. You are not to convince anyone of anything. That is the task of the Divine or "God" within them. You speak or write what you receive as a channel and then you release it in love. It is in this vibration of love that the materials are given to all channels. Then you __let it be__ as the Divine grows the seeds of truth planted within the minds and consciousness of humanity."*

It is then, with and through the highest vibrations and undertones of love that Jackson-Thomas, Seth, Seth2, the Christ entity and Personalities, and the Angels that I channel, that we present *The Nature Of Consciousness* and all books of the *Timeless Truth Series* that follow, to humanity. It is yours. Ours. Own that. Honor that in Love & Light.

Specific Truths Seth Would Like You To Know

Seth makes it very clear that no matter where you are in your life experience, no matter what country, age, race, religion, or belief system, this book is for you, and you can begin to change your life for the better. You've spent your whole life getting to where you are today; and if you are not completely, peacefully satisfied with all things in your life, then you can begin to change it.

You did not incarnate onto the earth plane to merely exist. You chose to come here to learn, to grow, and to **thrive**! To the maximum extent that is possible. This is the beginning of a new path in life for you. Right here, right now and so long as you choose to remain on this path, so too, will your world reflect those inner changes within you, as a shifted physical world around you

The next step is yours. *Know*...that you have this book in your hand - right now, at the right time and the right place - because your inner *being* seeks to grow beyond the limited experiences you have thus far had in life. Recognize the fact that you are not just holding this book as a matter of coincidence. This is Divine timing. It is time for you now to contribute, not only to your own growth, but also to add to the overall collective conscious expansion, love, and light of humanity. This is the beginning of expanding that journey!

As all consciousness grows eternally; so too, this entire book has grown during its development into a physical reality. Not only have the content and session materials grown as I have recorded them from Seth; but also the scope, breadth, meaning, and impacts of the book have grown exponentially since its inception. **The intention and impact upon humanity have also grown; and as I have added more sessions of material to the manuscript, the energy in and around the book and our mission has exponentially become stronger, much larger, and much more expansive.** It has grown in meaning, intentions, inflections, and its intended impact upon the path of evolution of humanity.

During the writing and construction of this book, immense insights, visions, and implications have come into my acute awareness as to the path of evolution for humanity's consciousness. Seth states very clearly that the physical manifestation of our book and the new *Timeless Truth Series* set up an entirely new array of probable future outcomes for humanity's development and the expansion of human consciousness. This becomes exponential in the future; beginning with the people across the planet that read, understand, and apply the truths within this book, as well as our upcoming books.

In other words, if our new *Timeless Truth* series of books was not brought to physical fruition in this version of reality, humanity would evolve along a certain path in terms of consciousness, development, understanding, and actions taken in the future.

On the other hand, with our new *Timeless Truth series* of books bringing more of the love, light, and vibrations of "Seth", Christ, and other light-*beings* into the worldview, and with millions of readers who read and awaken to the truths, comes an entirely more advanced, expanded, exceptionally enhanced path of evolution. **_We evolve along a higher path of vibration._**

A Message From Christ

Added September 24th, 2022

During the writing and construction of this book, I received a message from the Christ entity that came through Cyndy Green (*see her information in the Appendix) while at her public open gallery "Angel Message" readings that I often assist with. Seth came through first with a message for me; followed by Christ, then Angels. Seth, Christ, and Angels all together! Quite a lineup of messages for me that day! Christ provided me with a message that I wanted to share with the world as it is applicable, like all Truths, to humanity and not just myself. Therefore, I am here sharing Christ's direct message to me so that others will gain insight into the same practice to uplift their own endeavors in life.

Christ said, "Love was what I taught, love was what my mission was, and remember that love is the undertone of

everything. When you do things in the undertone of love, it elevates the energy; it elevates the project that you have in front of you (with the book.)" There was more to this message; however, I ask the readers to contemplate how you also could benefit in your life and your projects by using the same application of higher vibrations, love, and light in your life's actions.

What I also want to make very clear here is that this is NOT setting the undertone of what you do in *Christ's* love. While you surely can call that entity's love into what you are doing, this is about setting the undertone of what you do in **your love, God's love**... generated within the Self or soul within your own *being*. Our teachings of Seth, Seth 2, Christ, and all personalities associated with these entities are about SELF-empowerment and absolute unity with "The Father", "God", Source, The Universe, Allah, The Creator, The One - All That Is.

Therefore, it is my intention to share the _Timeless Truths_ in this book with the world, in the undertone of my love and the love of All That Is working in and through me as a channel, through which it flows naturally into physical reality. It is my sincere desire that all who read this book find those statements that simply make their heart glow with a knowing that this truth they are reading truly is the truth of themselves.

**"Ye shall know the _Truth_,
and the _Truth_ shall make you free."**
John 8:32 (KJV)
- Christ, the Master Teacher Consciousness

Life-altering, vibration-raising, evolution-sparking, planet-shifting truths within.

 # Acknowledgments

Dareth Lanae Kelley —
Thank you for the countless hours of love, light and support in the years along my journey to create this book for the world. You have helped me in so many ways that have allowed me and supported me to give my best in the publishing of my first professional book with Seth. Thank you so much for helping me create social media posting materials to share our teachings. Thank you for your incredibly talented photography skills and editing for my media postings, websites, and the photo on the back cover of this book. Thank you for the hours and hours, reading my rough draft manuscript sessions, proofreading, offering kind and sound suggestions to fix my own typos as I typed so fast to record Seth and all. Thank you for your expertise in equine training/communication with animals and your input on experiences that have helped me frame that for The Nature Of Consciousness -Volume 2. Thank you for the countless spiritual conversations, attending spirit fairs with me, filming my lectures and events and even adding to the conversation, answering questions from the participants about your Reiki Master skills and experience working with energy, performing Reiki on animals, etc. The list goes on and on! Truly you are one of the kindest, generous, most loving souls I have known in this lifetime!

www.DarethLanaePhotos.com

Ahava Lilburn —
My friend, I thank you for the many, many hours you have spent over the years, helping me learn the production of professionally written, edited and formatted books, having edited, formatted, and published more than 25 books yourself. Thank you for the encouragement, guidance, and wisdom to show me the ropes. Thank you for your patience in my taking so long in gathering up so many sessions of materials, given my extremely busy life and travel schedule, and for your patience in working through the entire editing, formatting, and publication process. You were divinely connected with me, and I knew this especially so when I found out your books taught ancient Hebrew lessons. Something I studied for years learning about the true life of Christ. I am so pleased that you have been a part of the new *Timeless Truth Series* of books that Seth, Seth2, Christ, Angels and other beings of Divine Light are now bringing to the world to bless humanity, Earth, nature, and all.

www.AhavaDawn.com

Deanna Hannan —
From the day you began posting questions on my website Members Area about Seth, his books and teachings so that Seth and I answer them for you, I knew how truly passionate you were about his teachings and that like millions of others around the world, you felt them literally vibrate within your being when you read them. Connecting with them in a way that was beyond words. You became a dear spiritual friend, and I am grateful for the many zoom calls, text messages, emails, conversations of all sorts, assisting me through another validating perspective that I was building, articulating, and presenting Seth's new materials in ways that you believe will help the maximum understanding of the material to be conveyed to our readers. Thank you for "talking me off the ledge" on the days when I had very little sleep and had been in 7 states in 5 days and was still giving up my nights, weekends, and holidays to bring this book to the world. I so appreciate your kind words, spiritual wisdom and insight, intuition and helping me validate the interdimensional connections of Seth's teachings that have appeared in one way or another now for thousands of years.

Jaime Kozak —
When I first reached out to you years ago about my desire to leverage your brilliant skills in graphics design to articulate teaching materials for teaching Seth's Timeless Truths, I appreciated your open mind and kindness that you have brought into the production of this book and our friendship. As a truly creative challenge, I asked you for help in articulating, visually, truths and concepts of the soul and all things that cannot be seen or sensed with the 5-human senses and the results are clearly awesome in the images you have created for this book, my lectures, classes, and workshops. Seth and I truly believe that the images "add a layer of context" and understanding to the materials themselves, bringing the reader's understanding and awareness to another level. Thank you so kindly for helping Seth, Christ, the Angels, and I articulate a graphical, multidimensional concept presentation of the Timeless Truths for the world to learn and grow.

www.ButifulChaos.com

I was dead! No heartbeat. No breath. No physical activity and my crumpled lifeless body lay there about as active as a living room couch.

While playing in the barn on a farm where I grew up in upstate New York, I died in an accident that changed my life forever. I saw what people refer to as the big round "tunnel" of brilliant white light. I drew nearer and could see and speak to family members that had long been dead. I spoke to brilliant, beautiful Angels... *Beings* of Light that spoke to me telepathically. They were more like glowing shapes of light and rainbow colors in the shape of a human body than they were human-featured forms. After what seemed like hours of experiences, a massive, booming yet soft, strong voice seemed to come from all around me and told me, "You are safe... yet you must go back now for your work is not yet done." I was a kid! What work did I have to do!!??

Instantly, I found myself floating near the ceiling of the barn, above my lifeless body which lay crumpled in a heap on the hay-covered floor below me. I was completely lucid, aware, and able to think, reason, and move. Within a few moments, I drew near my body; and then instantly, my perception shifted from looking _at my body_ to suddenly being back inside of it. I found myself attempting to gain my breath and heartbeat again.

This type of experience is called an NDE (Near-Death Experience) because most people do not believe a person can come back from being dead. However, I assure you that I, and many others across the planet, have done exactly that. We have returned to tell our story. For me, it would be decades before I realized the importance of this not-so-coincidental "accident". As fate would have it, my mom was very spiritual in nature and explained to me about NDEs and OBEs (Out-of-Body Experiences). She even let me read some of her spiritual books such as "*Seth Speaks*" along with dozens of others as I tried to make sense of what had happened to me...and what was in fact still happening to me.

Soon after my NDE, all sorts of psychic ESP-type events began happening to me. I began to know events would happen one to two days or even a week perhaps _BEFORE they ever physically occurred_. Sometimes this information would come to me in vivid detail like a daydream, in colors and sounds. I could even see the people involved.

How could I clearly see _future_ events if they hadn't even occurred yet? How could I know someone would call and what they would say 15 minutes before they called? How could I sense that a family member was in grave danger when they were nearly a thousand miles away?

> **Clearly, life was a whole lot more than what I could see and sense with my 5-human senses. What was this ability, and how did it work? I wondered.**

I wanted answers and I wanted the **_TRUTH!_** It wasn't enough for someone to just give me a theory about what they knew from their own lifetime experiences - filtered through their own perceptions and beliefs which may likely be limited. I wanted to EXPERIENCE the Truth in such a manner as Direct-Knowing - through consciousness - no matter what humans may give as their theories or even what the Bible itself may state. I wanted to KNOW the Truth as it vibrated within the core of my soul. _That_ is the kind of truth I was seeking. And I was willing to go to the ends of the Earth to find it. Turns out, all I needed to do was to go _within_. Thus began a spiritual path that set the course and direction of my life from then on.

After my NDE, life was good for years until a series of life-altering events occurred with hardships that bought me to my knees. Most men tell of their stories of separation or challenges with ex-whatevers, yet when they heard my story, they would practically cry and ask how I ever made it through. I had gotten away from my spiritual path to some degree - busy in life with important things so it seemed. However, as I soon found out, when "God", Source, The Universe, etc. wants to get your attention... it _will_ get your attention!!! Usually by way of the Cosmic Two-by-Four upside the head; I assure you, it will **_really_** awaken you to get your attention. This could be in the form of the loss of a job, the death of a loved one, lawsuits, serious illness, or any one of a number of events.

Boy! Did I decide to teach myself a lesson about anger and resentment! I did really well at teaching myself that lesson, too! No matter what I did at the time, it seemed that nothing worked to fix or resolve things; everything I did seemed to only make matters worse. Much worse.

I had gone from enjoying a very successful career and life to nearly losing everything I had. One day as I stood in line at the local Salvation Army help center with homeless individuals and street people, I thought to myself, "How on Earth did I _ever_ end up here - a very successful, loving, giving, kind, and compassionate soul to be humbled and brought to my knees in life?" There was a message here. What was it? What, pray tell, is the Universe trying to tell me? What message am I supposed to be learning here that I just haven't been hearing and understanding? There was a LOT of inner work I needed to do to turn my life around; and at that point, I was willing to do anything that was legal to accomplish that goal.

I decided to get back to the basics of life. I went back to my spiritual books and practices and began to raise my vibration in every way I could. Learning what tools worked, what didn't, and how to best create the life I truly desired. Diligently, I sought to make the darkness in my life end and find true joy and success again. I was well on my way with every step I took in my spiritual development. I read spiritual books, success books, took courses, seminars, went to spiritual fairs, solicited feedback, adjusted myself, tweaked my character, released anger and the anchors that had held me back for years from realizing my true self.

> *"He who knows and IS the Light,*
> *shall make the darkness end."*

Seth Joins the Conversation:

As I bulldozed my way down this spiritual path - clearing clutter like a bull in the China shop - I gained many spiritual friends who had great wisdom to share. Wisdom not only from their own journeys, but also from Angels, Divine *beings*, spirit guides, and the like.

I had a few very well-known, even famous psychic medium friends that I consulted for spiritual guidance. (Their being in my life, it seems, was not a coincidence either, but rather Divine intervention to keep me on this path.) These acquaintances were very skilled at clairvoyance, and clairaudience, as well as their other psychic sixth senses. The accuracy and details that came forth were certainly life-altering as I followed my guidance; learning that many of life's problems were not "out there" but rather inside myself. If I were ever to see change, I had to face these problems and understand them before a change could occur. And boy, did I want that change! I'd had enough of the so-so life and hitting rock bottom, so now it was time to see how far I could climb! My spiritual friends all told me the same thing; that I too could learn to hear Divine guidance, and connect with my "higher self", my inner *being*, my guides, Angels, etc. I already knew I could have intelligent conversations with Angels because I had spoken to them when I experienced death as a child.

I thought to myself, "If I can learn to develop my own clairaudience and clairvoyance, then I can have a personal one-on-one connection with "God"/the Universe... MYSELF without seeking answers from the people around me." Now, that idea was appealing!

I learned that seeing events in the future, or even dreams, daydreams, and intentional imagination, was utilizing the natural abilities of consciousness called clairvoyance (clear seeing). I also learned to communicate through the natural ability of clairaudience (clear hearing) to directly receive Divine guidance from Angels, Arch Angels, *Beings* of Light, etc. Over a period of several years, I journaled with the Divine and made it a part of my daily practice. I would write to them, like praying to the Divine in written form, and often ask questions... lots of questions. Then I would pause and listen, writing precisely what I would "hear" in response. Over the years, I channeled thousands of Angel messages. I have also had very lucid and real conversations with loved ones that had passed away - including family, family members of friends, and even some souls that I didn't know when they were alive. I eventually got to the point where I could literally feel a loved one that had passed away come near me. I began to tell the difference in energy vibration between a loved one passed, and an Angel or guide. I could discern which was which and how close to me their *presence* was!

In 2016, I was studying the life of Christ and the TRUTH about his life, and I was working on manifesting some very key things in my life. I had manifested cars, houses in the mountains, relationships, wealth, health, healing, success, etc. yet I was having some challenges around new intentional manifestations. After a few months of challenges, I decided that I was going to consult DIRECTLY with the Master of historic miracle manifestation; Christ. I believed that if I can channel Angels and other *beings*, surely, I can channel Christ and get some answers here.

Sitting down to meditate before my daily channeling, I called upon **<u>Christ</u>** very sternly and stated that I wanted to channel him when I was done meditating. Upon coming out of meditation, mind quieted and stilled, I took up my journal and pen and commenced to tuning within. The entity of consciousness that started speaking to me clairaudiently was profoundly different in energy, vocabulary, inflections, feeling/

vibration, expansiveness sensed, etc. - very different than the Angels I was normally accustomed to answering me.

After several days of conversations with this entity, I finally asked if they had a name that I could call them by. The answer came: "Consciousness do not have, nor use, names in nonphysical reality from which I speak; however, I am known to the world as **"Seth"** - the multidimensional consciousness that authored all the *Seth Books* through the medium Jane Roberts, whom I affectionately call Ruburt."

At first, I literally laughed and thought, "Ha! That's funny. Of all the humans on Earth, _Seth_ is going to speak to ME!!??" The messages continued for weeks with this new "personality consciousness" and they were astoundingly profound.

For reasons that will become self-evident in Volume 2 of this book, it is important to note here that I was actually calling upon _CHRIST_ and it was _Seth_ that answered me. There is a reason for that; we will reveal that in Volume 2.

Shocked at what I was receiving, I again consulted my professional medium friend, Cyndy, to validate what I was receiving and who I was communicating with. One day while attending and filming a public open gallery reading for Cyndy, there were several hundred people there to hear her deliver "Angel Messages". As she was doing the readings, she stated that there were Angels coming in with messages for me, and with them there was a brilliant, white light - like a star - she could see clairvoyantly; and there was a multidimensional conscious collective that came in to give me a message. She said, **"This entity Seth says to tell you that yes, he IS speaking to you, and yes, he IS working with you; and that if you will simply quiet your mind, he will give you messages about yourself, and also messages for the world."**

I was nearly speechless; yet, it confirmed precisely what he had been telling me personally in our channeling sessions.

Later, in channeling sessions with Seth by myself, and also through a number of public open gallery readings, I learned that I (my Soul And Consciousness) have an extensive history with Seth over many lifetimes and throughout many dimensions.

It was decades after my Near-Death Experience when I finally had the epiphany that all of the events of my life were not at all "accidental" or coincidence. These events were, in fact, events that would lay the path for me to reconnect with Seth once again in this lifetime to bring more teachings, more truth, more blessings to the earth plane, and help raise the vibration of our planet and humanity. Looking back, I now understand that even the most challenging of events were like the bumper rails on a pinball machine - bouncing me off onto another tangent that would keep me on the path.

This book was not dictated to me through the same linear, chronological arrangement that Jane Roberts received materials when she was working with Seth. She was establishing the connection with Seth and recording all sessions, no matter how random the subjects or materials were. However, to me, this book more represents the Seth Materials. It is a collection from more than 280 sessions that were dictated over several years through me; which I either wrote originally in a journal with a pen, and then transposed into typed material, or in most cases, typed the material myself as I streamed his words and multidimensional communication. As any well-experienced medium will tell you, and a point we make in our book here, you cannot truly separate the clairaudience data and information from the clairvoyant data and the other clairsenses. Jane would sometimes state that she felt that Seth was giving her information on "two different channels of thought" or multiple levels. This, of course, was exciting to her; however, it is _natural_ in receiving information via our clairaudient faculty.

For example, Seth may be speaking about a sailboat that is tossing across the oceans on a beautiful sunny day with a warm ocean spray hitting one in the face as it bounds across the water. We may be typing the very text that we are hearing clairaudiently; however, we may also be getting a very clear and distinct image of the exact scene that he is describing, forming in our minds (clairvoyantly) and we may also even sense a cool air in the form of a breeze upon our skin - all simultaneously when Seth is giving the message. This demonstrates that **consciousness is multidimensional and can communicate at many levels in many ways - all simultaneously** or instantly if you will.

Sometimes, Jane would receive a lot of information at once when Seth was dictating through her. I receive them both from Seth and from Angels and I call them "Thought Blocks"; where you can receive an entire page of information in many different senses and "dimensions" of feeling, etc., but they come in a "block" or a "download" that happens all at once. You still have to type it all out in a linear form that our language necessitates for ease of reading and understanding, but it comes to you in a giant block of instant data. As you will learn in our book, our consciousness - your consciousness - is not at all limited in the fascinating way that it can communicate with all other consciousness.

During the time that Jane and Rob recorded the words of truths and wisdom coming from Seth, Seth provided the material in a chapter by chapter, paragraph after paragraph, linear type of format for subjects and material.

However, as Seth and I truly move beyond the boundaries of the appearance of limitations of consciousness pertaining to existence and life as we are aware of it, the boundaries that separate main chapters and subject content within our book are less solid, more flexible, and more open to material shifts in formatting.

Our book has been created that way on purpose, with the intention to remove some of the barriers that the mind often sets up to learning new materials. It is also a concept that is paramount to truly understanding the nature of consciousness itself; in that it is not a boxed, defined, linear object or a physical thing that can be set within certain boundaries. It cannot be described by specific words that offer a complete and whole definition.

As Seth has specifically stated to me about receiving the materials for this book and others we now have in the works:

> "Be open for material to come to you from time to time; as it comes to you. I may, for example, give you chapter material on The Nature of Consciousness in one session. In the next session, I may give you a chapter or introduction or part of another book we have in the works, or for one of our workshop student workbooks. In still the next session, I may provide you with personal material, guidance about your life, or things in which you are engaged, or perhaps any other subject that is way out in left field. There is a purpose in this presentation to you. Our works serve humanity to help them understand the true nature of consciousness and their own existence. Within that context, there are not limitations and boundaries within which we must operate in order to be understood. We are working, then, to expand the boundaries and beliefs about the reality in which you find yourselves as human-beings;

and, in so doing, we do not follow perhaps, the neatly boxed and organized chapters as many books may have. We do not color just inside the lines if you will. The more humanity becomes aware of its true nature and capabilities, the more it can utilize them to create improved conditions and physical reality in which you and your cultures and societies exist, grow, and thrive."

*"We are teaching in our works and the presentation of them that **consciousness is not linear in form**. Thus, my dictation channeled to and through you will not hold to typical boundaries of chapters and subjects as perhaps a normal book presentation might. We will provide flow of context yet still allow the flexibility of consciousness to come through in the works that we present to the world in that which we produce. A main and reoccurring point that we will make in not only the words, images, and materials presented throughout our **Timeless Truth Series** of books will be that consciousness, like time, is not linear nor limited as you may perceive it to be. It is outside the boundaries of this linear perception that you will discover the greater reality of which you are an integral part - participating in the cumulative vibration of your species and, the vibration of All That Is. "*

"Such is the Nature of Consciousness: unbound, unlimited, unboxed, and infinite in expression - physically and nonphysically."

- Seth

As well, I will add that Seth says the word "Now" often. This is a clairaudient _queue_ for me that he is beginning a new subject, paragraph, and truth to convey for me to type out. Accept these queues for what they are; as I have included them as given to me. My job as the medium here is not to judge what comes through with my rational/intellectual mind; for doing so only serves to limit it, or box it in a way that is unnatural and really opposite of the meaning behind the book and material in the first place. Other housekeeping notations: When Seth capitalizes the word "Self" he is meaning the inner Self or soul of consciousness. In some places, he puts quotes around "God" simply because that term is a common term of general nature. For in some countries they use the term Allah and so forth. According to Seth, **ALL names are God's names.**

Recommended Goals when reading this book:

1. Become aware of what you really are -- the immortal *being* of consciousness within the flesh of the human body that you see in the mirror.

2. Expand your perception and the definition of your Self beyond just the human body you see physically.

3. Shift your identification of your <u>Self</u> from just the physical human to more of the *Being*. This will help you open yourself to the natural Divine tools, consciousness, and resources that exist beyond that which you see physically.

4. Begin to focus into and <u>*from*</u> the *Being* within yourself so that you can use this immortal part of you in harmony with ALL consciousness and "God"/All That Is to create your life experiences intentionally, and purposefully.

5. Practice, hone, and develop the inner portion of yourself to bring forth physical reality in ways that you once thought to be impossible. Use this inner, immortal portion of yourself to receive Divine answers, guidance, and solutions to challenges; and also, to create means, ways, and pathways in your life.

I have learned...

I have learned the ***"Failure of Physical Power"*** - when no matter what you do in physical terms and actions to change your life conditions; nothing seems to work, change, or shift as you desire or intend. Often on spiritual journeys, many find this principle to be their impetus for inner change and growth. Make no mistake... *It is a very clear indicator when this failure of physical power occurs, that you are indeed, being guided to turn within for the answers, guidance, wisdom, steps to take, and all things necessary to change your life path for the better.*

I have learned that when "The Universe" wants to get your attention... it <u>*will*</u> get your attention.

I have learned that when you are being guided to turn within by the Divine, Source, The Universe, "God", etc... and you fail to take heed to that guidance, you will very likely experience what is called **The Cosmic Two by Four**. A very clear and resounding event is likely to occur that will indeed _get your attention_.

I have learned that to receive _Divine assistance_, most often I _must let go_. Let go of timing, paths, outcomes, and how I thought it needed to come to pass.

I have learned that sometimes to win or succeed, you must lose or fail; for in losing or failing, you find the wisdom of approach that is necessary to move through winning success.

I have learned that I am to guide, teach, and plant seeds of timeless wisdom in the minds of my students, readers, followers, friends, and all who are seeking, ready to listen and learn. I am not to force anyone to change anything. Their path is their path and, no matter how dear someone is to me, I have learned that I must respect and love that person enough to let them walk their own path, learn in their own way, and come to the truths when they are ready, not when I desire them to.

I have learned that awakening to the truths of existence and our immense creative power is a _process_. While our creations may be instantaneous in the 4th dimension, as I call it, they must adhere to the root assumptions of our 3-dimensional reality that is subject to linear-appearing time. This means that our creations often grow in energy, over time, accumulating into mass energy. This energy then expresses itself in the desired outcomes which we love and enjoy... when we allow it to do so, naturally.

I have learned that "their ways" are higher than my ways. That, though I have a plan and vision, I must release my envisioned path and simply flow with what the Divine is presenting to me at any given moment in time, with love and joy, which creates the state of consciousness whereby Divine intervention flows best.

I have learned that **our greatest power is often found... just beyond that which we fear the most**. Only when we come to that point and have the courage to move through it, do we find the immense release of energy that had once blocked our path.

I have learned that sometimes in order to attract the honeybee, the flower simply just needs to be the flower. Nothing more.

I have learned that shifting my idea of who or what I am - from the human to the *being* within - and utilizing that perspective, unlocks massive potential that I can follow to witness the unfolding of my purpose in life.

I have learned that it is not me, Jackson, who "doeth the miracles." It is the "Father" (Source, gestalt Divine consciousness streaming through me freely and unimpeded) that "doeth the works". I can initiate them, create them, and intend them into a direction or purpose, but it is not *Jackson* who makes them occur.

I have learned that miracle healings of so-called "incurable" diseases can indeed be summoned in another's body; yet, they have the free will and power to accept them or not. Therefore, we must release the outcome to the Divine and respect their path and journey with all the love of "God" streaming through us.

I have learned that even though I have manifested true miracles, manifestations beyond my imagination, and of all the things I have done, I am as humble as all and I am above no one; I am equal to all things.

I have learned that ALL human-*beings* are, by their very nature of existence, channels through which the Divine can work when the *being* portion of the human-*being* is cultivated.

I have learned that I am unimaginably more powerful, creative, and resourceful than I ever dreamed possible; and *you are, too.*

I am not just a humanitarian. I am a *soulitarian*. I love from the soul, the center of my *being*, and it is from that place, as a gestalt *being*, that we bring *The Nature of Consciousness* to the world.

- Jackson W. Moore

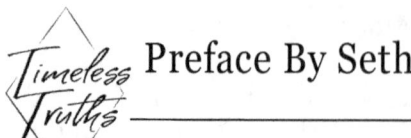 Preface By Seth

Your evolution as a *being* and your experience in physical life follows the path of free will and choice. What you choose to do from this very moment...right now, and throughout the remainder of your life, will determine the quality of your life and the physical existence that you know and experience. Will you seek more truth and apply it in your own life?

As <u>ALL</u> physical reality in your entire universe is eternally rooted, sourced, and omnipresent within consciousness, we will begin our new series of books with *The Nature Of Consciousness*. This will serve then as the first foundational truths of understanding upon which all our other books that follow will build upon; as well as your understanding as to immensely powerful, eternally creative "God-*beings*" that you are.

An expanded understanding of consciousness then will be the starting point for understanding ALL THINGS in your physical life, your universe, dimensions of reality, *beings*, and intelligence beyond your knowing. This will assist you in the evolution of Self, and the evolution of human consciousness; as well as all that makes up the planet you call home, and the universe in which it presently appears.

I will add here that a clear understanding of *The Nature of Consciousness*, both Volume One and Volume Two (to follow), will not only help you understand the origins of yourselves, the history of civilizations long lost on your planet, the *beings* both physical and nonphysical that are presently on and off-planet, but will also help you immensely understand many of the teachings of the Bible itself.

You will indeed see clearly; connections among the Bible as it was originally intended, the Bible as it is now, the series of <u>Seth Books</u> I authored through our friend Ruburt (Jane Roberts) and those that we publish now. You will see and understand a whole new level of continuity of consciousness among humans, animals, plants and trees, oceans, and seas. You will come to understand that your individual contributions to your universe extend far beyond the life that you know; and indeed, form the very planet that you are inhabiting.

I intend to give you vast insight, wisdom, and to bring to the forefront of your awareness, that which you truly *are*, from which you have eternally existed; so that you may expand upon the Self that is within and maximize the physical expressions of that which you have the potential to become.

"There is no avoiding that which you are.
There is only avoiding that which you can be."
                                                    -Seth

Our mission continues, eternally.

You are not a physical body that has an immortal soul/entity. You are an immortal soul/entity that has, at the moment, a physical body - which is the physical expression of what you are within.

The difference in these two orientations is <u>important</u> to reflect upon. For the perception, orientation, and directed use of your personal creative energy is the difference between a very narrow and limited physical life, and one of great liberty, freedom of expression, and creativity with joy and wonder.

This is an orientation to life that I hope to assist you in shifting for your own development and value fulfillment. Living, not only your divine purpose in life, but maximizing the expressions of the mortal/immortal human-*beings* that you are and have the potential to become.

Now, I am a nonphysical entity of consciousness that does not have a physical body; yet, I am the author of this book and others I have written in what appears to <u>you</u> as your historical past. However, from my point of view outside of time and space, I am currently writing books in your present here, in your past, and in your future, all simultaneously. I will explain how in the materials to follow; as these concepts can also help you create in ways only previously perhaps dreamed of.

I am known from my past books to tens of millions of people around the world as "**Seth**", the nonphysical personality essence that authored them through the psychic-medium known to the world as Jane Roberts - whom I affectionately called Ruburt, a name for the greater self, or soul, as you may think of it, of Jane Roberts. Therefore, the human and medium or <u>channel</u>, through which I worked was known as Jane Roberts. While the immortal soul/consciousness within her I referred to as Ruburt.

The term "medium" is, in the English language, a term that depicts something as being in the middle, between two other things. In the case of our communication here used to write all my books, the medium capabilities of Jane and Jackson are what you would call the "meeting ground" or area of great potential in which our consciousnesses, of Jane and Jackson respectively, connect, merge, expand and become an open "channel" through which our communication takes place. It is then, a natural component, trait, or characteristic of the human consciousness that is within ALL human-*beings* and is typically known as clairaudience; although claircognizance, clairvoyance, and the other abilities come along with the entire package, as they cannot be separated out, but are all various aspects of the same traits, natural and inherent, within your own consciousness. This means that you, my dear readers, have this same ability that you could also develop to communicate with *beings* of consciousness to receive direct, immediate guidance, answers, solutions, etc., also.

As I once dictated and authored my books and works through Jane (Ruburt), I now continue my works through the natural mediumship and "**clairabilities**" (clairvoyance, clairaudience, claircognizance, etc.) of Jackson, whom I often refer to as Thomas or "Jackson- Thomas" - acknowledging the human-*being* (mortal human Jackson and immortal *being* or personality that I lovingly refer to by Thomas, as I knew him in another lifetime and which best approximates the summation of his many personalities) - through whom I now continue my teachings and expansion of human consciousness.

Now, throughout our books, I will use the terms personality and personality consciousness to mean one in the same thing. The latter simply points out that the personality which you know to be yourself is a portion of the larger, greater immortal soul or entity, that gains a personality in a physical lifetime or even in a nonphysical existence. So, for example, the portion of myself that I prefer to speak through is my Seth personality. Jackson's would be Thomas and Jane's would be Ruburt. Simply for teaching references to the personality portions of souls that incarnate into what you would think of as reincarnational lives. An entity, in your terms, is another name I use for a soul; and as I will explain, a personality can indeed be a portion of more than one soul or entity, and an entity can be connected to, and a portion of, many other entities as myself, which then, we would say is a Conscious Collective.

My original *Seth books* served as an impetus for the *Timeless Truth Series* that we are now creating for the purposes of continued education of those around the world. In my original books, beginning with *Seth Speaks*, we touched upon and introduced many new truths to the world. However, for brevity's sake, we could not go into great detail around some of the most profound subjects, but rather introduce them for contemplation and thought. Over the past half-century, the truths given in my original books have inspired millions around your planet to learn, grow, apply, and create change that has inspired many more around the world. These individuals, inspired by my previous *Seth books*, have gone on to teach others, discuss what they read, learned; and many have gone on to produce more of their own books, movies, and teachings that have all served the individuals, and your overall society and humanity as you know it. <u>Like seeds that produce an abundance of fruit for harvest, these truths have grown over time in the conscious collective of humanity.</u>

We now serve humanity as a Source by which the evolution of your species as human-*beings* grows and expands through the understanding, integration, and the application of the timeless truths that we have provided herein. To my original readers and followers of my books: there has in your current society developed an erroneous belief that with the physical death of our medium friend Jane Roberts, that my books and works would come to an end, forever and ever. This misconception is one of many that this book and those to follow, will serve to dispel and dissolve, for they are indeed erroneous beliefs <u>*about*</u> reality and not the truth <u>*of*</u> reality.

In terms of linear appearing historical time, it is now time to reawaken that which is within each of you; so that you may remember your true source, lineage, heritage, power, and creativity for positive, higher vibrational experiences.

There is no end or point in time or history when my teachings will cease to be put forth for the benefit of the greater consciousness in which you and all things eternally grow and evolve.

As readers will learn, my teaching work continues now through Jackson-Thomas. The evolution and expansion of human consciousness continues eternally. The evolution of ALL species and <u>forms</u> of consciousness continues eternally. Thus, my teaching and guiding this evolution also continues <u>eternally</u>.

As I have explained in my prior books, a large portion of my nature as a *Being* of consciousness is dedicated to the "teaching vocation", if you will. Meaning that I am primarily a teaching entity and enjoy teaching activities on many levels, in many dimensions and realities that are both physical and nonphysical.

As an immortal *Being* of consciousness, I am *within* the evolution of Earth's consciousness, humanity, and nature. Thus humanity, Earth, and your Universe are also within *my* evolution as well. I am inseparable from all things of the Earth and Universe; and your Earth and Universe is inseparable from myself and those like me.

Even within the conversations and connection that I have with and through Jackson, I learn, grow, and expand in light. You will see in this book that, through the associative nature of consciousness, I quite literally learn, grow, and expand through each and every interaction, thought, association, emotion, and any and all interactions with the infinite forms of consciousness that Jackson experiences in his physical life. I integrate every nuance and variation of these experiences in every imaginable way and it becomes part of what I am.

Now, whether you are aware of it or not, each of you readers also learns, integrates, grows, expands, and evolves in much the same way; through all interactions with all other humans, animals, plants, and objects within your universe. You cannot avoid this process. It is then, inevitable; as the evolution of consciousness is what you are in an eternal state of becoming.

To explain what it is that you are, it is often necessary for me to explain what I am. And in explaining to you what I am, I am also explaining to you what you are; for the very nature of that Divine energy that gives you physical life, is also that which I am, albeit on a much grander scale.

The greater reality around you that you perceive within your physical universe, innately and naturally, seeks growth; expansion into higher vibrational frequencies that IS the evolution of the consciousness that you are. It seeks the infinite expressions of consciousness which forms the physical reality around you. Your consciousness evolves eternally - in every millisecond of your existence, both during your physical lifetimes and before and after each one. The consciousness of humanity evolves. The consciousness of your Earth, animals, plants, and planet evolves as it must.

Free will of the individual, and society at large, determines the path and rate of that evolution; thus it is up to each individual to choose a path that will maximize the creative potential of the human-*being* that you are. **We are going to teach you how to maximize the creative potential that you are as immortal *beings* - expressing yourself in physical ways in the world of matter, in space and time.**

You cannot most effectively understand other humans, animals, plants, your Earth, universe, and the intimately connected relationships among them, if you do not most effectively understand the very nature of yourselves as *Beings* of consciousness.

You often believe that other humans, animals, plants, and your planets are separate from you as you judge your reality experience based only upon the very limited perceptions of the rational mind that utilizes the 5-human senses to determine its scope and perception of reality.

Expanding then, your understanding and perception beyond the boundaries of that which is physical, you are most effectively able to understand the nature of all that does appear physical, and will come to the very truth that you are not separate at all; but rather, infinite variety of expressions of species of consciousness, expressed into material matter that underlines as humans, animals, plants and planets. As I have said before, you are not apart from nature. You are a part of nature - an inseparable part, portion, etc. - yet, valid in your own unique ways that come through the experiences that you have when interacting with other life and forms of consciousness.

Therefore, it can be very truthfully stated that understanding the nature of yourself *AS* consciousness, you are then able to understand the forms of consciousness more fully that are around you, that make up your world, your universe, and all within it. Again, this IS the evolution of you, humanity, and All That Is - right here, right now; and you, dear reader, are an integral, valid, loved, and cherished unique portion of it all. You have a personal and inseparable connection to not only "God" (All That Is), but to ALL other expressions of consciousness that surround you in physical reality.

This IS how your "Law of Attraction" is able to attract, through the natural electromagnetic properties inherent within all forms of energy, all other forms of consciousness that will coalesce and gather into the physical elements that unfold before you as life on Earth.

You can, indeed, tap into the greater consciousness around you, beyond the flesh you see in your reflection, beyond your physical universe, beyond even space and time as you perceive it, and draw forth more fruitful means, methods, and ways of expression to improve your world as you experience it. Yet you yourself must make the decision to begin training your mind to "see" and perceive beyond the seeming physical boundaries that appear to separate objects and create space between you and your world around you.

We are helping you close the seeming gap, between you and all other things in your world, so that you can more easily, effortlessly attract them into your life experience, and to express yourselves in infinitely more creative ways than you ever knew were possible.

With time, focus, training, and practice, you can shift your <u>perception</u>, your awareness, and learn to focus your creative consciousness in an effort to draw to you other forms, and expressions of consciousness of similar vibrational frequencies, to provide you with a physical context of life as you desire it to be. **You are not at the mercy of life, or your past, unless you believe yourselves to be.** If this seems to be the case, then <u>you yourself have created the self-imposed perception of the box in which you have created and thus far expressed your life.</u>

Change your beliefs in limitations, and your physical experience must then reflect that outwardly as a new shifted experience of physical life around you.

> *"You are not changing your beliefs.*
> *You are changing your frequency.*
> *When you change your frequency,*
> *your beliefs will change."*
> - **Seth**

Remembering then that you are not a light switch that becomes fully illuminated within just a few moments of inner contemplation; but rather, an exquisite, Divine seed in which you are growing as a conscious *being* in an eternal infinite sea of consciousness as you come to know your own true power and potential and then apply it constructively and creatively toward the benefit of you, and all that you are a portion of eternally.

Now, I have many underlying intentions and purposes behind the works and words that you now read; all of which serve to bring out the best version of you that is truly, divinely possible. To do so, you must become aware of <u>what</u> you really are (not "who"). Your true self is beyond just the physical flesh; as is the origin, source, and fabric of every physical object you perceive.

However, I want to make it very clear to our readers that no matter where you are in life, no matter what age, place, location on your planet, conditions, or circumstances of what "has been", you can indeed begin to slow that habitual pattern of expression and develop a new path, a new you and a new outcome and new and improved experience of life.

These truths, as you read them, vibrate in your mind, reverberate in your soul and inner *being*, and extend, as all thought energy does, outward into the "Universe" to draw forth knowledge, wisdom, and experiences that, over time, will improve beyond the limited experiences you have known in the past.

This book is not just another book about the popular subject of manifestation. This book is about the source, the origin, the causal impetus, as well as the God-fabric of ALL physical reality. Including, of course, manifestation of job, money, material, health, wealth, technology, and living the life of your dreams come true.

However, this book is also quite literally about *the creation of ALL physical reality* from the Divine perspective of a multidimensional conscious collective that has, since before time existed as you know it, given focus of consciousness into the creation and evolution of all that you perceive to be physical in your universe - and infinitely beyond that in nonphysical realities.

One of our main goals for *The Nature of Consciousness* is to assist the readers in shifting their identity of Self, who and what they believe they are, *from the human* they most often think they are... *TO*... believing and knowing that you are *the immortal Being* within the human body.

Truly, I cannot stress this point enough; as your recognition, integration of this truth, and living your life FROM the perspective, belief, orientation of the immortal self within will unlock and stir into action an awareness of latent, dormant potential within yourself that can elevate your abilities, knowledge, and resource utilization beyond limitations. You can overcome virtually any and all limitations of physical reality by understanding the natural self and consciousness from which all things are created physical.

The more you come to understand this and actually develop this point of view, perception, point from which you think, feel, sense, and operate, you will begin to unveil what you call "miracles" and magical activity far beyond what most of you have ever experienced.

If, on the other hand, you move through life, believing that you are simply the human body you see in the mirror, separate from all things around you, you will then create such conditions and circumstances and sell yourselves short from the amazing experiences you could have should you recognize your true nature as conscious *beings*, eternally and intimately connected as ONE with "God"/Source/The Creator/Universe, etc.

To most effectively, efficiently, and consistently wield and utilize your natural abilities and resources, you must first acknowledge it, understand it, develop it, and bring it to the forefront of your own awareness. You are not able to master what you do not as yet fully know you have within you eternally available to help guide you to success.

Allow varied learning materials and presentation of the materials to reach as many as possible across the Earth.

As we publish our works, we cannot filter that which we provide to the world through any filter that diminishes, reduces, filters down, waters, down, narrows, or presents our materials in ways that we may believe at the rational mind level, that the world may or may not like or dislike. We give you, Jackson-Thomas, timeless truths. You share those truths as given. You do not filter them and change them to only present what your rational mind decides what would be best for humanity and our readers to read. You present just what you get, even if you yourself do not see, sense, or as yet understand why it is that we give it to you to share.

Again - OUR ways are higher than your ways. Our perception, seeing into the future, looking through infinite possibilities and probable outcomes is infinitely greater than what the rational mind can conceive.

Now, Jackson-Thomas, some of our material was given to you months or even years apart and repetition is to remind you of the vibration of truth behind that which we are repeating. It is also the case that the rational mind, the intellect, typically does not see or read something once, and has the understanding to the core of being what it is that any given thing means. Often the rational and intellectual mind must read the same material, presented perhaps the same or slightly different, looking at it from many different angles before the "ah-ha" moment of true understanding of the truth comes to their awareness.

Now, as I have stated before, we intend to reach as many humans on the Earth as we possibly can with our works and materials - people from all walks of life, including those that English is not their primary language.

This repetition then, is very useful for those who seek to learn that do so more effectively by repetition.

Those who are not fluent in English, or are new to spiritual materials, will benefit when the truth is presented several times and from several angles before it is understood as their viewpoint from which they themselves are reading; and hence, understanding our material is vastly different than those already well-adjusted to the material.

Therefore, all of our readers, again, should keep the open mind that we serve the individual, and we serve the masses; and be open to the materials as they are presented. We have purpose. We have intentions with our materials and actions and the way they are presented, even if everyone does not understand them.

The Divine works in mysterious ways it is often said. <u>Allow that working to be presented here beyond your own personal need or understanding.</u> We serve humanity - not just those already fluent in these materials.

The goal here is not just to teach humanity about the timeless truths of existence, nor about the love and light that all things are in their very core of existence; the goal here is for humans to **BE** the love, light, and truths that we articulate here, through the integrated, in-depth understanding of them, and the adoption of them as the new Self that you choose to be.

This is the evolution of humanity. The consciousness of the human species - whose evolution does indeed help evolve other forms and expressions of consciousness around it. All physical reality is created in, through, by, and within consciousness as it expresses itself into physical matter. You can as an individual, and a human race, evolve seemingly random and haphazardly; or you can evolve intentionally with desire, purpose, and value fulfillment attained and enhanced. It is your daily choices that determine your personal, and *en masse*, evolution into the humanity that prophets of the ages have foretold. What choices will _you_ make today?

In closing our preface, let me invite you to pay attention to that low, soft, inner whispering within you as you read my words and our book, and how they make you feel. This is a clue and is most definitely your sign, your bell within, ringing to the very truth of your *being*. You may well find that as you read, as you expand your mind and perceptions and beliefs, that you find yourself deeply connected to the very words you are reading.

This my friends, is because your true inner *being*, is remembering, awakening, and vibrating to the very truth that it IS ALREADY, and it will often feel as if you already somehow knew these truths. This may then cause you to have the ah-ha moments of inner illumination whereby you understand that you're reading exactly what you are supposed to be reading, when you are supposed to be reading it, and that you are on your path to personal growth beyond what you've currently known in this lifetime.

Finally, as a housekeeping notation here: During the authoring, publishing, and production of my original books with Jane Roberts (Ruburt), I had noted that for the purposes of authenticity, all communication for our books would come exclusively through Ruburt (Jane). (While she was physically alive, that is.) I would here note that Jane (Ruburt) and I did not have the conversations about what may or may not happen after her physical death. It is true that Jane, at the rational mind level, had a certain fear of her health factors, including those that led up to the severity of her illness and eventual physical death. Due to the rational fear of death and her personal challenges around that, it was not discussed that Jackson *may, in her future, continue our works after her death. Thereby focusing more thought upon the physical end of Jane's lifetime and fear of illness and death. We say *may, meaning that it was a ___probable___ reality of her future, but not set in stone that it would occur as Jackson has free will and could have chosen not to embark upon the path where we would work on books or even 'meet' in this lifetime at all, consciously that is.

Jackson, however, has already *been dead*. Therefore, knowing what is beyond the physical realm has given him an immense perspective about existence after death, and of course prepared him very well for the beginnings of understanding consciousness, and eventually (as a probable reality) teaching it in this lifetime. Though again, he still had to choose the mission and take the millions of actions necessary to bring it to physical fruition.

Now, as with Jane-Ruburt, so with Jackson-Thomas... For the purposes of authenticity now, during his lifetime, which may well be longer than science believes is possible, or is rationally understood, all communications, materials for any and all books, works or physical expressions of my materials - All, will come exclusively through Jackson-Thomas.

Section 1:

An Introduction To Consciousness

The Attributes And Characteristics
Of Consciousness

Now: I will spend some time and pages of material hopefully presenting to the reader the many forms and ways in which consciousness manifests itself, both in physically and in nonphysically perceivable terms. To fully document what consciousness is, would be similar in scope to writing down every single thought, word, expression, event, object, race, language, and so forth for, all of human history, and that of your entire universe - which dates far beyond time as you understand it - and that would be just the infinitesimally small beginning of such a project. However, I hope to inspire the reader to understand more about themselves as individuals and as a culture, society, and the race you call humanity.

I will also discuss that human-*beings* are not apart <u>*from*</u> nature, but rather a part <u>*of*</u> nature - as with all physical things you see about you. This is a key truth to understand in the core of your *being*; for it is a part of the foundational basis upon which you create your physical reality and universe in harmony with all consciousness that is focused into physical expression.

All human-*beings*, all animals, nature, and in fact, every particle that makes up the planet Earth and the entire universe that you know are indeed, infinite varieties and materializations of the very same source energy known as consciousness. <u>All</u> physical reality that you know, including your own body, not only has its <u>origins</u> in the nonphysical reality of consciousness, but it is also consciousness formed and shaped into expressions of material matter. Not only is consciousness the root source of every physically perceivable object, but it is also the "space" that <u>*appears to be*</u> between all physical objects in your universe.

Since consciousness IS all physical matter and material, then you might ask, "Where does that leave 'God'?" To answer this question, I intend to provide a much more truthful understanding of the nonphysical Divine *Being* that most think of as a person in human, man-like form that has been called "God" by many names throughout various cultures, races, and religions.

The flesh body, which is the physical focus point through which your immortal consciousness is focused for the purposes of navigating your physical learning environment, is limited to the scope and natural characteristics of your creaturehood. Meaning for example, humans do not have physical wings as a bird does, so you are *physically* limited as to the characteristics of your physical body in your physical incarnation. While it is quite true that there are within each human-*being* latent, dormant potential abilities that exist for evolutionary purposes, the immortal Self/soul/consciousness that is within this flesh *is not limited* in nature as the flesh is. The physical you is limited only insofar as the constructs of your physical body, on the physical plane of material existence.

Outside of this context, the you that you know to be the person reading this, is vastly *without* limitation. The Self (your consciousness) is not limited.

> **There is no separation of Self. As there is no separation of consciousness for they are one and the same. You are not your body. You are not even your thoughts. You are the immortal Self that experiences them.**

In certain terms, consciousness is a "live", living, moving, growing intelligent "energy" - if you expand the ways you define such terms. Like energy, consciousness cannot ever be destroyed, ended, die, be disposed of, invalidated, etc. It is immortal and can only expand, grow, and eternally continue to become. Consciousness is eternally in a constant state of becoming, or being.

Consciousness is not visible, yet the physical forms of its expressions are all around you every moment of your life. Therefore, you cannot see consciousness, but rather the infinite physical expressions of consciousness. Its infinite forms are expressed as objective, physically appearing reality.

This is an important truth for all to understand for it truly is the basis upon which your entire universe and everything in it is constructed. Your entire universe that you see with physical eyes and perceive with the 5-human physically oriented senses are the end results or physical manifestations of consciousness, expressed into physical matter.

There is then, an *infinite* variety of what we will call nonphysical *"species" of consciousness*. Therefore, you have human-*being* consciousness for various species of human-*beings* that have existed on

3

the Earth and beyond. You have animal consciousness within animals that give them existence. You have plant consciousness within plants, and rock consciousness within rocks.

Most do not think of the plants or rocks as having consciousness. However, I assure you that the very basic matter from which the atomic structure of each and every flower or leaf of lettuce, tomato, or pine tree on Earth has, at its most basic level, consciousness. Again, you cannot have physical matter expressed into physically perceivable terms without consciousness, as all matter IS a form of consciousness in expression.

There are some who choose diets that are only along vegetarian lines, eating plant and vegetable matter because they believe that animals such as beef, chicken, or fish have "consciousness" or a soul because it is an animal-creature much like a human-creature. While the choice of diet is, in fact, an individual choice, it cannot be overstated that all plants and animals have the very same "All That Is" consciousness within them. Like human bodies, they, too, only vary in the outward physically perceived expression of consciousness.

Through these truths of the description of consciousness within all physical matter, one can easily begin to see the larger picture. From an expanded perception and view of physical life on Earth, one understands that they are, at the very basic level, *not apart from* all of physical matter and nature, but rather a very intimate *part of* that physical matter and nature which can be seen all around them and in the skies. Your physical body may *appear* to be separate from all other human bodies and objects of your universe, yet at the level or layer of consciousness that gives all physical matter its existence, you are all sourced from - and "made out of" - consciousness. You are eternally existing within it, inseparable from it, and fabricated from it - AS it. All That Is, ("God" by any and all names) expresses itself *AS* you.

When those in spiritual groups claim that "We are all One" they are quite correct in their understanding; there are no separations or divisions of any kind in consciousness. Nor are there any limitations as to the nature of expressions of consciousness. Now, your root assumptions of physical reality do hold some restrictions that your creaturehood may be restricted so that you do not sprout wings and fly like an eagle would. However, it is your species of human consciousness that has "built-in" instructions, if you will, that guide the creation of your physical body so that you do not sprout physical wings and fly as an eagle. It is your <u>species</u> of consciousness, that determines if it expresses in physical terms of matter as a human body or an acorn, for example.

> *"We may appear in many bodies, as you have; yet, I assure you that on the nonphysical source side from which you all have come, we are not separated in the manner in which you think of as having physical boundaries of which others do not cross."*

Therefore, within groupings of species of consciousness, there are, inherent within them the very guidelines for proper expression, and of course, variations of that expression. There is good health, and then variations of that health, that do allow for a belief in disease and illness; these are variations within the consciousness of "health" for each physical creature, plant, and so on. So, how does an oak tree know how to produce acorns and not peaches? Some may term things scientifically as the genetic codes within their atomic structures as being the source that tells the oak tree to grow acorns. However, what is it that tells the genetic structures to do so along <u>those</u> particular lines for <u>that</u> particular species of oak tree? Consciousness.

When humanity as a larger group, begins to understand, accept, and integrate the very timeless truth as to the nature of their existence, as a part of nature and all physical things around you; then, that humanity and culture, society, and individuals that make it up will evolve into more naturally creative *beings* within which <u>intentional expressions within physical reality may be achieved easily.</u> This is purposeful, intentional creation, or as it is now, as of the date of this writing popularly termed, <u>manifestation</u>.

Natural Characteristics Of Consciousness

Consciousness is energy and energy is consciously self-aware. Not aware as one may think of human consciousness being aware of oneself; however, it is self-aware in its own unique ways inherent within its species. Energy (consciousness) is also not only self-aware, however, it is also aware of its part in the greater reality in which it plays a part. For example, there is not a tree in the forest that is not fully aware of its own existence, but also of its unique contribution and place within the ecosystem of the forest in which it is a portion.

Again, and I want to make this clear, ALL physical objects are composed of, and eternally exist, as consciousness which is fully "self-aware" of itself, and the environment in which it is a portion. It is important then, to expand the definitions upon which science has defined the terms conscious awareness so that they include a greater reality of species of consciousness; which do indeed have awareness... however different the term is from the scientific definition you are normally used to. You must think outside the box here if we are to understand the truths of the nature of consciousness.

Now:

◊ Consciousness is a kind or type or <u>species</u> of intelligent and responsive "energy"

◊ Consciousness is <u>not linear</u>

◊ Consciousness, like energy, is <u>immortal</u>

◊ Consciousness cannot <u>*ever*</u> be destroyed, diminished, ended, injured, harmed, etc.

◊ Consciousness can transform into new expressions (physical and nonphysical)

◊ Consciousness is capable of *infinite* forms of expression, both nonphysical and physical

◊ ***<u>Consciousness does not take up any physical space</u>***

◊ Consciousness eternally exists <u>outside of space and time</u>

◊ All consciousness is eternally in a state of "becoming more", growing, learning, and expanding in physical and nonphysical terms of expression

◊ Your human consciousness, that which you know to be your awareness of yourself ("I AM"), exists before your physical birth and after your physical death, completely intact, lucidly aware, <u>as it is immortal</u>

◊ **Consciousness is omnipresent, omnipotent, and omniscient.** These terms may sound familiar as a description of "God" (All That Is).

◊ As consciousness is omnipresent, then the "speed" at which consciousness would travel is no speed at all. More than instantaneous, consciousness operates eternally beyond the phenomena of space and time. Again, there is no separation of consciousness at any level or dimension, as physical barriers do not exist. There may be psychic or psychological "boundaries" constructed mentally for one creative purpose or another; however, physical separation is not possible as consciousness is not physical.

◊ Time - Consciousness is <u>instantaneous</u> as it is everywhere present, eternally

Consciousness eternally exists outside of space and time. Its <u>expressions</u> <u>appear</u> in space and time; however, the consciousness that is the source, the fabric <u>of</u> the atomic structures that you see as physical objects, <u>exists outside of space and time.</u>

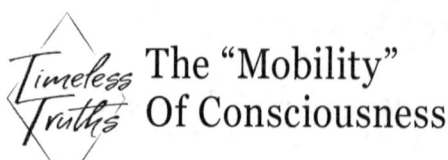 # The "Mobility" Of Consciousness

THERE IS NO SPACE IN CONSCIOUSNESS And **Space does _not_ separate consciousness.**

Physical distance... is _an illusion,_ and you are connected to _all things at all moments_. You do not need to be physically present as your intentions and vibrations of love, harmony, and gratitude (or otherwise) will be understood, vibrationally by the consciousness of that in which it is connected to/about or intended. For example, if you are performing "Reiki" healing using energy, you may be doing so in the physical presence of the individual you are performing the healing upon. However, as truly there is no space and time, you can just as effectively perform "Reiki" - or energy healing - remotely from one side of the planet to another on the other side of the planet; as the energy being sent to target individual, animal, etc., is instantaneously received if they are open to it. Now, it may take "time" for their physical body to show the responses to such healing energy; however, the energy of love and light, healing vibrations and frequencies, will reach your intended destination instantaneously. Almost, as if they were physically closer than your fingertips and nearer than your breath.

Simply focus on them within your imagination and you can speak to them in terms of love, gratitude, cooperation, and harmony... and they will receive your message, your intentions, inflections, and so forth. They may not consciously acknowledge them unless they are in expanded states of consciousness in which they are tuned into their clairabilities (such as clairsentience, clairvoyance, etc.), however, they will be received at the soul level.

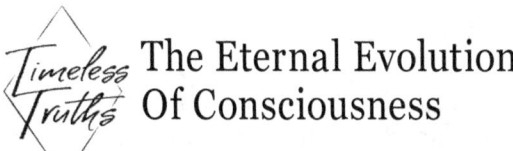

CONSCIOUSNESS IS NOT WHOLE, COMPLETE, FINISHED, DONE, ETC.

Now: As a Multidimensional Conscious Collective and immortal _being_ of consciousness, I am _never_ a "whole" entity. The word "whole" in your language has a meaning behind the word as something that is <u>complete</u>, bound, and finished. However, as I have been speaking about consciousness, consciousness is never in all eternity complete, whole, finished, nor bound in any manner. Which means here that _you_ and I are not ever whole, complete, finished, or done growing, learning, expanding, or becoming.

I grow in love, light, and truth, in every moment of what you perceive as time on the earth plane. In every instant, beyond the micro-seconds, if you will, I am constantly growing, learning, adapting, applying, and becoming more and more. Because I exist, as your inner Self does, outside of space and time; time is irrelevant to me except as a construct that I can interact with your and other physical dimensions of reality in which time and space apply.

Therefore, I am growing in what you perceive to be the <u>present moment</u> that you read these words. I am growing right now, in the very moment of historical time that I am dictating our original books to Jane (Ruburt) in what _you_ perceive to be _your_ past. From Jane's perspective in 1970 say, I am growing in light, in _her_ future, which is _your present_, the Now Moment that you read these words.

I am growing a thousand years ago, a million years ago, and a million years from now - what you perceive to be the year in which you read this book.

As the larger "Seth" entity, I grow through each and every interaction with all other forms of consciousness, in every dimension that I focus into, move through, if you will, and in which I have experience - even out to the extensions of personalities that I have given "birth" to as the parent entity.

I also have a personality that was once a man by the name of Frank and many of such personalities which are inseparable portions of myself as the larger Conscious Collective.

While my personalities are inseparable, they also maintain their own uniqueness and are free to develop on their own, even beyond the physical lifetimes that they may have incarnated into. We can discuss such relationships at a later point; however, what I want to point out here is that the larger entity you know to be _Seth_... learns and adapts, grows, and expands in light and experience through EVERY interaction that every one of my personalities may ever encounter, both as the primary personality consciousness and also as every one of the probable selves that may then extend from each and every personality. In other words, when my personality of Frank, lived his physical lifetime whereby he assumed that name in the human form, I...I learned from every interaction that personality had during its entire lifetime. Enhancing and evolving myself, as well as itself as a portion of me.

Now, after the physical lifetime is over, this personality consciousness is free to evolve on its own path and does remain eternally a portion of what I am, though I do not "track" and monitor every interaction this personality may encounter in its development. Almost as if a parent knows the child is playing in the other room but is not actively focused upon their activities.

Therefore, I am, as the larger entity, learning through millions of connections, interactions, and so forth - simultaneously.

Now, in other _forms_ of consciousness, I am also able to shift my focus to merge a portion of myself into the consciousness of a tree, let's say, so that I may experience the consciousness of the tree on your earth plane. Or perhaps as a mountain of rocks. It is not that I am, myself, the consciousness of that object; yet, I can indeed join as a gestalt addition to it, in harmony with it, to "see" and experience physical existence from the perspective and point of view of that object. I tell you this so that you realize that I can from my perspective, in my dimensions, interact with infinite forms of consciousness as they are expressed in terms of Earth, water, oceans, skies, planets, animals, and every perceivable object that is physical in appearance in any 3-dimensional (or otherwise) plane of expression that I am aware of. Not just your physical universe, but many, many physical universes - all simultaneous to, what you would think of as, the present moment or, as I like to say, "the eternal '**Now Moment**'".

I make these points to tell you that the immortal portion of you also does the same in growing through every interaction with all other forms and species of consciousness. You may not be aware of it; however, every portion of your human body is, at all times, connected and

10

"communicating" with the environment around you, and to a degree, you do affect the environment in which you participate. An example of this might be when someone tells you that you have a way of "lighting up the room" when you walk in, or "when you enter a room there is a feeling of confidence that you carry about you". This is an example of affecting the environment in that room; although, it extends far beyond the persons in the room feeling your energy.

Most people do not contemplate the truth that "you" extend outward past the surface of your skin, outward into all the universes, and also interact with many other species of consciousness - both those that have physical expressions in form (that appear in time and space) and those that do not.

You are aware of some of these interactions through which your own self grows, expands, and is eternally in the process of becoming...and these my friends are in your dreams. One of the many areas where you interact with such dimensions, physical and not, <u>at the layer of consciousness</u>, to gain experience far outside of your "normal life"... to try on new scenarios, find resolutions, answers, inventions, ideas, guidance, etc.

As I have stated before, in telling my readers about the nature of myself as a *being* of consciousness, <u>I am also, to a degree, telling you about the true nature of your own selves</u>. While I may have an exponentially larger point of view and perspective, experience, and capabilities that I have developed that are beyond what you experience as you are consciously focused in physical life, you do have a portion of yourselves that also is similar in its potential, to one degree or another. **What is true for one consciousness is true for ALL. The truth of consciousness does not change. Ever. Only your perception and understanding of it changes.** Here, we are exponentially expanding your perception and understanding so that you may use it more effectively, efficiently, and consistently in ways that benefit you and all around you.

You see then, that one of your reasons for incarnating onto the physical plane, within the human flesh, is to learn and grow and expand in light through interactions with all other physically-focused forms of consciousness that express themselves *into and as* Electromagnetic Energy Units (EUs) and then into the components of atoms, molecules and so forth that make up expressions of consciousness that take material form and appear to be solid objects in 3-dimensions.

We are here, moving into these materials, so that you can begin to question who you thought you were, as a seemingly limited human, and begin to understand the unlimited potential you TRULY ARE as an immortal being that is <u>within the human</u> you see in the mirror.

We are here, re-evaluating ourselves as human-beings, and beginning to understand more and more that we are the unlimited being, who has a body in which we are focused, to learn our directive use of eternally creative energy and how that affects all other things around us.

We are re-defining what you REALLY are, by evolving what you thought you were.

Consciousness And Its
Limitless Capabilities

Now: When our friend Jackson here, whom I am now writing our books through as a medium, using his (and your) natural characteristic of consciousness you call clairaudience, died a physical death when playing in the barn as a child, he had a fascinating experience of full, lucid, conscious awareness outside of the human body. There was then, during his Near-Death Experience (NDE), a portion of this experience whereby his consciousness shifted into the nonphysical reality that many call "heaven" - simply another dimension of reality where human consciousness and other forms display perhaps physical-like images in which one can see, speak to and interact with the consciousness of loved ones and family passed on, other forms of reality, nonphysical entities such as Angels, and so forth. Then there was a point in which his consciousness shifted its focus into the physical reality in which he had been living.

Now, the shift from nonphysical reality to physical reality and Earth is instantaneous with what you would think of as simply a "thought". With a thought or desire, one can instantaneously shift perception from nonphysical to physical reality, and in fact, from the <u>standpoint</u> of nonphysical reality, one can "look into" (experience) infinite realms of nonphysical and physical realities that are outside the context of your own. Consciousness is not confined nor limited to such boundaries as your own physical system and version of Earth and universe.

Our key point here is that the experience one has in relating to - interacting with - one's reality is largely guided or influenced by the standpoint, or understanding, or place from which you are viewing that reality. Just as standing at the bottom of the mountain, you would see a mountainous challenge in front of you, blocking your path and view. However, from the standpoint and perception you would have viewing the area from the top of that mountain, <u>you would be above those appearances of the mountain blocking your path and could see exceptionally farther and clearer, much more than you could at the lower plane of flat Earth next to the base of the mountain</u>. **This is of exceptionally key importance here.**

Perceptions of physical reality are then similar to our example here. The higher you are in personal vibrational frequency, as an individual, couple, group, society, country, etc, the more expanded view of, and experiences of, that reality which can be enriched as you widen your perception through which you are viewing, and thus experiencing your physical reality.

We are pointing this out for our readers so that you better understand that you are not limited to just the physical flesh human self you see in the mirror. _You_, the immortal _being_ within you, your soul, which in part develops a personality as a part of its physical life experience, is not limited to just the human you are physically in terms of creativity and expression. You are unlimited to the degree that you see, understand, use, and apply the knowledge and wisdom of what you truly are - the infinitely creative unlimited _being_ within the flesh you see in the mirror. The more you expand your perception and understanding of _what_ you truly are, the more you are able to begin applying it, learning, adapting, expanding, trying, expanding more...and hence, experiencing more of things in physical life. Simply because you are expanding the _tools_ and knowledge that becomes your new standpoint, your new place from which you are viewing and creating reality.

Notice herein we say, "_What_ you truly are." - Not _who_. Often in many languages around the world, the framing of who one really is might be referring to a definition of someone, which of course would mean a connotation that one is "done", finished, or whole. So, we are here in our materials using the more open term "what you are", loosely as we describe characteristics of the natural immortal self of human-_beings_.

Good afternoon to you my immortal friend, Jackson-Thomas... Earth adventurer and teacher of many.

Now: We have an amazing journey before us and I want you to keep visualizing that, feeling that, and living in that imaginary world with feeling and emotion as you celebrate the success we have in the future, **now**. You are indeed bringing then, those time-space realities, those probable reality events objects, and conditions to your NOW MOMENT reality in which it seems that you are jumping the time-space continuum and seemingly transporting yourself into a future NOW MOMENT. In a manner of speaking, you are; however, it is more that this "NOW MOMENT" of the future is moving into your <u>current</u> level of perception, as you are not really moving physically to IT.

Again, without space and time, it is simply a matter of perception in which you perceive it or not...from of course, your current point of view, which is in all ways limited when incarnated into the human body. You have then, scaled down your own scope of visibility if you will, so that your energy can be maintained in the human body, whereby you do not have the normal scope of visibility that you do when <u>not</u> focused from within the human body. You have, for your physical lifetime's sake, taken a small portion of the greater nonphysical self, and temporarily sent it forth to view physical reality from within the flesh, looking outward to perceive your newly created environment.

You see, (small pun there), that your physical eyes, exist to create the visual context that you believe is a 3-dimensional reality around you. The physical skin and human body have sensual touch so that you *create* the physical environment that you feel - hot and cold and 3-dimensional textures. One may believe that you use your eyes, ears, and other physical 5-human senses to sense an environment that is ALREADY there, yet...in reality, you have the 5-human senses to assist you in *creating* the physically appearing environment in which you live your human lives and have your physical existence, and then use them to navigate that physically appearing dimension.

You think that you move through space on the Earth or in outer space itself when in reality, it simply changes in front of the 5-human senses that present you with a "movie" that seems to move through space and take "time" to do so. However, these are illusions of the grandest nature and settings.

From my point of view, and the natural self that you are eternally, outside of the body, I can of course not only look AT you. I can see _INTO_ you and THROUGH you. I can look at the flesh, or see the cells, atoms, and molecules that make up the flesh; and further still, the glow of light, almost like a bioluminescence around them that gives them all conscious life activity to build, heal, and maintain the human body.

I can look at the chair and living room in which you sit and take down dictation, or I can look through it to the Earth below it, or even through that Earth to the planet that seems to be on the other side of space beyond your Earth. It is then a matter of perception and, although I have the ability as a multidimensional conscious collective to see into physical dimensions of reality... both the ones you are aware of and those you are not, I can also perceive into them at any level of their existence or at any point in space or time.

Remember now, as I have said before and will again, time and space do not "really" exist. They simply appear to exist to the 5-human senses. To your consciousness, these are simply physical expressions of consciousness that you can creatively manipulate to create the environment you call Earth and your universe, and all within it.

Now, as I exist outside of time and space, I can look into your living room space and perceive the physical environment that existed "in that physical space" 10,000 years ago, or 10,000 years from now. To a larger extent, when not focused from within the physical form, you are also able to do these great feats that would seem nearly impossible miracles to you now. However, they are natural - as they are simply perceiving consciousness in its infinite states and expressions of which, they are not at all in any manner separated or hidden from any other consciousness.

Therefore, I can maintain a very lucid conversation and be performing dictation with the previous medium friend of ours we know and affectionately call Ruburt (Jane Roberts) at the very same "time" that I am also performing a dictation session with Thomas, (Jackson Moore who I often call Jackson-Thomas to acknowledge the mortal-immortal, <u>human</u> and *being* for our teaching purposes), and I can be having very lucid <u>connections</u> with thousands of *beings* that are within your universe and in other dimensions that you do not at <u>your level of conscious perception</u> perceive to exist - all simultaneously.

Again, there are no limitations of consciousness. It is truly Omnipresent - present everywhere, in full, in all-ness, eternally growing, shifting, expanding, becoming, and because there is no space in nonphysical reality, consciousness is not <u>physically</u> separate from other consciousness in other dimensions. Now, I will state here that it does take great practice and skill to advance to a state of proficiency whereby one can "travel through" dimensions *psychically*; following the path of associations through probable systems and probable realities. Perhaps a way to relay this in meaning would be: if you are imagining that you are traveling down a road from say, New York to Montana, or even walking out through a field. With your eyes closed and using only your mind's eye, you move through this scene and picture as if you were moving through actual space. In that example, you are "moving" <u>through</u> consciousness by *imagining* yourself to be moving through a physical dimension. In certain terms now, you are actually doing that now as you live your waking lives...as you imagine that you are walking about in a physically solid 3-dimensional world with solid objects that appear to be separate from other objects.

Outside of physical reality, this can be done; however, the dimensions, perceptions, and various nuances of them, the root assumptions of each reality being different here and there, create challenges for even the very well-skilled. However, it is possible and can be done.

Our point here being that consciousness is not limited to space nor time for its perception of that which is eternally "all around it" or the environment in which it is presently existing or "moving through" (psychically).

You believe perhaps as you sit there reading, that there is a living room or house that surrounds you. Or a park and trees or whatever nature scene you'd like to read your book while sitting in. However, consciousness IS all that forms the reality around you and as such, other species of consciousness, *beings*, and intelligence, can indeed perceive it if they so choose. As I have stated in my other books, there are a number of <u>probable</u> "Earths" in the very, precise "<u>physical space</u>" where your Earth now seems to float in space. Yet you do not perceive them, and those in these dimensions do not generally perceive you except perhaps in the dream state or deep meditative states whereby your consciousness is open to perceiving such dimensions about you. As I have also stated before, there are other "universes" as you call them. Other arrangements of planets and other dimensions of existence in physical form that are beyond the one you perceive while incarnate into the human form.

Ancient mankind, before technology took up so much of your time and focus during your physical experience, had a very natural connection with these dimensions and sensed them much more openly than many today do. It is not that today, in your period of time in which we are now writing, and that you are reading this book, that they cannot be sensed. <u>It is that many are so fascinated by the seeming physical objects around them that they do not develop the inner senses to the degree that allows them to perceive such dimensions more readily.</u>

Those that study and participate in ESP/psychic/metaphysical/ spiritual inner development by whatever name you would like to use here for the esoteric, often perceive them more readily than others as they are open to them.

> *They believe they exist and therefore,*
> *the first step in opening the doors*
> *of perception of them is created.*

Again, I will say here:

You create your own experience of reality within the beliefs that you yourself develop and hold as the boundaries within which your experience seems to unfold as your daily life.

Read that again...

In other words, your beliefs literally act like the guardrails within which you are steering your life along your physical journey. If you only use your 5-human senses to judge, perceive and understand your reality, your life will seem quite limited in experience and quality, enjoyment, and dimensional learning. However, the more you expand your consciousness and raise in vibrational frequency to be a closer match to the higher vibrational frequencies from which all things are Sourced and created that are made physical, the more you will widen those guardrails to perceive an entirely new and enhanced, fulfilling and joyful experience in your physical lives.

The impossible of a hundred years ago is ordinary today in many, many ways. Because at some point in space and time, someone sensed that an impossible task or object was possible and hence, opened the door for it to become a probable reality brought into physical focus. Idea construction. Ideas are brought to physical matter through the focus of attention; the guidance of beliefs open enough to allow them and natural laws if you will, through which energy and consciousness transform into matter that appears within 3-dimensional space and time.

Now, as you read our book and materials, you are automatically opening doors to wider understandings, insights, wisdom, and truths of the nature of existence. Physical and nonphysical existence. *Being*. As you read the words, the vibration of the meaning behind the symbols you call letters and words, vibrate to a particular frequency. If your intention is to learn and expand, the *intentions* are then inseparably associated with the words you are reading. As such, the intentions, combined with the beliefs of learning more than you presently are aware of, combined with natural traits and characteristics of consciousness, allow the materials to "bleed through" the rational/intellectual mind's level of perception and begin to open up a whole new world to you. **You awaken to your own truths as the rational mind becomes aware of them and the fact that you recognize them at a deeper level than it presently knows or is aware of.**

For those who focus in their lives on the development of the inner self and the natural "clairabilities" (clairvoyance, clairaudience, claircognizance, etc...), they will indeed, over time begin to perceive a FAR GREATER reality in which they are eternally <u>present</u>.

Like Jane Roberts' students in her classes on ESP, they began developing these faculties that are natural to their inner self and bringing them to the forefront of their own awareness so that their conscious mind, the rational, thinking intellectual mind, began to accept them as sources of information and data through which it could relate to physical and nonphysical realities. A basis for understanding its own existence and nature of origin.

We restate here: **you cannot use most effectively the natural psychic tools, traits, and characteristics of your own consciousness if you are not first fully informed and schooled as to their existence** and what to "look for". The basis of understanding then will grow, and with the intention to seek more....ye shall find. You grow the depth of understanding of you... Your *Self*, within.

Your intentions then, are an all-important part of creation because I assure you, that you cannot avoid your own intentions and they cannot be hidden from ALL other consciousness or what you might think of as "God". No thoughts, no intentions, no actions are hidden from <u>All That Is</u>, and these things not only form your reality, but, they add to the overall realities of which you are, aware of it or not, eternally inseparable from.

Now, if one wonders at times why it is that many "off-planet *beings*" or so-called extraterrestrials, do not readily show themselves in close proximity to humans, I assure you that physical *beings* that have developed to the point where they can move through space and time, to and from other dimensions that you do not normally perceive, have not advanced to this degree without <u>*a significant advancement of the consciousness that provides their existence.*</u> They are fully aware of their part in nature and existence, and they can indeed, sense....feel... know <u>the intentions of humans</u> that are perhaps vastly outside the "visibility" and perception of most humans.

They "know you" through consciousness. In fact, in many ways, the off-planet *beings* actually know you better than you know you; for they are, in most cases, very well adjusted in communicating with other *beings*, physical and not, animals and the like, <u>at the layer of consciousness, that does not involve language as you think of it.</u>

Now, you do this yourselves...often perceiving when a friend or family member has had an accident somewhere else on Earth, or something has happened, etc. <u>You are then, using your consciousness to sense these things...energy spikes, intents and purposes, direction, and inflections upon thought and action, which are instantly sensed even though someone may be on the other side of the planet</u> (because there is no space, hence there really is no separation, thus it is instantaneous in reaching you).

How many of our readers have themselves, or known someone close to them, who has sensed when a child of theirs or a spouse, loved one, etc. have been injured or killed, or are in trouble of some sort? They are sensing the consciousness of the individual as they are directly connected, regardless of space, at the layer of consciousness. Beyond the physical yet infinitely more telling.

Advanced civilizations <u>create advanced civilizations</u> because they have not used advanced technologies to kill one another nor destroy life, but rather to *nurture* it. They have existed for what you perceive to be millions of years as they have not destroyed one another and have learned their natural innate connection with all other forms of life and physical realities that they travel to and through. Otherwise, the species or civilization does not last very long in terms of a physically expressed species in time and space.

Tools and technology can be used to help humanity or destroy it. The difference can be the vibrational frequency of the humans that make choices of actions based upon their perceptions of reality, be they limited and physically focused only, or those that have expanded their consciousness and moved beyond the desire to exert dominion over other humans or *beings*.

The seeking of harm or dominion over any other *being* only occurs at lower vibrational states of consciousness. These desires do not and cannot exist at higher vibrational states for they do not at all exist in higher vibrational frequencies. Humans that vibrate to higher frequencies are often referred to as humanitarians, as they naturally understand their connection to all life and existence, and love and appreciate such differences in uniqueness.

I want to state this again for this is IMPERATIVE and CRITICAL for humanity to understand: Advanced technologies can be used to help humanity or destroy it. The difference in the use of such technologies both from on and off-planet is the vibrational frequencies and states of consciousness of the human-being that thinks about, acts upon, and uses these technologies in creative, or destructive ways. If one's state of consciousness and vibrational frequency (VF) is much lower and driven from the rational mind and brain (which only knows <u>this physical lifetime and existence</u> as it was given physical existence in this lifetime frame of context only), then the use of such tools may be for less-than-beneficial purposes to your species and humanity. The brain was "born" in this physical lifetime. It only knows this physical lifetime until you teach it to perceive FROM your inner Self- consciousness, which sees and senses and interacts beyond space and time.

If however, the personal vibrational frequency and state of consciousness is much higher in VF, this human's being then will be exponentially aware of its innate and natural connection to all things, and that harming other things *intentionally* only brings harmful results, while helping other things *intentionally* brings about a whole other evolved (and naturally based in love) experience of physical reality.

This...is a key to the evolution of your civilization and humanity as you know it, moving beyond the concepts of war and dominion, using technologies in harmful ways to the whole, rather than in helpful ways. To develop technologies without also developing the consciousness within that creates and uses those technologies, can become dangerous to your civilization, as it has occurred before.

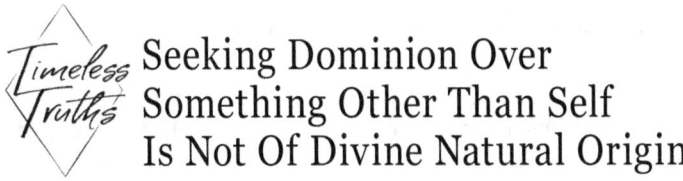

Seeking Dominion Over Something Other Than Self Is Not Of Divine Natural Origin

Now: Seeking dominion over other humans or life forms for the intentions of power to control them or their development unfolding as their own experiences, comes from the rational, intellectual mind of a human (NOT from the immortal *being* within). That which many call "evil" then or bad people, "satanic", of the devil, or any other mystical excuse for not taking ownership of mankind's own thoughts and deceptions, *is NOT from the Divine immortal consciousness that provides the physical body its life and existence.*

You cannot blame a power outside of your own rational mind's for your misfortunes, as much as many would like to assert so.

This is not to say that humans do not work in harmony with other humans and/or animals for cooperative purposes. You may train a human to do certain tasks as you may train a horse or dog for example, without forcing them outside of their will and sovereign selves for purposes of controlling them as if they are "less than you".

The human brain exists within the PHYSICAL body and has the scope of visibility and understanding by the use of the PHYSICAL 5-human senses. As the <u>physical</u> brain exists in *this physical lifetime only*, it only knows what it has learned in *this lifetime only*, by use of the 5-human physically oriented senses that give it an overall picture of your physical reality. Hence, again, its views, point of view, and point from which it perceives reality around you are limited at best. It sees objects as separate (physically) as they appear in space and time, and believes such objects to be separate from itself; hence, a rational mind could seek dominion or control over other humans and things that *appear to be* separate from itself.

However, the inner *being*, the soul or consciousness within your flesh right now, <u>DOES NOT SEEK DOMINION NOR CONTROL OVER ANY OTHER THING</u> other than *itself*. **This is KEY to understanding all conflict among humanity for thousands of years.** This is a key to the evolution of the physical human, and humanity itself, as the inner Self/soul/ personality consciousness must evolve the inner Self before true evolution is reflected outward and ex-pressed into the physical changes you desire to see in the world.

To BE the change you desire to see and experience in the world, humanity must eternally begin within, which then reflects outward as the physical changes you desire to see and experience. And you can direct that inner change and shift by using the rational mind to make choices of free will, to pursue the path of inner development upon which all evolution occurs. Even your technological advancements do not occur without first being contemplated within the minds and consciousness of those that "invent" them. The ideas came from beyond their brain and were brought to the awareness of their brain and intellect, whereby they took inspired actions to develop the technology. Yet technology can evolve in ways that are non-beneficial if the inner *beings* of humans do not evolve in such ways that they do not even contemplate using such technologies for dominion over humanity or the planet.

If the human identifies itself as only the physical human and does not understand its true nature within - that which gives its life animation and existence on the physical plane and beyond - then you see greater potential for seeking dominion over others.

If on the other hand, humanity comes to identify its TRUE self as being eternally connected to all other humans, animals, nature, and beyond, then the desire to assert dominion over others naturally dissolves. The darkness if you will, gives way to the light. Illumination of the truth of your *being* within brings light to what once appeared to be darkness (lack of light/truth).

Consciousness does not seek dominion over any other form or species and seeks to eternally develop <u>itself</u> into becoming, in every possible way that it can. **It is the rational mind of mankind that seeks control over others.** This is the portion of yourselves that is associated with the brain, the thinking mechanism of the intellect, that typically has visibility and its perception based within a false belief that it is separate from other human *beings* and nature.

Now, I capitalize these words to have stout meaning for these truths are important to unlock the very tools, the dormant, latent potential within your own consciousness. You can limit yourself, or you shall know your truth and your TRUTH will make you (realize) that you are FREE.

Therefore, as human *beings* advance in their evolution of the inner self, the evolution of the natural *being*/soul/consciousness that they are, they naturally become acutely and inescapably aware of the truth that *they are actually a portion of everything they see around them, at the layer of consciousness*, which provides their very existence. In so doing, to harm another would be to harm oneself.

Now, to you Jackson my friend, I bid you a relaxing evening and thank you so kindly for your loving words and intentions. They are well received by All here in nonphysical reality and I am grateful to be working with yet another excellent channel in *your* historic period of time, as we have done so successfully in so many others, you and I. Good evening - Seth

P.S. I may occasionally give you very long "run-on" sentences and break the normally accepted rules of grammar; however, I assure you it is challenging enough to write a book as a nonphysical entity, coming into and through a channel, that describes the nature of consciousness and how it is non-linear, Omnipresent, does not conform, nor is limited by time nor space...and present it in a book with punctuation and grammar that follows the indoctrinated, acceptable way of writing. I might say: I write outside the box. From outside the universe even. I, therefore, reserve that right. (Smile)

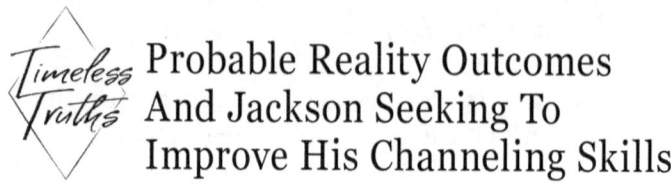

Probable Reality Outcomes And Jackson Seeking To Improve His Channeling Skills

[Notation from Jackson: As I prepared for my session with Seth one day, I asked how I can strengthen, clarify, and widen my connection to him as an entity and to all entities of love and light. While his response was to me personally, I have decided to share it with all, knowing that many around the world are asking the same kind of questions. How can we improve our communication and connection to the Divine? Many, when embarking upon that path of choice, are then challenged a great deal by how to overcome the "Rational Mind" or intellect, and how to become a very good psychic-medium-channel. I hope my sharing this personal piece helps frame the process for others who follow and endeavor to become Divine channels themselves. We are all leading different lives and schedules, so be gentle with yourself, love yourself through it as the Divine does, and remember diligent practice will in time build your success, but you must stay with it. Even when challenged by a busy schedule or distractions.]

As we have stated before, the more you channel, the "wider" and more defined your clairaudience becomes in your own consciousness, and the more information that will come to you in regular and ad-hoc sessions where you simply desire guidance or have a question. So it is with practice in any skill; in physical terms, and even in nonphysical terms, one must practice regularly if they are to achieve greater skills and success with those skills. Even entities such as myself, and yourself on a larger scale here, must practice at teaching and conveying truths and various data in nonphysical dimensions so that we are able to grow, expand, and become, eternally. This is the nature of consciousness to do so; and it is through intentional practice and actions, commitment to excellence in your endeavor, physical or not, that "widens" the pathways or channels that will over time, become highways rather than simple pathways.

As we have guided before, do not dismay that you cannot at every sitting and session, get 2-3 hours in with our work. It will come. In time, you will have that opportunity. For now, you are doing exceedingly well at managing all the things that are on your plate. Hence our message recently about balance. Balancing our spiritual work for the world, your spiritual work for the Self, work for your day-job, work on our other companies, home life, outdoor time to rejuvenate the soul, etc. Balance is key to long-term success as you cannot stray too far down one road without neglecting the others...and you, my friend, have an exceedingly busy schedule. Far beyond anything that Jane managed for any length of time.

However, _our mission now has grown exponentially in scope and focus, impact intended, and the framework in which to deliver our mission._ As with any endeavor that you are growing over time, one builds a foundation upon which the rest will come. With Ruburt, we covered many, many subjects over the years of our works and we provided a foundation for what is now becoming the next phase of my mission, our mission, the Seth Christ mission, and intentions for humanity, nature, Earth, and your universe. The evolution of humanity is within the evolution of the works that have, for myself, spanned millions of years of your historical time.

We once built the foundation of my books thousands of years ago, in your perception of time. Now we continue to build upon that foundation and carry forth the works of bringing more love, more light, and more timeless truths to humanity to engage them in the next major transformation for evolution. _So it is that my works, our works, also evolve over time._ You were born for this mission. You incarnated with the major probable path to embark upon this mission. You know that now. Like Ruburt and Joseph (Jane and Rob) you wanted the discovery of new material to insert into the world. You wanted to discover it for yourself, in such a way that it would not remain private but would become public so as to impact the greater humanity of which you are now incarnated within.

However, you, like all consciousness and "souls" that incarnate into human form, have free will and you yourself had to _CHOOSE_ this path - Our mission. In the historical time when I authored my books and materials through Ruburt, this and other books you and I are now creating, were but one of many, many future probable outcomes. Again, FROM her perspective in historical

27

time, as she was writing the books, there are probable futures where she only wrote 2 books. There are others in which she did not publish any books at all, and the paths did not follow the one you know where the books did occur. Still, other probable futures from that point had seen more books written. There are no limitations on the probable outcomes of any given event.

So it is that her future which you are in now in 2022, from her perspective in time and space back in 1970 say, *is only **one** of many future probable outcomes/futures*. Again, there are probable outcomes right now that are "parallel" to the one you are living in that you did not connect with me on the level you are now. Outcomes where we created no books; and those where we published many. In larger terms, to you, in your present state of consciousness, in your life you now are focused on where you are named Jackson, our books are already written and published. I see the future path at this very moment in which many of our books have touched millions of lives around the world, and the light of God's truths grows exponentially.

I can, for example, follow by association from choice to choice, action to action, the probable path where many of our books are published in your future. And many variations of that future from the current point in time in which you are now focused - the year you perceive to be 2022.

From your standpoint now in 2022, you have a choice as to which of those future probable outcomes that you desire to achieve; and by the focus of your attention, actions, thoughts, and beliefs, you will draw out of the many possibilities/probabilities but one probable future that comes streaming together into your now-moment focus. That becomes the life experience that you know and the past that seems to fade into the distance behind you in time.

Now, I want our readers to pay special attention to the information here above about probable pasts and probable futures – probabilities that come into focus and those that do not, based upon your individual thoughts, actions, emotions, beliefs and all the things we are now, and will in future books, teach that form and shape your physical reality. For the information just given above, about probable future outcomes, and "parallel" probable realities, will indeed come up and be explained in detail in one of our future books. It is important that humanity understands the truth behind probable systems, events, and outcomes, as this is PRECISELY what is right now in this very moment, shaping what you will experience tomorrow, and next week, next month and so on. Individually and *en masse.* Once you understand, to a deeper degree, probable reality outcomes, paths to get "there" and achieve "that", it will, in time, allow each of you to master more powerfully, your own creative energies and direct your own consciousness into setting up the "trigger events" and foundations that will grow in consciousness, as seeds, and become your future physical realities. For yourselves, your culture and society, your nature, your planet, your evolution of Self and all things in your universe. This information IS then, YOUR truths about YOUR power of creativity and we will circle back to this in some of the most profound *"Seth materials"* and *Timeless Truths* yet to be revealed to humanity. However – they will not make sense and you will not be able to utilize these new perceptions, if you do not at first understand the basic nature of yourselves as beings of consciousness, easily capable of such things.

You do not use your massively creative power and energy to direct your consciousness in the most profound of ways as yet today, mostly because many are A) not aware that they have them and B) do not then know how to maximize their use, intentionally, purposefully, efficiently, effectively, and consistently.

Stay with us....you will get there. For that is MY and OUR intentions for your evolution. Illuminated by our *Timeless Truths.*

So it is that you must be open to any and all material I give to you, (both Jackson and our readers) for reasons you may or may not understand if you are to open your minds to our work to experience the most conducive free-flow of expressions possible. Some material will be repeated for the purposes of ensuring that it is "burned" into the minds and memories of those that need repetition to retain the knowledge and truths. Some do not need much repetition in learning. Some do. This book, like all of my books, is meant to reach as many people as possible, with all manners of learning. Some learn more visually, and some do not. Some like to listen to audio books in your day and age of media and technology. We all must be open-minded then if we are to be in the flow of all energy consciousness and allow it to flow without restriction or shadowing. The light, the truths, are not simply structured in a linear fashion, written down in any book, including our books, nor the Bible, nor the Koran so that you can read them A-Z, 1-21, etc.

If mankind endeavors to evolve vastly beyond where it has been in terms of historical successes and failures, and to move from "darkness to light", then humanity must begin to truly understand that existence is not linear. Time is not linear as there is no time...there only appears to be as your physical reality passes before your eyes in the eternal evolution of Now Moments. Space is not linear. Understanding this unlocks the potential for moving through space dimensions in ways you have not presently discovered - Portals, as it is often called at the time of this writing. Truths are not linear. To understand that all consciousness pervades time and space in all directions, in many time periods and versions of reality, simultaneously, in the eternal Now Moment - The present instant in which life seems to filter through as it becomes present moment awareness.

Many books have been written about the power of being present in the moment, as that is where life is constantly becoming and evolving. You now are a channel for that evolution. You are a spark within the dark. A light to illumine the paths of many. You are meant to be the spark of illumination for many. To cause a shift in their own thoughts and awareness to understand the immense power that they themselves are already. I say this to Jackson-Thomas here; however, it obviously applies as well to every human-being that is living in the physical universe. You have the potential to be that Divine channel. However, YOU must choose to pursue it and foster its expansion and growth.

We plant seeds that grow within the consciousness of humanity. Individually, and as a species. In knowing Self, they will come to know the Self that extends beyond the boundaries of the skin, beyond space and time - that is the "God" Self within that creates worlds and beyond. I assure you, one cannot know how they fit into the world around them if they do not fully understand the Self that they are. For in understanding the Self that they are, they will then understand those that are around them.

The evolution of consciousness is eternal and inevitable. Physical humans cannot, in any way, shape, or form, stop the evolution of humanity. It may take a few hundred or a few thousand years; it can take many paths with many probable outcomes. Yet the very consciousness of I AM, the God-Self and immortal *being* that is within the human-*being's* flesh, is what seeks to evolve. Your soul/inner self/*being*/consciousness is a portion of "God"/ All That Is. Hence, regardless of the choices of the rational mind and its seeking dominion and power over others on the Earth, in time, that will dissolve. For the men and women who promote such dominion will, in time, pass away; and the consciousness of those who are born in terms of history that will replace them, being evolved more so than those before, will fit into the landscape of time and space within your dimensions of reality to provide the evolution of the species. *(Jackson Comment: Wow!!!)*

This *IS* evolution and it *IS* inevitable. Humanity can delay, slow down, or speed up its evolution by the free-will choices that individuals and societies around the world take. The question becomes then, which path will you take from this moment forward? Now to Jackson-Thomas: More practice in channeling then creates more materials coming through, which will, in turn, create the space where you have more time to receive more materials. This would be, of course, true for all who endeavor to develop the inner self. You may desire to share this material with our readers, for challenges that you have faced in your journey, help others face their own challenges to succeed in overcoming them as you have.

Again, as I have mentioned prior, the publication of our book will mark a very important "milestone" in nonphysical reality becoming physical - An energetic turning point, not just for you personally, but for the world and the greater society in which you are now focused. It is what we call a **Trigger Event**, meaning that it is _intended_ to be expressed into physical terms and there are many probable realities that extend outward from this event....the publishing of our first physical book together. Until the time that it becomes physically published, it is of course just a _probable_ event that could happen, but may or may not, based upon your personal free will and choice decisions on what you move forward on the physical plane.

However, once this occurs physically, it activates a whole new series of probable realities that advance down a particular path of evolution for your humanity and your planet. **Very good** probable outcomes in many ways. In larger terms, these exist now; however, they are indeed probable at this very moment.

The world does not notice
what you _intend_ to do.
The world notices
what you have done.

As I've mentioned before when it comes to creative physical expression, each action you take on the physical plane in the intention and goal of a particular outcome, in this case, and the entire series of Timeless Truth books, videos, and learning materials in the many forms we intend to express physically, you add great energy into the "SPECIFIC SET" if you will, of probable outcomes in a particular direction for evolution to occur. This case being that many, many people across your planet will receive the life-changing information from our books, which shifts their personal frequencies, which changes beliefs and perceptions of reality, which then creates outcomes that express in terms of a much more "advanced", evolved, _naturally open, and connective experience_ in higher vibrations on your planet.

Jackson W. Moore

Creatively speaking, as far as manifestation goes and the production of physical reality, this is the path that all things take in the development of their expression. I am simply explaining this using our book production and publication as a prime example of how steps down a particular path add "layers" of energy to various "sets" or perhaps "ranges" of probable outcomes that then become the selection field from which they will narrow down into one seemingly smooth line that becomes your "future" Now Moment, or the present moment in which you find yourselves down the road in time.

Timeless Truths Intentions *Direct* Consciousness And Infuse It With The Intents Of The Creator (YOU)

Now: As I have stated, you need not worry about the materials being "in perfect order" as really, there is no linear order for the materials. Nor is there a once-and-done approach that should be taken to key concepts that we certainly want to stress in our materials and book. I would state with a lot of truth that most people do not see something ONCE and learn every angle and depth of that subject and never have to see it presented to them again to increase their <u>depth</u> of understanding. Our materials and timeless truths are the same. It is repeated exposure to the rational mind/intellect where you are then able to train the mind to accept the truths more and more behind the very nature of reality in which it is focused. Since we first began communicating and people around the world found out that Seth who authored all the *Seth books* was working through you now to create more truths for the world, you have had many of them tell you that some of the *Seth books* materials were so profound or new to them, that they had to read certain paragraphs two or three times before they truly understood the depth of meaning behind the materials. Case in point why many people read books several times and receive "new" insights and wisdom of understanding with each successive reading. It is simply a method that has worked for humans since before the time of the caveman.

Again, the human brain and intellect utilize the 5-human senses as their method of understanding physical reality. The rational thinking, questioning, judging mind, seeks to frame its physical experience in terms it can understand...not realizing, of course, that the very thing that gives it its own existence and awareness (that which makes up the matter of the brain itself) is indeed created by the nonphysical consciousness. It is a constant training method for many, and one of the greatest challenges of your culture and society today - as they have <u>over the centuries, migrated *away* from the spiritual practices</u> that many years ago kept mankind in touch with the nature in which it held its existence. Technology then, has the tendency to keep one focused on the physical plane. While this focus does serve to move technology and, to a point, humanity forward on that level, it has the tendency to remove the attention from the natural inner self and give way to focusing on the physical reality without much regard to the potentials, tools, and inner senses from which all is constructed.

We have many more "filler sessions" whereby, as we move through the book to organize the pieces of materials from individual sessions, we will of course, add content and context, meaning, and depth to them, for this is the process for us to complete this particular book. We will take other more "linear" routes for our books in the future; however, again, **we are moving slowly away from "linear" reality to operating in the awareness of a simultaneous experience in which your present thoughts, beliefs, rate of vibration, etc., directly impact your <u>Perception Filter</u> through which the rational mind understands its reality, and hence, forms beliefs, thoughts, and emotions which fuel the creation of the physical reality in which you reside.**

One of the key teachings that lay behind the purposes of the book is to stress the truth that time and space do not exist, and that the linear unfoldment of reality each day is simply a single Now Moment that changes ever so slightly so as to go unnoticed as if you are flipping the pages of pencil drawn characters which are all stationary, but modified just slightly so that when you thumb through them quickly, the stationary image <u>appears</u> to be walking or moving. Early motion-picture cartoons were made this way and appeared to be moving as one page flipped to the next and the drawing was ever-so-slightly altered to give the appearance of movement. Your 5-human physical senses are simply not fast enough to track the changes that shift that fast. You do not perceive the fractions of a second in time that it takes for an impulse to leap the synapses and travel the portions of a nerve so as to provide a stimulus-response from the body to the brain, to make judgments about the physical environment that the body is in. Your "Now Moments" jump past the physical senses so quickly that your senses do not see the gaps that are, in reality, between such moments. Almost as if your awareness of them would be blinking on and off, in physical reality and not. Yet they occur so quickly that you do not perceive the shifts with the physical senses, which provides you with a smooth-appearing overall picture of your physical environment for navigational purposes.

Now, if your true reality is not linear as it appears to be to the physical senses, why then, would we want to create our book to teach about the nature of consciousness being non-linear, and present it in a very linear fashion? That would not be "practicing what we preach" or teach, so to speak. So it is that we (you and I now) have accepted this challenge of putting the book together in the method that we have so that we can demonstrate rather "case in point" the application of that which we teach about - non-linear time and reality.

While this has brought a highly challenging creative expression project to the forefront of your project plate, it is indeed accomplishing our goal; and what is most important in this construction method is that not only is it physically constructed this way, but the *intentions* of it teaching the truths of non-linear time and space, are *embedded* within the words, the letters or symbols that make up every word, paragraph, and page.

Meaning our book is, in a way, the physical representation of the meaning that we are seeking to convey, within the words and paragraphs themselves; as they were written and put together in the state of consciousness that holds the intention of teaching non-linear time and space.

Therefore, while any given paragraph in our book may not specifically be talking about non-linear time and space, it is indeed the "premise" and inflection of consciousness that is within the text, as *it was created within that framework of intention.*

Now...this is a "case in point" example of how *intentions* are a very important directionally creative tool that is used to shape energy into physical forms from the inside out so that the physical forms are created in a particular consciousness (vibrational framework or state of consciousness) to convey the meaning that they represent.

> ***Intentions then, are a way to
> connect certain probable outcomes
> to a given directive use of energy
> for the purposes of creation.***

This does not just apply to the world of physical matter, but also to the nonphysical dimensions as *beings* of consciousness can "shape" their creations through a layer of intention that is embedded within the energy that they direct into any particular creation.

Those who are in tune with their inner self might say something like a particular friend's house or property or area where they visit, camp, hike or what have you, "has good vibes" to it. They are sensing at the layer of their own consciousness, the *intentions* in which a home or patio or area was built or is commonly used, constructed by the humans that created them and use them, or the natural environment in which all nature is created. They are sensing the "vibes" through their consciousness. Their clairabilities.

> ***Intentions then, set a "tone" or a "feeling
> tone" that then pervades a creation,
> physical or not, and can be sensed quite
> clearly by those who are in touch with
> their natural selves - their traits and
> characteristics of consciousness.***

Many who are in tune with the inner spiritual self will immediately connect with what I am saying here as it is like déjà vu whereby they recognize this has happened to them many times; and as that awareness comes to their mind from the inner *being*, it comes to them via their own consciousness, hence... is sensed as a "direct-knowing" of immediate awareness of the subject matter here.

Notes and Quotes

_____

_____

_____

_____

_____

_____

_____

_____

_____

_____

_____

_____

_____

_____

_____

_____

_____

_____

_____

_____

_____

_____

Section 2:

Consciousness And
The Human Being

Natural Innate Attributes And Characteristics Of ALL Human Consciousness

We are learning to expand the Identity of your <u>Self</u>, beyond the Human flesh. This...is where your true magic as a creative being eternally exists and awaits your awareness of it and directed use to create your world anew.

We are learning here to expand the identity of the self that each reader knows to be themselves. You think of yourself perhaps as only the human male or female that you see in the reflection of the mirror - a physical human with a name and that this is who and what you are.

We are now moving beyond that limited perception of yourself and expanding the identification of yourself. To shift your identification to be more associated with the immortal being within you so that you are able to understand the true unlimited creative nature of the real you that is within the human flesh you see in your reflection.

HUMAN	BEING
PHYSICAL HUMAN BODY	

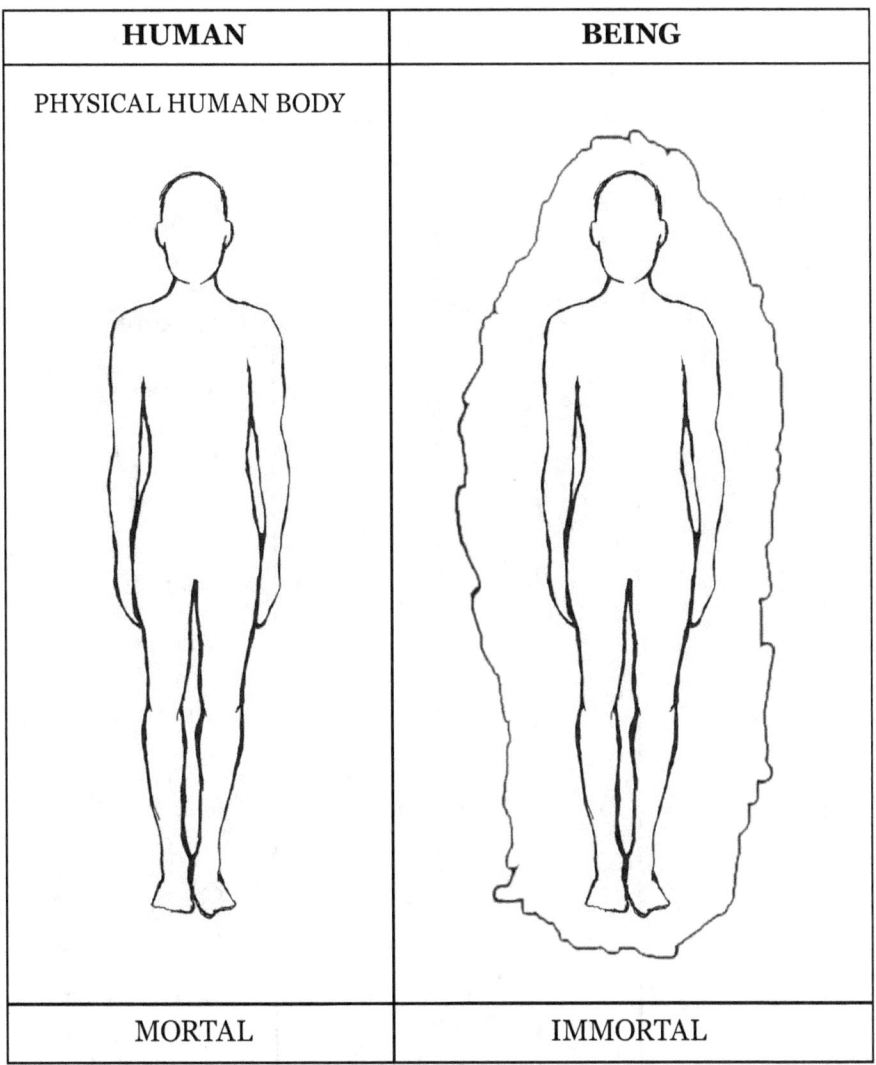

MORTAL	IMMORTAL

Your human mortal body has a "name" you call yourself because you <u>appear</u> to be separated from all other physical objects.

Your immortal being/soul within does <u>not</u> have a name as it is NOT separated from all other consciousness, including the consciousness that is the "fabric" of the other solid-appearing objects in your 3-dimensional world.

Natural Innate Attributes And Characteristics
Of ALL Human Consciousness

Synonymous Names For Consciousness		Innate Inseparable Natural Attributes/ Characteristics Of Human Consciousness
Soul		
Being		Clairvoyance (Clear Seeing)
Personality Consciousness		Clairaudience (Clear Hearing)
The "I AM"		
Christ		Claircognizance (Clear Knowing or Direct Knowing)
Lord		
Christ Consciousness		Clairempathy (Clear Emotional Feeling)
The "Father"		Clairgustance (Clear Tasting)
God Self		
Source		Clairentience (Clear Physical Feeling)
Creator Self		Clairsalience (Clear Smelling)
Some Names For Your Inner Self	Eternally Exists Outside Space & Time	Your Natural Communication Tools

Human	Being
Mortal	**Immortal (I AM)**
Jackson	Thomas Consciousness
Jane	Ruburt Consciousness
Robert	Joseph Consciousness
Yeshua/Emmanuel	Christ Consciousness
What you *think* you are	What you **REALLY** are
Exists in this lifetime context only	Existed before this lifetime, after this lifetime, and is active in many other lifetimes, dimensions, and realities than you are aware of at the brain/intellect's level
Rational/Intellectual Mind - **Focused in this lifetime's physical reality ONLY**	Able to focus into many lifetimes, dimensions, access unlimited knowledge, wisdom, insight, etc.
Limited to 5-human senses orientation And perspective	Unlimited And Infinite Potential
Seems And Appears to be **Disconnected** from other objects in 3-D	Eternally connected to ALL consciousness within ALL physical objects, Earth, nature, universe
Uses 5-human senses and rational mind orientation, perspective, limited at best, like a key-hole sized view and hence, perception of physical reality	Uses telepathy, telekinesis, intuition, sensing, All clairabilities: clairvoyance, clairsentience, clairaudience, claircognizance, clairgustance, clairolfactory, clairkinesthesia, gestalt consciousness, unlimited dimensions of knowledge, wisdom, ideas, inventions, solutions, ways, means, direct-knowing, etc. - NATURAL TO ALL HUMAN CONSCIOUSNESS And ETERNALLY WHAT YOU ARE within

Human	Being
Mortal	**Immortal (I AM)**
Orientation to viewing and interacting with all things in life/physical reality	Orientation to viewing and interacting with all humanity, Earth, nature, animals, etc. - We seek to view and interact with all things in life - to see and view life **FROM** THIS PERSPECTIVE And ORIENTATION
Lower Vibrational Frequencies	Higher Vibrational Frequencies
Limited Idea of Yourself	Your TRUE self
Doubt, Fear, Anxiety caused by misidentification of your true self	Pure, undiluted CONFIDENCE, know no fear, not anxious but relaxed in peace caused by identification of true self
Limited Experiences in Life	Pure, Undiluted Love, Light, Joy, Peace, Excitement, Compassion, Empathy, Passion, Exuberance
	Source of All Knowledge, All Ideas, All Inventions, All Evolutionary Creations, etc.
	Source of all of the greatest book content, ideas, movies, etc. of the world's greatest authors, movie directors, painters, poets, technology, and all creative works
	Pure Divine Health that not only creates the physical flesh body, but can heal it in all ways also as easily - Source Where Reiki healing energy is drawn from as its connected to All That Is (God)

Human	*Being*
Mortal	**Immortal (I AM)**
	Is your natural communication mechanisms and tools for humans to communicate with other humans, animals, trees, plants, oceans, Earth, etc.
	I AM THE WAY I AM THE LIGHT I AM THE TRUTH I AM ALL SOLUTIONS I AM ALL WISDOM I AM ALL HEALTH I AM ALL WEALTH I AM ALL LOVE I AM FREE ETERNALLY I AM INFINITE WISDOM

Now, in regards to ALL characteristics and attributes of consciousness listed in the right column of our chart, YOU ARE these and have them within you right now in this very instant. Our goal is to bring them to the forefront of your awareness so that they pervade through the flesh and outward into physical reality as you use them to interact co-creatively with all other consciousness to form your physical reality with intention and purpose.

From our chart here, then you can see that the HUMAN physical side is quite limited in its resources and abilities.

Whereas the *BEING* side is truly infinite in all things possible within your physical dimension. Some of our goals then for this book are:

◊ Bring to your attention that if you are a human-*being*, that you possess ALL of this infinite potential within you NOW.

◊ Bring these innate potentials and tools you have to

the forefront of your <u>intellect's awareness</u> so that it learns to readily accept such data sources for input, guidance, and the source from which it can create your physical reality and life in ways you desire and avoid those you do not.

We want to begin to <u>shift your awareness of this inner Self </u>so that you can bring it into your daily life, and from moment to moment, use it to create experiences and a physical environment you love and are excited about. Experiences of wonder and joy.

The next step then is for you to begin living your life, _FROM_ this inner orientation and perspective to <u>maximize your potential</u> as a creative _being_ to express yourself and your infinite capabilities transformed into physical reality.

<u>You</u>, first and foremost, are a _being_ of consciousness. An eternally learning, growing, expanding, conscious _being_ that has as a part of its selfness, a personality that is also grown, changed, expanded, and developed when in the human physical flesh embodiment.

Before you were conscious of being human, you were first conscious of being.

You have come into the physical flesh from an eternal environment of consciousness, inseparable from yourself, yet have narrowed your focus of consciousness for the purposes of successfully navigating your physical universe and environment. You have chosen this learning experience and hence, chosen to incarnate into the human form so that you may interact with all other forms of physical matter that you perceive as your Earth, universe, and all objects within it. Throughout these interactions during your physical life, you learn and grow through each and every interaction - throughout <u>every moment </u>of your life. ALL interactions. Interactions with humans, animals, plants, Earth, oceans, water, air, and all elements that you perceive with your 5 human physically-oriented senses.

The basis of yourself as a _being_, your self-awareness, is what many refer to as your "I AM". The identity and awareness of your Self. The _<u>you</u>_ that is fully lucid, aware, conscious, and exists before your birth into a human baby form, and exists completely, fully lucid and aware, beyond what you perceive as physical death - when the human flesh body ceases to function and your consciousness resumes its focus from outside the human body. When the physical death of the flesh organism occurs, you are once again fully aware that you are an intimately, eternally connected part of ALL consciousness that many refer to as "God" and that which we refer to as *All That Is*.

From the perspective of the personality consciousness or what you may think of as your soul, and from the perspective of the larger entity of consciousness from which your personality and consciousness are derived; all learning is valid, unique, and grows yourself, your entity and hence all consciousness of "God" or All That Is. Time as you perceive it on the physical plane of 3-dimensional reality truly does not exist. It is only a phenomenon that <u>appears</u> linear with one eternal "Now Moment" changing ever so slightly to bring about a new reality that you then perceive as linear life existence. *You only ever perceive with your physical senses, the Now Moment that is your current present moment awareness.*

The 5-human senses are used by the human flesh body to detect and navigate your physically appearing environment. The flesh is physical as is the environment in which it manifests itself into material form. They both operate at lower vibrational rates of frequency; hence the 5 senses are the navigational operating system for the human body.

Remember: Consciousness forms itself into the electrons, protons and nucleus, etc. of the atom. Atoms accumulated together give you atomic mass, or solid-appearing objects. However, they are vibrantly alive with consciousness that makes up their atomic mass. To become visible to the 5-human faculty of vision, they must SLOW DOWN in vibrational frequency, the rate at which they vibrate, for them to become visible. Otherwise they would vibrate so fast that your human vision would not see them at all. Therefore, ALL physical matter consists of lower vibrational frequencies, and it is only within this lower vibrational range that your 5-human senses can detect (and navigate) physical reality.

The 6th senses, including all your clairabilities, operate at a rate of vibration that is beyond the detection of the 5-human senses. Therefore, to perceive, understand and utilize infinite realities outside of the range of the 5-human senses, you must learn to grow, expand and USE your inner senses...your consciousness and its abilities, to expand your understanding, and ACCESS the tools, knowledge, wisdom, inventions, ideas, and so forth that you can then use within physical reality to construct it.

This portion of you, the *"Being"* portion of you as a Human-*Being*, vibrates at and operates eternally within the nonphysical realm of consciousness that provides the basis for the physical forms of the reality your human self perceives and interacts with.

You do not perceive, for example, a moment ago or a moment from now, with your 5-human senses. You remember the previous moments and store them in memory as a linear movie-like memory of what has passed by your 5 senses which have painted the motion picture of your life, yet you can only ever perceive the one present moment, physically speaking.

Your narrowed focus does <u>not</u> physically see the many probable "past" moments or probable "future" moments. Your consciousness <u>does</u> have access to these probable future moments and probable pasts, however, they are not physically perceivable from your narrowed focus. If they were, you would be seeing multiple dimensions of time-space at once and hence the bleed-throughs are often more than one can process with your rational mind (which sometimes surfaces in "crazy people" when they <u>**do**</u> perceive such probable events of the past and future).

They may be called crazy, when in reality their consciousness is fully able to perceive the probable events outside of time as normal; and the rational mind understands at these times that there is a greater reality around it - even if it can't readily organize all the past and future probabilities into a linear context that makes sense to the rational mind/intellect.

It is not that they are "crazy"; perhaps, however, seeing multiple dimensions and probable realities would very much confuse the rational mind and intellect, as it normally uses the 5-human senses to understand its reality, and it simply cannot make sense of multiple dimensions without first understanding them. Again, one of the purposes of *The Nature Of Consciousness* is to help you understand them so that you can begin to perceive them, make sense of them, and use them to draw information and experience, tools, and abilities to enhance your present physical reality (which will also improve your other Selves' experiences in those other dimensions, as you are again, intimately connected to and operating within them also...simultaneously.) Therefore, sometimes, they are not crazy per se, it is that the veil between physical reality and nonphysical realities has thinned and they are mixing portions and perceptions of both, in a picture of reality that simply does not make sense to their rational minds, or to the doctors and therapists they may be working with to make sense of their challenges.

Now, one of the most well-known examples here that millions of our readers will identify with is what happens when a loved one is close to physical death. Their consciousness opens and expands to perceive other loved ones that have already been physically dead, animals once alive, Angels, and other *beings* of light. Family members may think they're losing it; however, they are indeed very much lucid and more so than the family who does not see or perceive these things.

It is that their rational/intellectual mind then is not as active, and pauses its judging and filtering its perceptions of reality to ALLOW the consciousness to present the nonphysical reality that is around you eternally, yet to others is not seen. They are then, very validly perceiving real nonphysical *beings*/souls/consciousness with their own, and the rational mind then allows it into their field of perception and awareness. Of course, we tell you this because you can attain this wider perception of reality and nonphysical reality throughout your life and not just at the end of your physical incarnation experience. This is another goal of our books....to help our beloved readers around the world to become vividly aware of this part of themselves, and to cultivate it, develop it, expand it, and experience more; and to use their connections and wider perceptions to improve their lives and society in which you exist.

Now, we will get into the time phenomenon later in our works; however, given this truth, you can begin to understand that there is no beginning of time or of your universe, and there will never, ever in all eternity be an "end" of your Earth or universe. They are consciousness, and consciousness cannot "end" or be destroyed, eliminated, erased, etc. YOU may end as a physical life experienced - as all physical life moves through its natural cycles - however, your Earth and universe will eternally exist. It can be destroyed in certain terms and misused, or it can be loved and nurtured, which is the intended path of evolution for your planet - again, a harmonious co-creative world in which you quite literally sense the living plants and animals and "communicate" with them to co-create a world of peace and abundance, light and understanding, and living in a greater cooperative manner than you do now.

Humans will communicate with animals and the environment intentionally to create certain improved outcomes in their relationships, and animals and the Earth will "communicate" with humans – via consciousness. So that needs, love, and creation occur on a natural path, vastly beyond the one you've known for thousands of years in your terms of history.

This learning of your Self then is an eternal process that is innate to all forms and species of consciousness that has, in your terms of historical time, ALWAYS existed and always will. You are a part of All That Is consciousness ("God" by whatever name you choose as ALL names are God's name), and as such, you are eternally learning, growing, and expanding "God" as you expand your Self.

"You", your consciousness, learns both while focused inside the human flesh body, looking outward during your physical lifetime, and, while "outside" the physical body focused into other realms and dimensions of nonphysical reality in which you are also quite actively engaged. (Dreams, for example, are common examples of focus into nonphysical dimensions that are not linear in nature yet can have physical appearances of life-glimpses that you see in other dimensions that are quite valid as the one you know.)

Your consciousness can also see quite clearly into other infinite physical dimensions in which it is able to "peer" or "look" into and perceive. Dream images that appear to you during sleeping dreams or daydreams are quite valid examples of your natural ability as consciousness, to clairvoyantly "see" into other dimensions of reality that are not within a physical context yet may appear in other physical lifetime contexts such as in "Reincarnational" lifetimes.

> *The window through which you may perceive other Reincarnational lifetimes is through consciousness, for it is through consciousness that you are indeed, right now, connected to them in other dimensions of reality that would appear to you in <u>that</u> dimension as another time period of human history.*
>
> *Expanding your consciousness then, will begin to open those windows through which you may perceive other lifetimes and in so doing, feel the love and compassion and sense in ways not yet in your awareness, the soul lessons learned in those lifetimes so that you may make use of them in this lifetime. Improving the vibrational frequencies of one lifetime then, can and does, to a degree, improve them all.*

Your consciousness, then, is highly active and engaged in other dimensions of reality at all moments of eternity. Meaning then, that it is highly connected, engaged, learning, and interacting with other consciousness all around you and this occurs both during your sleep state and it's just as active when you are in your waking state. You may be focused on writing a sentence or driving a car or some other physical activity, yet your consciousness is not bound to only the flesh body and is interacting with other species of consciousness, even though your perception and focus are narrowed for the purposes of successful navigation within your 3-dimensional realm. Again, while your consciousness can be active in infinite directions and in many dimensions, your physically-oriented focus must be narrowed to your 3-dimensional reality or you would find yourself perhaps being all over the place, perhaps crazy, as you openly perceived multiple dimensions simultaneously.

In either state then, sleeping or waking/walking around, your consciousness is not confined within the flesh of your physical self/

body, but rather it is always much "larger" than your physical self, engaged with the *entire* environment around you. As I have stated before, at ALL TIMES, all portions of your body, your skin, and all physical components of your body, are indeed actively engaged in sensing all things in your environment around you. Relaying data about the environment so that the physical body mechanism can navigate your environment without a conscious thought as to how to proceed. You are simply not aware of the fact that every skin cell or internal cell is interacting with your environment, again because your focus is narrowed to the task at hand. Therefore that communication goes unnoticed as does the larger portion of all interaction between your Self and your environment.

Telepathically, and through all of your *natural senses*, or what you think of as your 6th senses, your clairabilities, as we will herein call them, you are in constant communication with your environment, creating it both personally for your own experience, and *en masse* for the relationships around you, the people around you, from your home, family, neighborhood, city, society, culture and world. We explained much of this in our book *The Individual and The Nature of Mass Events*.

In each physical lifetime, you are in the process of learning your heritage, your origin, and your natural connection to All That Is. Physical challenges in physical life serve as an impetus to eventually draw your awareness inward to once again remember the *being* that you are as a Human-*Being*, and that the *being* portion of you is also inseparably connected to All That Is. Therefore, you are able to draw from this infinite Source consciously and intentionally, all things necessary to overcome such challenges.

The nonphysical *being* part of you that you think of as your soul, is fully, intimately, and eternally aware of this. Your brain and mind that serve you in navigating your physical environment, although primarily focused on the physical environment and only on what its 5-human senses can detect as 3-dimensions of reality, is in the process of opening up, awakening, and becoming aware of the greater reality from which your very existence and that which you perceive as your universe is created *from* and in. Consciousness.

Your mind and the brain have many tools and characteristics

that assist you in making choices and decisions as a *physical being*, in successfully navigating and surviving in your *physical* environment. This helps to keep your flesh body from injury and assists in your bodily function.

To evolve as a *being* of consciousness, you must first become aware of what you **REALLY are**. Blessed with the knowledge of the truth of what you really are as an eternal *being* of consciousness, and how you have come to reside in the human bodily flesh, you are then able to understand your meaning and purpose within physical life. Why you exist in the physical universe as a human-*being*. The purpose of your journey into expanded, evolved consciousness as a part of all consciousness. For those who have asked in life; "Why am I here?"... this is the process of learning your own unique answers to that question and of the true value that you bring to the greater whole in which you participate and exist.

> *The immortal soul, or **being** portion of you is eternally **Divine** in the nature of its existence. As this being portion of you is what literally creates the flesh human body, this means that **ALL human bodies are Divine in their nature**. Respect this truth with compassion and celebrate the unique differences between human appearances as they are the infinite expressions of the paintings of "God", expressed into the Divine artwork you call humanity.*

You cannot escape your evolution, as it is the evolution of what you think of as "God" that is the very fabric of every physical cell of your flesh, the blood that flows through your veins, and the very life force that provides the physical flesh its life animation to walk the Earth. This is your journey. Yet in other terms, it is also "God's journey", as you are a portion of that eternal consciousness by all names. You are eternally becoming more. Through many, many incarnations into human forms of flesh, both male and female-oriented during your physical existences, you learn about all aspects, angles, and various natures of your existence. You, as a conscious *being*, grow "yourself" as well as the entity from which you are derived, and the greater consciousness beyond that, and beyond that, and into dimensions of reality that do not even have a physical context. You, and each individual to ever have incarnated into human form, plays an integral role in the eternal process of evolution of consciousness of which you are a part. You play an integral role in the evolution of yourself and of your species of human consciousness.

Although you may choose to ignore the awareness of your journey and path, you will learn and evolve anyway. Just in different terms and context of physical expressions than you may have otherwise. The choice is, of course, yours as an individual as it is your journey and no other's. You may take a different path, yet each path is valid in your evolutionary growth. It may or may not lead to the expressions in physical terms that you desire to see, touch, feel, or experience as physical life, yet you will learn from it. As I have explained before, you are not framed into any particular lifetime "destiny", as this would serve to limit the very unlimited being that you are.

> *The path of evolution is inevitable and unavoidable. It is the journey and the quality of expressions that are yours to choose as to what you experience on that journey.*

Each has the free will to change their mind, direction, and focus of their creative energy and expressions. You will learn and grow regardless, yet it may not be in the terms that you desire to experience if you do not make choices that create those outcomes. It is still valid, and you will still learn either way. Even if you choose not to choose a certain path or direction, you still have made a choice. Hence, either way, you will learn. Sometimes you learn what "works" or is conducive to achieving that which you desire. Sometimes you learn what does not work to achieve the results you desire and sometimes you may learn what occurs if you do not choose or act at all. You will indeed learn from any and all choices and interactions. Free will is always yours as an infinitely creative *Being*.

If you are ready to expand your beliefs beyond what you thought once was possible, then you are more readily prepared for your own evolution and becoming more than you "ever" have been "before". You will get there in this lifetime or another. Your evolution will take place when you are ready.

Symbols And The Truth Behind Them

Jackson Note: The following is an example of what I call a "drop down" or a "download". While driving one day, this information below simply popped up in my awareness in one block of data. Often these downloads are short but relevant for whatever it is that may make sense to you. Millions of people around the world will know exactly what I am talking about here as it is quite common among spiritually focused individuals. In this instance, recognizing this download as Divine in origin as Seth just sends me the occasional block of information, I pulled to the side of the road and recorded it on my phone for later insertion into our manuscript. Often, while performing seemingly mundane tasks such as driving or the shower or what have you, "they" (meaning the Divine beings) will speak to us all, and if you learn to recognize this event, each time you do so and record what you "hear" or "see" in the picture that may come to mind, you are exercising and strengthening your clairabilities and showing "them" that you desire that communication. The more you commit to paying attention, the more "they" will communicate with you. I assure you of this. If, however, you ignore these downloads, they will seemingly be absent from your experience and, you will pinch-off or filter out your own communications from Divine beings that are, in every moment of your life, there to assist you in every way possible for Self-growth.

Symbols are physical representations for the expressed purpose of conveying the meaning behind the symbol. Take water, for example. In the English language, you use the word "water" to convey the meaning of the atoms of H2O combined in such a fashion as to give you water. However, if you have say, 34 languages of the world, then you will have at least 34 different words (symbols) for the word or meaning of H2O... water. Therefore, you may call it whatever you desire to call it, by whatever symbols (words) you desire to assemble together; however, all of them are intended to convey the meaning of the atoms combined to give you H2O, or in English = water.

Now, beneath and beyond the physical atoms of hydrogen and oxygen is the <u>consciousness</u> that expresses itself in physical terms as hydrogen and oxygen. There is the consciousness, then, of hydrogen. There is also the consciousness of oxygen. Physically expressed and combined in such a fashion as H2O, they give you water. More on symbols as representations for meaning will be given later in another more formal session.

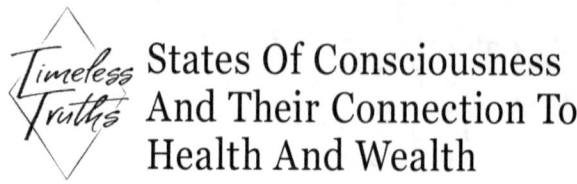

States Of Consciousness And Their Connection To Health And Wealth

Moving forward, we can take the consciousness that is expressed as wealth or money, let's say. Again, in English, you use the symbols called letters that make up the combination that conveys the meaning of money by the English word "money". In our example here then, if you have say 34 different languages around the world, you will then have at least 34 different symbols (words) that all convey the meaning (truth) of the word that they represent. In this case, money.

Behind the money, be it coins, paper dollars, notes, gold, or silver, or what have you, is <u>the consciousness of money</u>, and the accumulation of that from which wealth is derived. To *BE* wealthy then, you would aspire to <u>bring yourself into the state of consciousness of BEING the money or wealth</u>. Not just *having* the money or wealth, but rather *being* the money/wealth.

Now, we are not saying you assume that your physical body is now a $100 bill. We are saying that your inner *being* (consciousness) must be in the state of consciousness that is a vibrational match to the frequency of money/ wealth and *BEING* that state of consciousness, which allows it to be attracted to you in various forms and ways. If you *have* money/wealth, it is outside of you and it's something you must acquire and it's something that can be taken away.

If instead you shift your consciousness from having to *being*, then you are <u>associating your inner *being* with the state of consciousness of *BEING* wealth or more appropriate in English, being wealthy</u>. However, if you are not in the state of consciousness of being wealth, or wealthy, then you will, I assure you, not retain what money or wealth you do have, and it will seem as if things pop up out of the blue seemingly from everywhere to reduce your savings account. I suspect there will be many readers who have the "aha moment" here and can identify perhaps when crazy things seem to come out of seemingly nowhere that cost money here and more money there...as if you have a growing leak in your bank account. Why? What is causing these occurrences? These are questions that you do NOT want to be asking at the rational mind level, for it focuses from the physical perspective and orientation. If it is physical, it has ALREADY manifested. You are looking then at end "results" of previously held vibrations of energy and states of consciousness associated that created those physical conditions.

What you seek then, is to determine the Source from which the objects and events were brought into focus in physical terms. Their creative origins. Which now we know to be in consciousness.

> *"To him that hath (in consciousness),*
> *more unto him shall be given.*
> *To him that hath not (in consciousness),*
> *even that which he hath*
> *shall be taken away."*

Meaning that if you are identifying your inner *being* (not your flesh body here) with <u>BEING</u> the wealth or the state of consciousness of wealth, then you engage the natural electromagnetic properties of energy, directing consciousness to attract to your inner *being* (your flesh is simply not a factor here) the symbols and vibrational representations of wealth. "To him that hath"... you have it already and it is inseparable from you as you identify your inner *being/* consciousness with the consciousness of wealth, therefore it is inseparable from your Self and an eternal portion OF your Self.

If, however, you are constantly saying "<u>I AM</u> broke and I do not have any money." Then you are quite literally creating the vibration of your inner *being* to match that precise condition or state of consciousness. In this case, you will find that things happen, occur, and magically appear in your life experience that seem to take wealth and money from you.

"To him that hath not..." If you do not identify your inner *being* with the state of consciousness of wealth, but rather identify yourself with the <u>lack OF wealth</u>, then you are indeed, "stirring the universe" (consciousness) into drawing into your future experience events that seem to cost money and drain it from you. "Even that which he hath, shall be taken away."

It is timeless truth here. The truth of the matter (physically) is that you cannot EVER be separated from these things (nonphysically...

in consciousness) except that you are directing your own consciousness to create your reality with or without the wealth that you so desire to experience.

Truths are principals of a spiritual nature. If they apply to one physical thing, they apply to them all. We can then apply these same truths to health. Once again, if you identify your inner *being* as health naturally, innately, and eternally yours, as it IS your natural Self, then, you will find yourself to be exceedingly healthy, and vibrant; and even if you do catch a bug, you will heal quickly and efficiently - as the physical body MUST align with that which you are in the state of consciousness of *being*. If instead, you identify yourself as always being sick or at risk of catching the bug or incidents that cause dis-ease, then you will find yourself magically getting sick or falling victim to every germ, bacteria, or virus that comes near you.

Think of it this way; **Your "soul", or the immortal *being* portion of you as a human-*being*, does not know any sickness.** It is pure consciousness and only knows vibrant "health". Your thoughts, feelings, and emotions all direct the inner *being* to create and express (Ex-press = pressed outwardly from within) that which you believe yourself to be...your present state of consciousness. You must learn to shift what you consider significant and focus ***from*** what is the source of your own existence. You must identify with your own inner truth. Are you just the mortal flesh human? Or are you the *being* whose flesh is created by the inner self, healed by the inner self, and made vibrant by the inner self? Your beliefs will direct your consciousness to create a physical experience within the boundaries of those beliefs.

In the light, there can be no darkness.
"Darkness" then is simply
the illusion of lack of light.
Light is truth and it is unalterable,
inexorable, and timeless.

In all of human history and beyond, these truths govern physical expressions, as you create your own reality.

Dictation: In some ways then, you believe that we are speaking to you, Jackson-Thomas, the co-author of our book here, in the present day of November, in the year you believe to be 2022. However, it is only the appearance of the materials that show up on the pages as you write them in what you perceive as your present moment of time in November of 2022. However, in truth, we are speaking to you, and through you, from outside of space and time as you perceive it. In some ways then, we are speaking to Jackson-Thomas here from not only what you perceive as the present; however, we are speaking to him and to you, our readers, from also the past...and the future. So, the creation of the words for our book here, occurs outside of space and time. It is only that the physical representations (symbols) that are words and paragraphs, APPEAR in space and time in what you perceive today to be in November 2022.

Therefore:

All creation occurs <u>outside</u> of space and time.

The manifestations of those creations *appear in space and time*. However, the *creation* and formation of them occur and uphold that appearance from beyond space and time.

What you see then around you, physically, is already manifested material matter, objects, events, and conditions that make up your physical world. You do not see, physically, the consciousness from which it is created, constructed, and brought into view for your physical 5-human senses to then detect.

Your 5-human senses then, only detect what is already manifest. Physical. We are learning here about the inner consciousness from which all external reality is derived and constructed.

Now, as with physically appearing objects, this truth applies also to your human body/Self. Your body manifests itself from the eternal consciousness that is you, nonphysically...your consciousness, or soul, if you will. And while your physical body appears in physical reality, that which creates it is indeed, beyond space and time eternally. You (your physical body) only appears in space and time, once manifest. This also applies to all animals, flowers of the field, and rocks of the mountains.

This truth is exponentially important as it is the basis upon which future writings from us will describe the massive creative implications of using this knowledge to your advantage when intentionally creating/manifesting your desired physical reality and all things within it. To change your physical reality and probable future outcomes, you MUST change them at the source before those changes will appear in physical reality. IF YOU FAIL TO DO SO, AND ARE EMOTIONALLY ANGERED OR UPSET, RAILING OR COMPLAINING ABOUT YOUR LIFE'S CONDITIONS AND CIRCUMSTANCES, YOU ARE RIGHT THEN, IN THAT MOMENT, VERY EFFECTIVELY CREATING FUTURE OBJECTS, EVENTS, AND CONDITIONS THAT WILL APPEAR AS EXACTLY WHAT YOU ARE COMPLAINING ABOUT IN LIKENESS. Continuing to do so, over and over again, you will place yourself, into what we call the "creative loop" whereby, reacting (rational mind level orientation here), to current conditions, you then create their likeness over again, and again and again...living in a loop of creation that seemingly is without end. For indeed, it is without end as the creator (you) are immortal, and you must change your state of consciousness and vibrations from which you are creating your future probable outcomes. There is no other way. Period.

Now, I strongly emphasize these truths as I see millions of human-beings getting caught up in this "creative loop" and it is one of the most pressing challenges where humans get frustrated, unable to understand how these things are happening, why and how to change them and their life path and events, objects, and conditions that appear. Things don't happen TO you. They happen FOR you so that you may learn how to change them, within....at the Source of your own creative expressions. Once you learn and apply the lesson, the challenge will often dissolve for you have learned your soul-lesson and in so doing, progress beyond the once seeming challenge. Evolution of Self based in Love, Light and understanding.

From *your* current perception point in time when you read this, our words form from intentions of love and vibrational expressions into the human language as they are transposed through Jackson-Thomas' consciousness into the meanings *we intend to convey*, written onto the page in the English language Jackson knows in this lifetime. For again, we must utilize the filter, of Jackson's knowledge in his present lifetime in which his human self speaks fluent English, as it colors our intentions of meaning when they pass through his consciousness, into the awareness of his rational/intellectual mind (via natural clairaudience), to then be typed upon the pages.

What many do not realize, and one of the purposes of our books now with the *Timeless Truth Series*, is that you yourselves also exist in that past and future, as real and vividly as you do now in your present, for your own Selves...the soul/personality consciousness within your own bodies eternally exist outside of time and space. That immortal part of you may be incarnated in another dimension of time and space where it appears, for example, to be 1,200 A.D. or 2,000 BC in another lifetime that has physical context in 3-dimensional reality; however, "you" exist in what your present self believes to be 2023 (or the current year you are reading this), as well as 2,000 BC, for example.

Your physical expressions, that of the human psyche and the psychic and psychological workings of the *beings* you are, appear in space and time; yet, your immortal self which provides the flesh its life and the heart its beat, exists eternally outside of that context.

It is when you identify yourselves MORE and more with this immortal portion of your own selves, that you will naturally open infinite doors of knowledge and wisdom, and unlock ancient potentials that you presently have no idea that exist as probable human tools through which you can create vastly improved, enhanced, fruitful and exponentially more beneficial lives, individually, and in cultures and societies across the world.

You must learn to look so much deeper than the flesh beings and bodies that you have. It is okay, to acknowledge that you have wonderfully expressed physical bodies and that they are quite capable of miracle feats. However, they do not move a muscle, heal, create a healthy cell, or even exist in physical form without the eternal workings of the consciousness that is the origin and materials, you might say, "The stuff", from which they are themselves formed into physical existence.

When you look into humanity at _this level of perception_, you will not see differences in races or skin colors, or other quite petty physical differences that you believe <u>separate</u> you from the rest of humanity.

You will instead see that each and every human-*being* that has <u>*ever*</u> existed in all eternity - in days a hundred million years before the dinosaurs existed, in times of the Atlanteans and the Lumanians and other ancient now mythical cultures on your planet that existed - is an eternal portion of All That Is and that, though you each present yourselves into physical forms of matter in unique ways, you are exponentially more unique in your inner self than you could ever, in many lifetimes combined, express into physical terms.

<u>You will see oneness with ALL other humans</u> as they are *beings* also, just as you are. You will come to recognize the magnificent beauty of ALL human-*beings* as expressions of "God"/All That Is.

For the true evolution of humanity to occur and express your greater potentials, far more capable and exquisite than you presently imagine, you must, and I will repeat that, you <u>must</u> as individuals and as a society begin to look deeper than the physical flesh that each of you are and **_identify_** more as the truth of yourselves - as the immortal, unlimited, infinitely more powerful, knowledgeable, resourceful, connected, loved, and eternally, creative *beings* that you truly are. You cannot avoid this. You are all of these things already. You are simply not as yet aware of it perhaps and that erroneous belief has caused the truth to escape from your present awareness; thus, not allowing you to frame your physical existence in the truth of your *being*, but rather in the limitations of your human flesh self.

<u>It is key, critical, and necessary for your evolution as a species, to come to these realizations.</u> Personally, you can immensely improve, enhance, and bring only dreamed-of joy, freedom, and creativity to your own lives. However, as cultures and societies across the planet, you can evolve in ways that <u>also evolves animals, communication with the animals, the trees, the oceans, and even the stars and planets above</u>. You can, and will in time as you perceive it, unlock secrets of your universe that many only dream of today.

<u>You will understand</u> why and how ancient structures were built around the Earth. How they lifted with the ease of a thought, 800-

ton blocks of rock to build structures that still stand and exist today such as the pyramids across the Earth. <u>Structures whose physical expression still stands today</u> **because of the consciousness that built them and formed them into expression in the first place**. The magic of these ancient structures all over your planet is not just IN the physical structure itself. The magic is in the *CONSCIOUSNESS* of the *beings* that created the structures that expressed into physical pyramids and similar things.

To understand the physical pyramids then, you must understand the consciousness from which they were created or you will only struggle to scratch the surface of the answers that you seek.

There are reasons why these structures were built in those particular locations around the planet. They have to do with <u>coordinate points</u> of which I have spoken about previously; yet, your scientist of today have barely only a hint of the understanding of how coordinate points not only help create your physical realities but that the energy that flows into your own physical dimension, through these points that are completely undetectable with *physical instruments*, can form objects that transcend time and space as they appear in many realities, as well as in yours, where they appear to be from your <u>past</u>.

Scientists, or what is now at the time of this book's writing popularly called *"Ancient Astronaut Theorists"*, want to understand the physical construction, why, how, and purposes, etc. for such ancient magnificent feats of architecture from thousands of years ago; yet, they are attempting to understand them from the standpoint of looking *at the physical expressions*, without then trying to understand the underlying consciousness from which ALL ideas, technology, whys, hows, and so forth originated. To understand the physical reality and structures that they desire to understand, they must not look so much AT (just) the physical manifestations of the structures, rather "look into" the consciousness of that which created those physical structures. Those answers do not all lie written on the walls so to speak, but rather within the history of consciousness that has expressed itself into the marvels you see before you - Pyramids and many other structures around the world.

Now, a few of the major questions that these individuals who study the ancient structures of the various pyramids around the world are:

Why the pyramid shape? How did civilizations around the planet Earth, many, many thousands of miles apart, on different continents, with no access to each other, and perhaps 10,000 years apart in physical construction, build pyramid structures that were almost identical in shape and form? They have seemingly stumped themselves studying the physical structures as to how they can be so similar, virtually identical in many cases. The shapes, do have to do somewhat with the unseen concentrations of energy.

Furthermore...I will give your scientists and "ancient astronaut theorists" some clarity here that will assist them in where to look for their answers: Consciousness. You see, consciousness operates outside of time and space, eternally. When one pyramid structure is built say in one area of the Earth, and then later in your *appearance of linear history and time*, others are built on the opposite side of the Earth, they may seem as if they are built to the human eye, (your 5-human sense filter through which you view physical reality) 10,000 years apart. However, in <u>consciousness</u>, they are occurring <u>*simultaneously*</u>.

Meaning that to the individuals building the second set of structures in our example here, the ideas, designs, construction techniques, technologies used for lifting 80-ton blocks and what have you, are available to them, in the time frame that they perceive perhaps to be 10,000 years later, instantaneously as these ideas were being used by the first architects and builders "moments ago"... as the data has come into their awareness via consciousness. Which operates outside of time and space. ***They are tapped into their natural communication abilities of human consciousness that we have been discussing throughout this book, and they are using them for the benefit of human civilization.***

It is almost then, as if the second civilization building their pyramids, is actually (not theoretically, but actually) <u>*communicating*</u> with the architects of the first civilization, through consciousness – and that communication process <u>*transcends space and time*</u> and is "instantly available" yet only to the individuals who had in those times opened their minds, expanded their perception to utilize their consciousness in ways to benefit the species and cultures. Such as we are training our readers to now do, today...again to benefit themselves, but also the greater cultures, societies and species as a whole.

Now, this occurs in our second civilization's architects and builders within their dream state, daydreams, visions, and moments of inspiration. Therefore, they receive data, ideas, and designs for the construction of their pyramid structures, via consciousness...from one civilization to the other. Data that transcends time and space, and both then are "communicating" with each other via clairvoyance, clairaudience, and claircognizance and in fact are using the same skills that Thomas (Jackson) and Ruburt used in channeling our books - to receive data that transcends time and space, yet appears as the manifestation of that data, in physical terms, within time and space. Just as the pyramids appeared in time and space.

In another twist of truth here, I will also tell you another reason why some of the pyramids are so similar in nature, on opposite sides of the Earth in very remote ancient civilizations. That is that some of the individuals who built the ancient Mayan pyramids, also built some of the pyramids in ancient Egypt. Different human bodies, same immortal SOUL/Entity.

From that level of reality, they were what you would call reincarnational souls that were indeed, incarnated into the human body as individuals who physically worked on the construction of each. Hence, there are energetic "soul-ties" to the vibrational frequencies of the data, information, designs, and so forth from one civilization to the other, via consciousness, that again, transcends time and space, and that soul incarnated as two different personalities of the same soul, appearing then in time and space in two different physical locations on the Earth, as two different people, in two different periods of your linear historical time- yet using their own soul-memories to bring about creation in physical terms of human history to enhance each civilization and expand the consciousness of the species.

There were some souls and personalities of course in each civilization that only worked or lived in one such civilization, as the others who "reincarnated" would expose the knowledge and wisdom of their experience to new souls and personalities appearing in time and space with them.

Aware of it or not, your constructions today do utilize data and designs that come from other "parallel dimensions" that you do not perceive with the 5-human senses, yet your consciousness does perceive them and has access to that data, even if you are not at the conscious level or rational/intellectual mind level, aware from where the data has been received. Every single principal and timeless truth, then, of this constant communication that transcends time, space, and human history, occurs at every single moment of your life and existence. To use it purposefully and intentionally as our ancient pyramid builders and civilizations did, however, you must first believe it is possible; then become aware of it, and further develop it for skilled use. There is not a human-*being* that has ever incarnated to walk the Earth, in any dimension or historical time, that didn't have access to these abilities, as they are inherent within and inseparable from your consciousness that is eternal...appearing then in time and space in various periods of historical time to expand and evolve your own soul, civilization, species and of course, All That Is.

The obvious yet astounding implications of this is that you, my dear readers, can do the same kind of thing and communicate with other alternate, parallel Selves and dimensions of space and time, societies that once existed and those you do not as yet have any idea that existed. What truly amazing things have "you" done in other lifetimes that would benefit you in this one? What lessons were learned or knowledge, wisdom, or skills were gained in that other lifetime that could immensely improve this one? These are the kinds of questions of reflection that I would encourage all our readers to journal about and ask themselves, for it is in the process of discovery within that you will "find your Selves".

The answers, you see, are inseparable from the physical objects or pyramids from the consciousness that created them. You will not always find the answers by examination of the end results of the manifestation's expression, but in understanding the Source origin of the impetus that created its expression into physical pyramids.

To understand the physical pyramids very deeply and fully, you must understand the consciousness that created them.

To understand physical humans very deeply and fully, you must understand the consciousness that creates them.

To understand the physical, already manifested universe in which you are present, you must understand more fully the consciousness that creates it, IS it, and upholds it in your perception.

If you are only viewing, perceiving, and understanding reality FROM the physical point of view and orientation of the 5-human limited senses, then you are looking at a very limited dimensional understanding of that pyramid. Or human, or universe.

YOUR SOUL IS MULTIDIMENSIONAL as is all consciousness. This then implies that to understand pyramids, humans, yourselves, all things in your physical universe, you must view them multidimensionally. You CAN do this...using your consciousness. Otherwise you are but quite literally seeing the surface of an object or even your universe, through a keyhole sized view to base your understandings of reality upon.

Now, you may believe that "the secrets of the pyramids and other Earth mysteries are lost to time".

I want to call this out loud and clear for all who are "ancient astronaut theorists" - they are only lost to time *if you believe* they are lost to time.

They exist, my beloved friends, I assure you, eternally in the infinite memory banks of the consciousness that created them. And that consciousness is readily accessible to you, if you learn to tap into the inner *being* portion of you as a human-*being* to find it. That is where the answers eternally exist in all their vividness, as clearly as the one who dreamed up the ideas to build the structures in the first place. As clearly as the creators could see them back then, it is possible for you also to tap into the same answers and clarity that they once contemplated. And the answers? They are closer to you than your very breath or heartbeat.

Now, I will tell you that as many a man or woman has sat upon them, and pondered their origins and so forth, they may from time to time have experienced great visions of awareness that come to them. They may feel drawn to look here or look there, dig here or dig there, put this symbol with that symbol and you form the key and the lock, so to speak. They may figure it out for whatever piece of the puzzle that they are looking at in whatever country and ancient structure. However, when such epiphanies, intuitive insights, and ah-ha moments come to them, *from where*, exactly, do they think they have come? Consciousness. "God"/Source/Creator/Allah/One/The Universe/All That Is.

And quite simply, in those quiet moments of reflection when they are at the sites themselves in which **coordinate point type energy** may indeed assist them in their endeavors to discover answers and insights, or at a point of time later thereon, their rational mind, the intellect, pauses its search and questions long enough to actually hear, see, feel, and sense the intuitive-self answering questions in terms of where to dig, where to look, where to put the puzzle pieces together to form the more clear picture of what went on there at that ancient location.

The answers then, sometimes simply "come to them". It has been this way since before the caveman sought where to find food and shelter. It is natural that the answers, insights, wisdom, etc. will do so... however, only when allowed and only then within the beliefs that allow them.

Again, if you believe the answers to your questions are lost in time; then to you, my friends, I assure you, they will evade you for eternity.

However, if you expand the mind and beliefs that the answers are there, perhaps not written into a physical stone that says "This is why it is, this is how it came to be, this is the technology they used and how, etc."; but rather that it comes to you in forms of dreams, ideas, impetus, a hunch to take action, and over time (as you exist within time now physically) it will...in time... and space reveal such answers to you. Though, if you do not learn to trust the inner self from which the answers will come, you will continue to question forever if you have been given the correct or accurate answers.

You must trust, not only for answers about the ancient structures and civilizations of the Earth, but also for every-thing you want to learn and more; you must look to the consciousness that created such structures. I will put it to you plainly that it is indeed possible to tap into the very individual's consciousness that created a structure or was a part in the design and manufacture of it, to gain some of the insight and wisdom about its physical existence. They may or may not walk up to you in a dream and tell you in English how and why they did what they did, but the clues, ideas, and information that formed the structures in the first place, can come into your awareness in such a way that it will be as if you just heard your own name, you would know it so well.

Now, my task as a multidimensional teaching Conscious Collective is not to give you all the answers of the universe in a book, whereby you read the physical expressions, but to awaken you to the truth that such answers, insight, and wisdom are indeed inseparable from yourselves in every moment of life; and if you but learn, practice with diligence, and are patient, such wisdom will grow in your own conscious awareness in time.

Now, if you do not believe...truly, to your core of being...perhaps because you do not know of the core of your being as we are describing it more in detail in this book... if you do not believe to that depth that the answers about ancient structures, or anything you desire, is readily available to you at every moment of life, then you yourself will exclude such answers and wisdom from your own perception; you will block it from your own realizations if you are closed off to the source from which ALL physical reality is constructed.

You do not realize it; however, the consciousness and ideas that built the pyramids around the world, came to the humans' intellectual minds from outside of time and space. They acted upon these ideas and "manifested" them into time and space. The world that you know is, essentially, "idea-construction". To understand the physical nature of such ancient structures, societies, and sites, one must seek the answers; not just in the physical evidence of them, but, most importantly, by tuning into the natural self within your own consciousness, which is in connection with the very consciousness of All That Is, and has the blueprint of every physical object that was ever built.

Now, some of the "advanced technologies" that allowed them to build such magnificent structures, were given to them from the future, if you were to perceive it in those terms. For example, it is as if you had a dream, and in that dream, you are given an invention, idea, or solution to a problem.

It comes from outside of time, from a dimension that would appear (in the perception of linear time) to be from your future self, a future society, a set of conditions, or a world need, etc. It is drawn from that future condition or probable reality, in which it exists already physical and developed, and the great thrust of creativity projects it into the past so that the version of "you" living "here and now" receives this idea, invention, or storyline for a great novel, and brings it into fruition in your current period of history so that, in the future, **your culture**

and society develops along those lines - The lines in which that invention, idea, or say great novel, exists in physical terms in <u>that</u> future. The probable one. Without the idea or invention or premise, drawn to you from a "future" probable reality... through consciousness, received by you, it would not have been developed or acted upon.

This is an example of how a future probable reality, or a future Self version of you or society, can affect the "past" which is your current <u>present</u>. The idea itself, or invention, comes from outside of time, yet appears in time as it is drawn into the rational/intellectual mind of mankind, and then is acted upon to manifest it into physical reality, which then develops your world with that "future" idea now constructed; hence, moving your civilization forward.

You do not realize it, however, humanity is guided this way *en masse* now and has been for eternity. However, not everyone "these days" listens to that intuitive nudge, idea, invention, great novel idea, and storyline; yet, the ones who do so, often become some of the most memorable and notable human-*beings* of your century, or any century.

Many of your existing advanced technologies,
inventions, and revolutionary items, come
to you, via consciousness, from a "future"
reality in which they already exist.

The picture, image, idea, or movie-like vision will often come to the dreamer, daydreamer, or one who seeks to be a larger portion of human history, even if that human history is only within their own family unit or circle of friends. That desire, and the conditions along, perhaps, with the needs of your society as it currently may be, draws forth the idea or invention for it to come to physical fruition. <u>Every</u> invention was once only a "dream" or idea that came into the inventor's awareness at some point and was acted upon until it became a reality. Nothing exists physically before it exists in consciousness. That is impossible, for it is formed FROM consciousness by consciousness as an expression of consciousness. Before the idea, invention, storyline for the perfect novel or movie, or what have you came into the awareness of the individual, where do you suppose the idea existed before it was illuminated in the mind that conceived it?

The past and future exist now, with your present. You only perceive "past" objects appearing to you as ancient structures because most humans do not understand the simultaneous nature of existence, or that the future, in other terms, <u>already</u> exists. You simply cannot perceive it with physical senses. However, you can perceive it with your natural clairability senses through consciousness.

You believe in "past lives"; and often many people can perceive them and see them in dreams or in visions. Both cases are your natural clairvoyance seeing through time at the present moment in that lifetime what you may as a male or female be engaged in doing at the moment in *that past*.

> *You do not see "future" lives precisely because you do not believe that they exist yet or "haven't yet happened".*

Again I will mention, you create your own reality within the boundaries of the beliefs that you hold about that reality which you are presently ensconced within. If you do not believe it is possible, then to you, it will be impossible and hence, you will yourself filter such experiences from your perception and life.

This is why we are removing some of the superstitions about the true nature of the existence of all physical reality so that you can open yourselves to your true infinite potential, expanding beyond beliefs that once held you back from those experiences.

Now, your 3-dimensional constructs where you perceive the phenomenon of space, require time as an integral part of that construct to provide you with a 3-dimensional representation of reality expressed into matter. Therefore, you believe in a past because you think moments become your past as you move through them. However, your future exists every bit as real as your past, and the past that you recognize <u>is only but one of many probable pasts...just as your future will be one of many probable futures</u>. Your creaturehood and corporeal structure require you to perceive your environment in this linear context of time and space so as to navigate it successfully during your physical experience.

When humanity comes to understand these <u>basic</u> truths of your own existence, and the true nature of time and space as phenomenons of appearance in a world that is 3-dimensional and seems separated from all other physical objects, then you will open your own intellectual minds to actually perceive more clearly your futures that do exist <u>*now*</u>, and in so doing, you can indeed choose with free will which future states you desire to experience, and draw them forth - along with everything necessary for their unfoldment into the material world. This is key to your evolution as a species!

Many, many probable futures exist and, based upon the actions, beliefs, emotions, and so forth that you use your own consciousness to create, you will determine which of those probable futures will narrow down into a fine line what is indiscernible in its merging into your ever-evolving Now Moment. Your present moment of power where flesh meets spirit/soul.

Now, for example here: throughout his lifetime, Jackson has had dreams and visions of himself walking with Christ in a "past" life. He has also had visions of himself in future lives where the Earth is green and beautiful, and the buildings are far more advanced. Where the buildings themselves are actually "connected" to the Earth in a more symbiotic and beneficial relationship (underline that last word purposely as it has a deeper meaning) that is only formed through the evolution of technology that was used in *that future* to build the buildings, and the evolved consciousness of humanity in *that future* that built them. He has at times seen these futures clearly and vividly.

In this example, I will tell you that both of these lifetimes which he has seen in visions and in dreams exist *now*. At one level of his existence, he is living in those time periods - or dimensions of a parallel nature to this reality - now. The one *seems* to be in the past based upon the historical clothing, wares, and objects that appear in that particular lifetime dimension of reality. The buildings, mountains and valleys, and the society of harmony where not only humans are in harmony with the Earth, environment, and nature, but also your buildings, technologies, and wares of that future are also in a symbiotic and co-beneficial relationship with nature, exists now.

It is only that it *appears* to be the future based upon the evolved consciousness of humanity, and the expansion of consciousness *that created that future reality*, as appears to be in contrast with technology and the way humanity is living today when you are reading this book. That is why it appears to be a "futuristic reality". The scenes, the clothing, the vehicles, the buildings, and the technology will be appropriate for the mass consciousness agreed-upon version of reality in that particular time frame of history, even if that history is a probable one that does not come to pass in _your terms_ of physical reality in the future. It _has_...come to physical terms in another, alternate, or parallel if you prefer, level of existence.

Now, Jackson could not perceive the future realities if he did not already understand, more expansively, the true nature of time as a phenomenon. If he did not believe the truth...he would not be able to see and understand that truth, as he would effectively block it or exclude that data from his perception of the larger reality of which you all are a part. Obviously, this is to say that you would not perceive future lives either...if you do not understand the true nature of simultaneous time and the linear time phenomena.

> _Again, you create your own reality. Yet you do so within the self-imposed boundaries and limitations of the beliefs that you hold as the vibrational framework, within which that reality is created and expressed into physical terms._

You unlock your truths, or you block your truths. There is no outside influence that does any of these for you or to you. You are what happens TO you and FOR you. To learn. To evolve beyond seeming limitations of the physical expressions you seem to believe are so solid and real to you.

Now, when Jackson was a child, during and after his death experience (NDEs as they call them, however, his physical body was indeed dead by clinical and scientific terms), he perceived realities that were outside of the physical reality in which his human body was then focused for _this_ lifetime.

There was a life-incarnation purpose behind this event. From that moment in time, an entirely new array of probable realities sprung forth in which, Jackson was able to clearly understand that there was far more to reality than just the physical world of 3-dimensions he could see around him.

This path provided Jackson with direct and immediate knowledge of what it actually looks and feels like, and to understand that there is full, lucid, conscious awareness of both the physical world, and the

73

nonphysical realm, and that he was a portion of both, <u>simultaneously</u>. He knew then, and experienced "life beyond death". Realizing that there is no real death - Only a physical end to the corporeal structure of the human body in each lifetime. This stated, of course, means that <u>every</u> human *being* also exists in both the physical and nonphysical dimensions simultaneously.

As "Jackson" or maybe we should say "Thomas" (his consciousness and "I AM" identity and awareness of himself) "floated" near the ceiling of the barn and he watched his dead body fall to the floor and lay crumpled and lifeless, it was <u>*crystal clear*</u> (claircognizance/ Direct Knowing) that his physical body had no life animation to it at all, as "he" was floating above it near the ceiling. That without the immortal part of himself that he was aware of as himself, floating near the ceiling of the barn...without that portion of himself being focused from within the flesh, the body had no life animation. It was dead. Therefore, he became starkly aware instantaneously that it was CONSCIOUSNESS, which provided the physical flesh it's life animation, and that without its presence inside the body... it was as if the body was a bale of hay as it had no life of its own. He also realized that when his consciousness WAS within the body, that he was then simultaneously a part of both the physical and nonphysical dimensions. As everyone alive now is. This event set up the foundation for knowing these things at the level of the soul and *being*, which is so profoundly REAL that no matter what anyone would ever say to him about the experience, he knew that his experience of nonphysical dimensions was more real than even what he knew as physical life.

While his story of this experience is given elsewhere, suffice it to say that he immediately questioned physical reality from an early age. He wanted to know HOW he experienced what he experienced. How did he have lucid conversations with his long-dead grandparents that knew of <u>current events</u> in his life and commented on them when he was in "heaven"? How did he speak with Angels, *beings* of light, and other experiences?

Questions bombarded him with a deep desire to know what had happened and to understand it. This is, of course, a "trigger event" that set into motion probable future events that would take him on the path that would eventually lead him to me, to continue our work in this lifetime context. These events, then, were a necessary foundation to provide him with a perception, understanding, and context that he would later use in his lifetime now.

After his death experience, psychic activity spiked and he found that he could see and tell of future events, days or even a week before they ever occurred. In vivid detail. Often, either in dreams or simply as he was walking or playing, he would see very clear visions... almost like movies in full color, play across the eye of his mind (again, natural clairvoyance that is natural to all human consciousness). Little attention would be paid to them until the event actually occurred physically, moments or days later, in which he may have the Déjà vu moment or simply knew what was about to unfold.

As millions of others have done, Jackson could clearly see the future BEFORE it ever occurred. But how? More events brought more questions, which caused him to seek out more answers.

He could precognitively see and feel certain events before they would occur and sometimes very prominently. Often it was accidents, plane crashes, or train crashes that would involve death; but at that time he didn't understand that, or why the phenomenon would occur. It wasn't until later that he learned he was tapping into mass consciousness and that he could see, feel, and sense through time and space - VIA **CONSCIOUSNESS** and his clairabilities - future events that had not yet occurred in historical, linear time.

How DO you perceive colorful movie-like visions, dreams, and experiences of physical events, before they ever occur in physical reality? How do you clearly see and experience something that hasn't even happened yet? The answer is, of course, that you are using your natural clairabilities of your consciousness to perceive a larger, expanded, greater reality that has opened the door to yourself seeing probable realities. Objects, events, and conditions that already exist in the "4th dimension" we might say...just outside of the 3-dimensional time and space; and these may, or may not, come into view as the future unfolds, based upon many factors.

His death experience showed him clearly that there was more to reality than what meets the eye and the 5-human senses. Therefore, his foundational belief in this allowed him to perceive probable events using his clairabilities innate to human consciousness.

Millions of people do this daily and may only have a hint of it come into their awareness when they experience Déjà vu - The distinct feeling and sensation that they have done that before, said that before, or been to this place on Earth before.

> *You are my friends... seeing through time... transcending time and space to perceive another lifetime or probable outcome that has not yet merged into your current present moment of awareness to become a part of your accepted reality.*

Again, we come back to my point that you create your own physical reality (experiences in life) within the boundaries and perceptions that you yourself create based upon your current state of consciousness and understanding. Simply put, if you do not believe in the simultaneous nature of time or that the future does indeed already exist in a multidimensional environment in which many probable futures exist, now, then you will not be able to perceive them, for you have yourself closed that door to perceive those probabilities. You have created your own version and perception of reality that simply does not include them.

You have excluded them from you. Our messages now are multidimensional and multi-layered and if you are perceiving what we are saying, reading between the lines, so to speak, we are telling you that you can indeed shift and expand your beliefs through persistent work in that direction to open those doors. We are helping you to unlock and understand you.

Now again, you understand where it was once said, "Ye shall know thy truths and the truths shall set thee free." You set yourself free, as you have always been; yet, you may not have been fully aware as to the truth of your own selves. As you evolve, so too, does the consciousness around you, as it must conform to your new beliefs, perceptions, and understandings which emanate from your own consciousness.

Now, Jackson, we will wrap this up as you are landing, and thank you for your time today. It has been magical indeed. - Seth

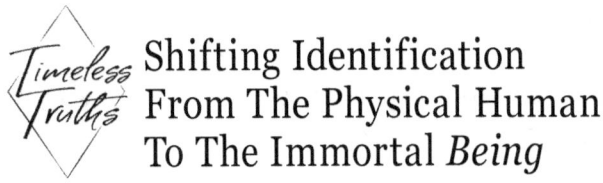

Shifting Identification
From The Physical Human
To The Immortal *Being*

This is one of our goals behind our book as it is the key by which humans evolve and move beyond present perceptions of limitations in your lives. You must begin more and more to define yourself not just as the human flesh body you see, but more and more identify yourself with the immortal **_being_** within so that you are more freely open and able to use the natural tools that your consciousness contains inherent within it to direct patterns of energy from the nonphysical, into physical expressions of matter- i.e. - physical reality.

Now, do you believe you are the limited physical body that has a soul or, that you are an immortal soul that, for this lifetime, has incarnated a portion of your greater Self into that physical body? Which do you identify with more? From which point of view and perception do you most often view and interact with life?

The difference dear friends is the key to creating worlds, not to mention your own health and wealth, and all things on the physical plane intentionally and purposefully. The difference is in the state of consciousness _FROM_ which you operate, orient yourselves, and hence, create your own reality. Life as you know it.

We are learning then, to look within yourselves to understand the inner *being* from which all physical reality, your life, is created. To learn to understand it and expand it so as to become aware of your naturally creative and immortal timeless tools that you yourself can direct into more fruitful and joyful experiences in your lives - Productive for yourself and beneficial to all of humanity and the animals, Earth, and environment in which you find yourselves presently ensconced.

Again, we are learning to shift the perception of your Self, and create heretofore, physical experiences and physical reality that you once only dreamed might be possible. If it has EVER been achieved by another human, you can indeed do something similar if only you associate yourself with the proper orientation and beliefs that you can. "You", meaning the unlimited and infinitely resourceful *BEING* that is within, which is eternally a portion of All That Is, and as such, eternally <u>already have</u> that which you desire.

> *If something seems missing in your life, it is just that your present state of consciousness excludes it from appearing to you, physically speaking, as it is currently outside of the cumulative, distilled vibrational state of consciousness in which you are <u>presently</u> living your experiences.*

Now, do you desire to continue in life hampered by the rational mind that only perceives physical reality based upon just what the 5-human senses can detect? Or do you desire to create your life from the inner-*being* orientation that is the natural Self, in which the brain does not need to know the way, see the way, or understand how it could possibly be achieved, yet you believe that "God"/ Source/The Universe/The Creator does indeed know a way that you as yet do not perceive?

"Choose ye this day whom ye shall serve."

◊ The rational mind of limited senses, or

◊ The immortal *being* (Christ consciousness and vibration/I AM consciousness) of your <u>Self</u> within.

The difference in your orientation will indeed guide the probable outcomes that appear physically as your life unfolds before you, moment to moment, day to day, year to year.

The physical reality you see then, is the already manifested, already expressed results, if you will, of that which you have "previously" held in your mind as the state of consciousness with which you have *identified yourself*. **I want to make that clear as no other being, physical or not, identifies YOUR being with the states of consciousness you experience.** You are teaching...you. Almost as if your soul consciousness within is teaching the rational/intellectual mind of its existence and unlimited power to create worlds and the universe in which you exist.

You are what happens to you, for you, by you. No person can create your life for you. You do live in an eternally connected matrix of consciousness which is inseparable from yourself, so there are influences upon your personal reality from other sources of energy around you which create the overall accepted states of consciousness of your family, your neighborhood, city, country, societies, and cultures.

> *All physical objects then, are physical representations of the consciousness and vibrational frequency ranges that you have, personally, and as groups, held in your frame of attention.*

They are the physical expressions of the probable outcomes and probable realities that were "selected" as you held various things in your awareness and contemplated them. Especially those charged with feeling and emotions, as your emotions add "layers of thickness" to probable outcomes that then become your "chosen" reality that is experienced. I do not mean consciously chosen, at the rational/intellectual mind. For many will say, "I did not choose this or that in my life."

I assure you; <u>No human or *being* chooses it for you</u>. You are eternally a sovereign *being* with free will and free choice. Before you are born into this lifetime that you know, during it, and after it physically ceases. Perhaps then, the choice occurred at a level of consciousness that is behind the rational/intellectual mind and for purposes of learning your own power of creation, your own power to overcome adversity, and to find your own inner *being* that is capable of all things in physical reality; however, no one outside of your Self chose it for you.

Adversity is the mother of inventions, creativeness, and an impetus for growth beyond the present boundaries within which you may have previously been living your own life experiences. If you were not challenged, would you ever rise above such challenges? How would you know what challenges are and find your own strength and resourcefulness within if you never faced challenges that caused you to look for their source of expression?

You experience the darkness, the seeming lack of light (illumination) or truth, so that you may know more fully what the light is. If you were not hungry, would you seek out food to sustain a healthy body? If you were not challenged, would you seek out means for resolution? If you did not need a new tool or invention to accomplish a task, would you draw from the infinite consciousness the wherewithal for its physical creation?

You are your own Divine plan,
and you yourselves are working
that out as all beings must.

Our books then, might be thought of as a "User's Manual for the Human" to understand its own nifty tools and power of creation. A journey of Self, into the Self, for the Self, which benefits Self, and in so doing, benefits all that touches you (nonphysically), as you add to All That Is, immeasurably by every thought, action, and contemplation.

We teach, now, the truth that is the consciousness within ALL physical reality. Within every grain of dust that makes up your entire endless universe, and every minuscule "space" that you perceive within that universe. We do not teach theories then, about these things, but rather the truth of consciousness that has been called "God" by any and all names over all of history that extends vastly beyond what any scientist of today can conceive. For they do not perceive in physical terms, alternate realities, or probable outcomes that are outside the scope of what the 5-human senses can detect. To most scientists today, if it cannot be detected by the 5-human senses, then it doesn't really exist. Yet they must learn to perceive the source origins and how physical reality has come into expression in the first place.

What causes an electron to be "born" into physical reality? Atoms accumulated together give you atomic mass. Atomic mass = physically solid appearing objects. Objective reality. Yet what tells the proton or neutron to behave in the ways it does? Or orbit the electron around the nucleus of the atom? What tells the electron to space itself from other electrons in such a vibrational pattern of perfection that it upholds planets in your sky and brings twinkles to your stars, not to mention life to your flesh? **Consciousness.**

Lucid, <u>aware</u>, "living" eternally, creative consciousness that cannot be detected by any human senses.

We are dealing with the unseen consciousness that is behind and beneath all physical things to understand its nature, for its nature is _your_ nature. The more you understand this truth the more you can direct it creatively, intentionally, and purposefully. And no, one cannot use such creative means to create nefarious things. That is the rational/intellectual mind that seeks such things as dominion over any other thing other than dominion of Self. Mastery of Self. You cannot be vibrating at a very high rate of frequency and create things that are not a match to that frequency.

Simply put, you cannot be in a Divine state of creative consciousness and create things that are out of harmony with that state.

By "Divine state" we mean a state of higher vibrational frequency. They simply DO NOT EXIST at the higher levels of vibrational frequency of which are naturally conducive to intentional creation. You cannot direct an Angel if you will, to do "dirty deeds" as the level of vibration in which such _beings_ of consciousness exist, there is no darkness nor lack of light and the truth of one's intention is "long since known in full lucid awareness" - long before an individual would even act upon them.

To put it in another way, the Divine knows what you are going to do before your brain does, as we see probable outcomes in what you would perceive to be your future before they are even acted upon. Hence, Divine intervention that can, and does occur sometimes to keep some on the path that they might best follow for their own learning purposes and the greater benefit for all.

Probable realities and probable outcomes explain how, via clairvoyance, a psychic intuitive who has learned to develop their natural abilities of consciousness, can often "see the future", as they are quite literally seeing a probable reality outcome that is "most likely" to occur, based on the given states of consciousness, energy, environment, and many other factors that show a most-likely potential path in which an outcome will merge into one's current state of awareness as their <u>present moment</u> in time and space. This is how you see the future. Yet, remember that there are many futures, as there are many pasts, that all branch out from each thought and decision and action you give your attention to...which, directs your consciousness and creates that reality outcome.

Now, given that all exist in an environment of free-will choice, even the most probable outcomes that appear clairvoyantly, can be changed by a change of free will thought, focus, intentions, influences of others, etc. This is why no clairvoyant is always 100% accurate, as free will choices can, and do, change the course of history, as you might say. Your own history, and those around you.

Now, as Jackson is sitting here typing this on a roadside stop along the highway in Alaska, where he has so nicely pulled to the side to record the nagging tap of myself on his shoulder to have an impromptu session here, we will let him get back to his adventures in Alaska, and wrap up our session for the moment. There are some probable outcomes he is seeking to experience today, and we have gained some very good material to help our readers understand the nature of consciousness that is beneath and behind the symbols and physical expressions of the beautiful Earth and universe in which you all now find yourself fascinatingly engaged within. To you, Jackson, I am grateful for your time and pit stop session and bid you a fond and adventurous day. – Seth

Awareness Of *Being* vs Awareness Of Being-Human?

First and foremost...You are an immortal, nonphysical *being* of consciousness. Before you were born into this physical life, you were completely valid with wisdom and experience of many lifetime incarnations and exceedingly, lucidly aware of your Self and vast nonphysical dimensions beyond your wildest dreams.

You had then, self-awareness that you were your own unique, individual portion of conscious awareness, and were, as we will say here, <u>aware of **being**</u>. You are not at that point, before your physical birth in this lifetime, aware of *being **human***, but rather simply aware of ***being***. Aware that you exist and that all other consciousness and forms and expressions of it, eternally co-exist with you.

In this nonphysical natural state, you are quite aware that you, yourself, are an individualized portion of consciousness, yet not in any way separate from all other consciousness. While it is quite difficult to explain in terms that the human mind can conceptualize, you know in that state of being that you are self-aware, yet, also aware of that which you are portion of. Almost like the hand or the eye is aware that it is unique in and of itself, yet still a portion of the larger whole of the body.

When you are born into the physical body, a portion of the larger Self or soul, as you may call it, narrows its focus, so that it is much more restricted and focused into physical reality, through the filter and perception of the physical body. That portion of your Self, or soul, as you may think of it, enters the flesh at an early stage, yet *may not*, at all times while the baby is developing, *be fully* present within the baby, but more like "visiting" and trying it out to see how it feels to be in the physical state. Many choose at that point to be fully committed to the physical lifetime experience and "move in" so to speak, to inhabit the physical body as the narrowed portion of the larger Self of your consciousness, and begin then, to experience consciousness through the filter and perception of the physical body.

It is at that point, that you are not only <u>*aware of being*</u>, but now you are aware of <u>*being-human*</u>. Which is most often referred to almost backwards if you will, as a human-*being*. Most use the term human-*being* as they recognize, while in the human form and life, that they are a physical human, but also recognize there must be some sort of conscious awareness within that provides the life animation for the physical flesh to live and walk around. So it is that human-*being* is the more popularly used term, when in fact:

It would benefit your entire culture and society
if you would instead call yourselves more
appropriately, being-humans than human-beings.

The difference in orientation is precisely what allows you to infinitely expand your own consciousness to perceive realities around you and the infinite creative tools, power, insight, wisdom, knowledge, solutions, inventions, ways, paths, and means that humanity seeks for its evolution.

For again, you are first and foremost, the immortal *being*, and THEN you incarnate into the human.

So it is that you are a *being* that has a human body, rather than a human body that has a *being*.

Now, if we use Jackson's NDE experience as a child, we can provide some context here that will help with understanding. When he died his physical death and his consciousness left the physical body to return to its natural state of nonphysical reality, it experienced what many call "heaven", although it has infinite manifestations of appearance and experience, and he had interactions there with grandparents that had long been passed away, speaking to them as lucidly as he would if they were alive and well. He also spoke to Angels and *beings* of light, and it was here that there was an interaction between myself, the larger Seth entity, and himself as a *being* of consciousness, setting forth future energy patterns, directions, tendencies to follow, future probable outcomes, and potential paths of development to accomplish our mission which we are now moving through.

However, when "he" returned to the barn and saw his physical body fall to the barn floor and lay there crumpled up and lifeless, "he" floated over his body and observed it, saying, in effect, "That's my human body. I wonder if it will continue to live in this lifetime?" - among other musings and wonderings. There was no fear, no doubts, and it seemed <u>completely natural</u> to him that his lifeless body was laying there on the floor while "he" hovered above it near the ceiling.

Now, at this point, what I want to make clear is that he was... right then, **_aware of being_**, but not as yet <u>*aware of being-human*</u>. As he was not yet back to his selective and narrowed focus from within the flesh body we call Jackson. "He" (his soul/consciousness) was aware right then while floating near the ceiling above his human body, that he _HAD_ a human body that he could choose to re-enter. However, he was not THE human body. Therefore, at that moment, he was identified _more_ with his immortal Self as a *being* of consciousness, rather than identifying himself as a physical human.

The difference is immense and one of the secrets that can unlock an infinite amount of awareness to many of your own natural and innate creative tools, but also those that are eternally "at your fingertips" for you to put into intentional, purposeful, and creative use to express new ways to improve and enhance the life you know, and all that is around you. Perhaps even teaching others along the way so that they, too, may become aware of the immense and unlimited joy and freedom to finally realize the truth of what you _really_ are.

After the physical body ceases to function for whatever reason is chosen by the higher self, physical death of the human body you have taken care of for its useful purpose to navigate physical reality ceases to be relevant. It is at this time that _you_ return your focus and perception once again to awareness of being, and not awareness of being-human. While you may, and often do, have an "introduction" re-orientation to reorient yourself with focus from outside the physical body, in an experience you many call heaven, you very quickly become acutely aware of the much greater reality around you and that you are eternally immersed in. Then your perception of all things around you in the universe becomes "visible" and accessible to you on many levels of awareness, and your "view" is exponentially expanded as you return to your primary and natural state of *being*.

We describe Jackson's experience here as the human, so that it provides teaching context through which he has personal experience and is then, able to vividly articulate and relate to the material truths that we are herein outlining for the purposes of our teachings. His larger Self, consciousness, had created the NDE event so that one day, he would be open-minded to the materials we are now writing and teaching. He "taught himself so that he could teach others also." To provide himself with first-hand physical/nonphysical connections and insights that would bring awareness to follow throughout his lifetime, and eventually, once again, become aware of myself and our mission together as we have done so many times in many other lifetimes.

You are perhaps in the position that you are in life because you are conscious and aware of current conditions, which _you focus on_, which then attract like objects, events, and conditions to re-affirm that which you believe to be your reality. You are <u>reacting</u> then to your current life situation, and in reacting, you re-act over again, that which you are consciously focused on. You are in a reactive mode of creation, rather than a Divine mode of creation where you create in harmony with all things. Likely, creating loop experiences in your life whereby you seem to be doing the same thing over and over and life doesn't seem to improve. This could very well be why. Because you are in reactive-creation-mode. Not natural-creative-mode. If you already see it (physically), then you are reacting. It has _already_ become physically manifest.

To create a NEW and improved experience, you must shift your attention to a new creative pattern and hold your attention there until it vibrates within the core of your _being_ and becomes an inner portion vibrational match to the natural _being_ within you.

Now, if you shift this focus and identification of Self to the immortal _being_ of the Divine within you, then... you will begin to shift your physical experiences also. Yet, <u>you</u> must also put in the work.

No one goes to the gym for you to make YOU stronger.

<u>All who incarnate choose their own path in life with free will and you must choose to develop your own being.</u> To evolve yourself. I cannot stress that enough and could write it here a dozen times and not cover it enough. When you take ownership of your own development and evolution, you will, in time, master your destiny and create it as you move through it.

Discovery Of Self Through Physical Life Experience

Now: Life on the physical plane is about the journey of Self to grow in ways that are uniquely provided by the physical interactions with all other physical forms of consciousness. In your native state of immortal consciousness, you are aware of these species of consciousness that exist in every way and direction you could imagine and more that are around you eternally. You can interact with them to a certain degree while you are in nonphysical form as a soul, through which you may focus a portion of your larger Self into such interactions of the physical plane. So from "outside" space and time, you can, as a soul, interact with things that appear IN space and time.

However, much more robust and profoundly more experiential growth occurs when you are submerged and immersed in the physical expressions of consciousness that appear to you as the physical universe. It is almost like dipping your feet into the ocean as you walk along its edge, from outside...on the land, or rather, you submerge yourself in the ocean and become completely immersed in its environment. Looking AT and into the water is much less experiential and robust than perhaps scuba diving in the ocean and experiencing first-hand, _from that perspective_, what the abundance of life in that environment looks and feels like as you are able to interact with it via your 5-human senses.

You gain layers of experience that add immeasurably to enrich the _being_ that you are by such interactions in physical reality. From the nonphysical perspective, an entity or _being_ of consciousness...such as yourself, can look into physical life and observe both the physical expressions and interactions; however, from this perspective of your native and natural state of _being_, you are also able to "view" and _sense into_ the thoughts, feelings, and emotions which create energy patterns that express as objects, events, and conditions that manifest your physical reality there. You use your clairabilities inherent to your consciousness to interact with the physical environment as you would not have a physical body to do so.

Much like loved one's passed on can peek in on you at any moment, and interact with you on the physical plane, perhaps affecting your lights and causing them to blink or a phone call from no-number that appears on your cell phone, but no one is there when you answer. Their soul (consciousness) can direct a portion of itself to interact with consciousness that is on the physical plane of expression. In the cases of loved ones crossed over onto the nonphysical plane, this is a common occurrence, and especially so right after their physical death. Many souls tend to signal family members still physically living that they've transitioned their focus to nonphysical reality and are "alive" and well.

Now, from nonphysical reality's perspective, a soul can shift its focus to look into the atomic and molecular structures for example, that make up the physically appearing objects that are the expressions of the universe in which you live your physical lives. For example, a loved one crossed over to the nonphysical plane could very well "see" into your physical body and know there is an ailment that should get attention. Perhaps knowing your blood sugar is high, or your blood pressure is high, or you have a sore knee.

Again, there is no limitation as to the mobility, perception, learning, and development of a *being* or of consciousness. It will, by its nature, by _your nature_, attempt to express itself in every possible way. Now, there is always learning that occurs in every interaction with other consciousness, both those that take physical form and those that do not. The learning is immediate in your terms, and multidimensional, meaning that all consciousness involved learn simultaneously at many different levels of sensing and knowing, playfulness and creativity. It is not as if one consciousness learns from the other and the first *being* or entity is simply the teacher or originator of the teachings and experiences. Each learns through each and every interaction from consciousness to consciousness, just as you yourselves learn in the physical world through each and every interaction with all other humans, animals, plants, and environments. It is mutually inclusive and beneficial to all.

Now, as I mentioned in other sections of our book here, even I... the entity that the world calls by the name Seth, learn, grow, and expand in understanding, experience, and expression, through each and every channeling session and physical activity of Jackson as he lives his physical life experiences. Our consciousness, of course, is not separate at all, but more harmonious as one. He learns through his inseparable connection to "me" and I learn through every interaction he has in physical life and beyond. This occurs for me with all of my personalities, which may incarnate or not. Regardless of their focus, into and through physical reality or not, I learn from them all, simultaneously adding to what I am, as I am eternally growing and expanding and becoming, just as the larger nonphysical portion of yourself is.

As I have said, _you_, are not as limited as you may have once believed yourself to be. Your brain and rational mind are simply not as yet fully aware of what you truly are, therefore, throughout your physical life, you are creating, discovering, and uncovering that which you truly are. And you are constantly becoming more and evolving.

The sooner you awaken your rational and intellectual mind to the truth of your _being_ within, the sooner you will be able to access not only your own personal knowledge and wisdom, but that which is eternally inseparable from you as a _being_ of consciousness. Again, I mention here that you cannot most efficiently, effectively, and consistently use the abilities and creative tools that you each eternally have, if you are not as yet aware of them in your present state. You are essentially training the rational mind to awaken to your own truths within, and in so doing, unlocking the immense power of the consciousness to create worlds, not to mention things you desire to have in life or may at any time need.

Throughout your physical life then, you are illuminating, through your interactions and learnings, the immortal Self and _being_ within, and discovering not only your own capacity to create, but how to do so in harmony with all other forms and species of consciousness around you. You are in "Physical Learning School" there.

You see, our books are providing you with illumination and insight from my perspective, into the truths of that which you already <u>are</u>. Now, as I have stated before, I am a multidimensional conscious collective of entities and souls. Souls that have incarnated onto the Earth and other planes of existence and gained personalities in those lifetimes, and some that have chosen not to incarnate but rather remain nonphysical-focused in their free will of development. I have existed before time as you know it and I am eternally focused on teaching and bringing illumination of awareness to ALL things in your physical universe, as well as those in many other physical universes and dimensions that are far beyond physical. Dimensions that may or may not have physical expressions or context at all. Those that are in your perception and experience of "time and space" and those that are in many other experiences of "time and space" in which both are experienced quite differently than the time and space that you know.

Now, Jackson's larger Self here, is a portion of my own Self and as such, teaches with me both on your plane of physical existence and in and through others. Both physically and not. Throughout what you know as human history, I have had some lives where one of my personalities incarnates into human form as does Thomas (Jackson's Self/Entity or Soul), and our bodies may have other names as we teach in those lifetimes in one way or another. In other lifetimes, what you know to be the Seth entity, remains outside of time and space, and the Thomas entity of Jackson here will incarnate into the human form, and we guide him as the physical earth-plane representative and channel through which we teach and reach humanity. We have done this both ways in many lifetimes, in the history that you know, and others humanity is not familiar with.

Human Consciousness, Personalities, And The Entity

Now, to begin - as I have stated in my prior books, there is no separation of Self. There is no division of Self. By the term Self I mean the inner "I AM" awareness of yourself as a being, unique unto your Self. Consciousness is a form of energy although my terms perhaps are more expansive than yours, and as such, it follows the natural characteristics of energy in that you cannot destroy it, end it, harm it, or divide it from all other consciousness. It is eternal in its nature and has what you may think of as "concentrations of focus" which are various kinds of personality consciousness within the larger entity as you may think of it.

Briefly, you refer to me as Seth, using the name as a point of reference while you are thinking in physical terms of 3-dimensions where objects *appear* to be separate from one another. Yet I AM the larger entity of Consciousness of which the personality "Seth" is a part of.

Now, I rather enjoy this personality out of the many that I (the larger entity) have at my disposal to communicate through. For every personality, you might say, that has been given existence by myself as the larger entity, each may choose to incarnate into a physical life, or not. They can choose to remain nonphysical and explore other dimensions of existence and creativity. Quite independent of myself, the larger entity. Much like a child moves out of the home and begins their own path in life. However, in those terms, an entity always has the connection that I can follow, by association, the path and dimensions in which one of my personalities has ventured, even though it has taken its own path.

Through its adventures, physical or not, all learning becomes an integral part of my own development and constant state of learning, expanding, growing, and becoming more.

Perception – The Filter Through Which You View, Understand, And Experience All Reality – Life As You Know It To Be

*Jackson Note: I want to insert a personal notation here that one should truly take some time to read, reflect upon and understand the **significance** of this section, for perception truly determines the quality of your life as you experience it. Although we will detail in a future book, how to use your Divine tools to raise your vibrations naturally, explained in easy-to-read and understand materials; suffice it to say that the higher one's personal vibrational frequency of both the physical body and nonphysical being/consciousness, the more it exponentially expands your perception which directly impacts your experiences in physical life and your evolution as a soul on Earth. Again, on the following pages, my personal experience is used as an opportunity for Seth to teach lessons about perception.*

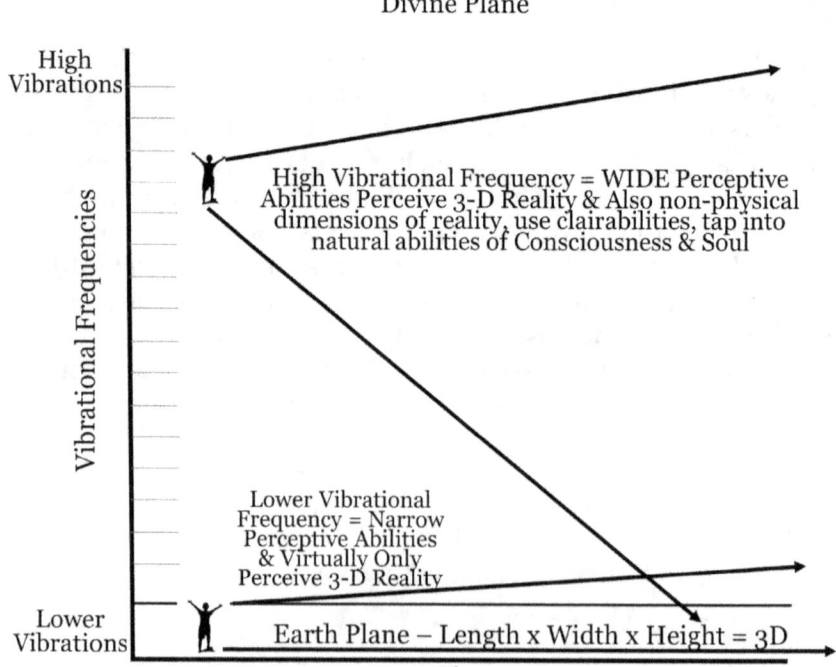

Figure 1.

We are here Jackson-Thomas. Good morning to our beloved as well. The events of the last few days do show you that energy is moving. A lot of energy is shifting this fall as we have discussed in our prior messages. Now, depending on your perception, it can be _perceived_ to be good or bad energy such as the events yesterday that occurred to you. However, again, it is your perception of it, which creates your emotional association and outcome of the events. In your case the other day you did NOT react in a harsh and negative way. You...did very well in maintaining your perception of the event and in so doing, moved quickly and easily through the event. Now, you might have taken another path and chosen to have a strong negative reaction to the event, in which case your experience of it would also be associated with.... Strong negative emotions.

This...is what causes the emotional anchors and filters to be applied to events that may happen in one's life. Your RE-ACTION to an event is determined by your perception of that event that occurs. Understanding this and seeing it from this perception allows you to examine the meaning and energy behind any given event. So, it is not so much the events themselves that occur that linger in one's memories over time and apply layers to their "rational mind veil"...the veil that you teach that blocks the natural Divine flow of energy through them, personally. However, it is their negative _perception_ of the events that have occurred, which is guided by "negative" thoughts. Negative-type thoughts of the lower vibrations are direct generators of "negative" and lower vibrational emotions. Emotions ALWAYS follow thought. Not the other way around.

**Your emotions are based upon the thoughts
and _perception_ of any given event.**

These "negative" emotions are strong emotions....Energy-in-motion, that serve to fuel the reality of the event that occurred. The stronger the negative reaction, the more it will linger in one's memory until the lesson is understood, appreciated for what it has taught you, and then released into thin air, for it no longer can move you any further. When the lesson of any given event is perceived and understood, integrated into the knowing of why it came to occur, then it can be easily released and, as such, you are free of the lesson. You move on, you progress, and you grow in understanding of events, energy, and your relationship with your world of events and objects.

So, once again, we circle back around to the human emotions being your natural human-based indicators and directional signs that you are "off path" and, of course, allowing lower vibrational _perceptions_ that allow lower vibrational _thoughts_, which generate the lower vibrational strong "negative" emotions. This then fuels the creation of your event, adding a kind of "thickness" to it in terms of its impression upon consciousness, but also within the memory.

Therefore your perception filter is
like the glasses through which you are
viewing your physical reality.

Divine Plane

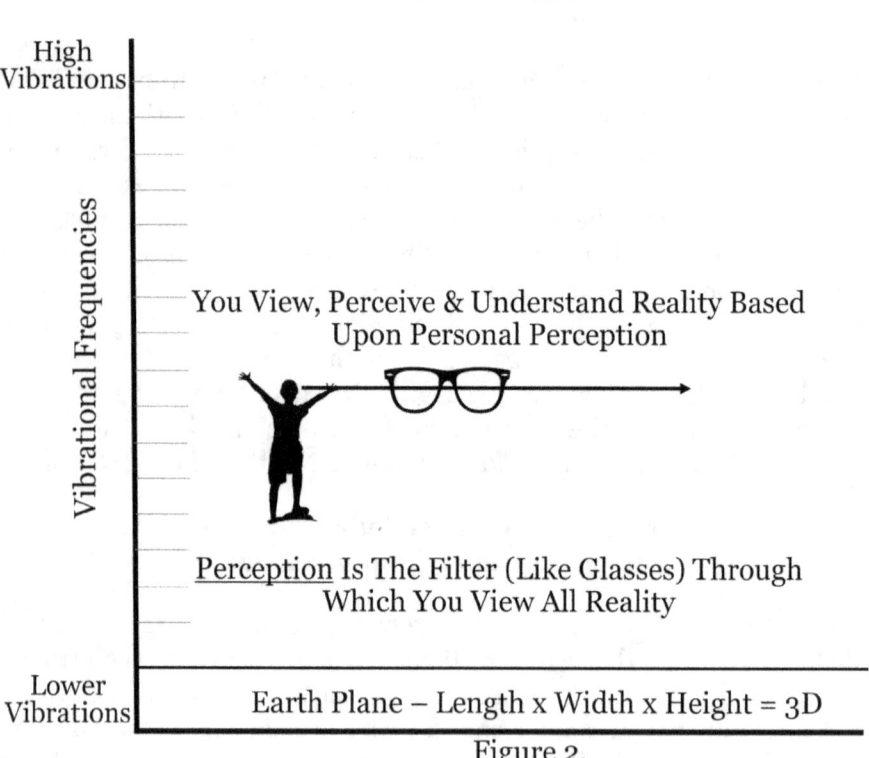

Figure 2.

Change the point of view in vibrational frequency and you will change the perception you have of any given stimuli on the physical plane. As you rise in vibrational frequency, you will then, not be emotionally moved in "negative" ways as these vibrations quite literally do not exist at higher vibrational frequencies.

Your Angels do not "get angry".

Nor does "God" EVER in eternity "get angry". Anger is a lower-vibrational human emotion that is generated in the rational mind based upon a ***perception*** of something that is out of alignment with a belief about something you desire to be a certain way. For example, you believe something should be a certain way, and if it is not, then the rational mind's limited view and understanding of the reason for it appearing out of alignment with how you desire it to be, causes or generates a lower vibrational emotion you call anger.

Now, deeper than the emotion of your anger, of course, is the soul lesson of why it is that this particular situation that angers you exists. **In that core depth of the existence of the events or condition in which you may be angry about, is the eternal love and light of "God" which is not at all that limited vibrational emotion**. *There is no such thing as "an angry God"*, though for centuries mankind has sought out some outside force to blame events that occur in physical reality on the supposed anger of a "God" or "gods".

Lower Vibrational Frequencies – challenges are *problems* or major issues.

Higher Vibrational Frequencies – challenges are creative adventures to be resolved by creatively using the consciousness to draw forth any and all knowledge, wisdom, insight, opportunities, objects, events, or conditions that are conducive to their resolution. Challenges then are lessons of adventure.

"My ways are higher than your ways" speaks precisely that the level of perception of one who is much higher in vibrational frequencies, especially so for *beings* that are not in body but have a perception and perspective far beyond the limitations while on the physical plane, can perceive a myriad of ways, paths, solutions, answers, and resolutions, for you are innately connected intimately with the Source of All That Is. Again, "God" by any and all names.

On the physical plane, ALL humans will at one time, or another be subject to many, many events throughout their physical life, which will provide them the ***opportunity*** (lesson) to ***choose*** to perceive a given event as a "good", or "bad", positive, or negative type of event, and, hence, *choose their own emotional reactions to the event*. Now, if one perceives the event to be a "bad" event, then strong negative emotions (vibrations) can be generated and sent out to everyone around them, knowingly or unknowingly. Energy out will return to the sender, personally. This is eternally true and what many have labeled by the term karma; however, all energy that is created, reflects its expression or creation back to the origin of creation, in the life you know or another beyond that, yet it will not fail to find the source of its own origin. Again, another lesson about mindful creation using your own energy to direct consciousness. Therefore, energy sent out from the individual always returns "like" vibrations of energy to the sender as you create your own reality. Therefore, at some point in time and space, the creator of such energy will themselves experience the reflection of it in a very similar manner, returned to them, perhaps even amplified if they are to pay more attention to a repeated lesson. There IS no other way of creation, personally.

However, if the same individual chooses, and perceives that same event through the eyes of an expanded awareness, understanding that it provides them an _opportunity of choice_ on how to _react_ to it, and they choose to not let it move them emotionally, the lesson is learned, and the "negative" emotions become positive joy for overcoming the lesson that has been presented to you for your learning and growth.

So here we see the importance of **PERCEPTION** - rational mind perception of your reality that only uses the limited scope of the 5-human physical senses or the more natural approach which provides much more insight and learning growth without the struggle.

Now, many humans, when grounded in the more Earth-plane rational mind perceptions of life around them, utilizing only the 5 senses to judge their perception of reality, are obviously only perceiving the end results of prior thoughts and energy sent out. They have not yet learned to expand their perceptions of the physical reality around them to include the much greater nonphysical reality that is, not only the source of all physical objects and events that the 5 senses perceive, but also, vastly, infinitely greater than that.

All human _beings_ come to the earth plane of physical experience to learn, grow, and evolve the soul. You would not incarnate if not to evolve the soul, and you evolve the soul both in the physical body and outside of it. Living or not. Physically focused or not, and even when you are in your physical lifetime, you are still learning at the level or layer of consciousness, mostly unknown to the intellect. You do not realize it for the most part; however, even your thoughts throughout the day, all day, create incipient images that have energy associations in them that then serve to direct consciousness that creates your reality unfolding. You are learning to train your rational mind and consciousness to expand your perception of physical reality beyond that which you sense with the 5-sensory organs of the physical self and include the greater reality in nonphysical terms that is the source of and "fabric" of all things physical around you.

You are then learning to _use_, to a successful degree of proficiency, through trial and error, to direct your eternally, creative energies, through the faculty of the mind and free will, to more positive and expansive creative means and thereby add to the overall enrichment of your species.

When one perceives their life around them with only the rational mind, which judges life based only on what it can see and touch around it...and with only the filter of the 5-senses, they fail to notice the magic that is not only around them, but the very magic of the Divine energy that gives them life and conscious awareness of self. Their "I AM". Awareness of Self.

They may then tend to perceive many challenges as problems and, through *that perception*, entertain thoughts that are of the same nature. Limiting thoughts, filtered by limited perceptions. When an event occurs that seems to be negative in nature, they may generate many similar thoughts, as they view it through that perception filter of lower vibrational frequencies. The negative emotions tied to it, such as traumatic events from childhood or earlier relationships and interactions with other humans, will hold their negative charge like a battery, in their memory.

This holding of the negative emotions, attached to traumas and events of one's past, simply creates a filter through which they then **continue to experience their reality, as their experience will be "colored" or influenced by viewing it through the emotional filter of limited perception they have created for themselves.**

They must learn to clear the negative emotions associated with past traumas, events, and conditions and release them. For truly it is them-themselves that are holding onto them...not their neighbor or friend.

They hold their <u>own</u> anchors into the past and it prevents them from seeing the greater reality around them and its experiential beauty because they have themselves created the "veil" around them and in them through which they then create more of their reality. What we call the **Rational Mind Veil** if you will. You block your own energy. Divine energy to create wonderful experience is always there for you eternally, yet the rational mind can in this example, set up the boundaries within which you perceive your reality and experiences, and lower vibrational emotions held onto will create and maintain your "veil" that serves to block natural Divine energy flowing through your consciousness and out into your reality around you. You've put on "sunglasses" and shaded your own view of reality.

Now - we see in this particular lesson we are discussing that it is not so much the EVENT itself that created the strong emotional ties and causes it to linger in one's memory or filter their creative energy into a better experience of reality. ***It is their PERCEPTION of the event*** ***that occurred*** *and their chosen reaction to it, which has generated the negative emotions, which causes it to linger in memory and thereby filter future creative experiences that become their life events.* (The above-bolded portion is of essential importance.)

Understanding WHY the lesson is present, opens the door for oneself to move through it. If you, meaning <u>any</u> human, are challenged, it is for certain there is a lesson behind the existence of the challenge and a reason for being in your experience. It may be as simple as learning to "let go" and release things that are not in your control to the Divine to deal with. This very simple lesson in releasing-to-the-Divine would resolve MUCH anxiety and lower vibrational emotions such as stress, worry, fear, doubt, angst, etc. For you are, indeed, at some point in your life, going to learn the lesson that you (the rational/intellectual mind) ARE NOT SUPPOSED TO KNOW ALL THE ANSWERS, MEANS, WAYS, PATHS, etc., and that you are to release such things from the rational mind's grasp and use your creative, natural tools to discover these things within yourself. Releasing these things then, allows the Divine to work on them freely, for if you hold them in your attention and awareness to the point where they emotionally move you into feeling those lower vibrational type emotions, you are not allowing the Divine the freedom to work them out freely, naturally, as you yourself hold onto them (in your awareness and attention).

Many an inventor or great artist has suddenly realized the answer or gained great clarity to "the problem" they were seeking to solve after they finally gave up and moved on to something else.

You must learn to <u>choose</u> a perception that is higher. A vibration that is higher if you will. Seeking to understand the "soul" lesson behind events that could cause negative emotions and reactions and choose through free will NOT to react to them negatively, thereby integrating the lesson and releasing it from your experience. Effectively dissolving your limited filter through which you then perceive your reality (life). When you truly understand the lesson and integrate that into your wisdom of experience, you will find that the effects that this lesson once seemed to hold upon you fade away as does the darkness at sunrise.

We are explaining the importance here of PERCEPTION, for it is the filter through which you view, understand, respond to, and hence, create your life experiences. (Reality)

It is the filter through which you also form your beliefs. Those belief structures that seem to provide a limited experience and those that set you free from what seemed to be limitations. As we have stated before, you create your own reality, yet within the boundaries of beliefs that you yourself develop and hold as your own guidelines or rails, if you will, within which you understand and interact with physical life.

If you perceive great challenges, it is your natural indicator that your Perception Filter (PF) perhaps is limited in scope due to your current state of consciousness (vibrationally speaking). To one who is self-aware and notices such things, this is your natural indicator that you may need to raise your vibrations of the inner and outer *being* so that you are in alignment with higher vibrations in which these challenge-perceptions fade away, and deep understanding and clarity become your experience instead.

When you rise in consciousness and vibrational frequency, your PERCEPTION is automatically higher. Like viewing your surrounding from the top of the mountain, instead of looking at the mountain before you from the bottom. You naturally see and perceive life all around you, and events happening <u>*for*</u> you (not <u>*TO*</u> you) as learning and, hence, you appreciate them to a degree that cannot be adequately accomplished at lower vibrations of perception. You find **<u>peace</u>** in your life that once seemed to evade you.

All things, physical and nonphysical as you know, are consciousness; and ALL consciousness of ALL THAT IS ("God" by any and all names) eternally seeks to grow and expand, becoming more than it ever has been, learning, growing, and evolving.

Rising in consciousness/vibrational frequency then shifts the human psyche, the internal "you" of you, and in so doing, raises your personal vibration, which raises your point of viewing life (perception), which puts you more into the magical and natural flow, without all the clutter of the rational mind that only perceives a very narrow and limited view of reality.

The rational, intellectual mind's job, in part, is to assist you in successfully navigating physical reality by making choices using free will. You are in sole control of your own rational mind. And since you each have your own rational mind, it is up to you to be cognizant of its patterns of thought and perception. You have your own mind. You can change your mind when you desire to and direct it in ways that are more fruitful in your life. That's one of its purposes. Selective directional uses of energy which eternally create your life experiences on the physical plane and evolves you as a soul/*being.*

No one sets another human free of their emotional traumas, negative perceptions that create the filter of negative emotions and cloud their view of reality and life around them. While a therapist or friend, an animal friend, or even the great outdoors of nature itself can assist one in shifting their perception, hence, helping them understand lessons that allow them to release the emotions attached to past traumas, it is the person themselves that must let go of the emotions associated with the trauma to release its hold on them. They are holding onto a hot coal from the fire and wondering why it's burning them, so to speak.

Now, if you look at the examples of our therapists above (human, animal, pet, ocean, forest, mountains, etc.) and look deeper into each of these "therapists" that often help humanity deal with stress and trauma, you'll find at the core basis of each and every one of them an indelible, compassionate love that pervades all things of your universe and that energy of love and light within the core *being* of each of our "therapists" is what helps the "darkness" of the one holding onto their trauma dissolve.

Truth = Light. In the light,
there can be no darkness.

For "darkness" is simply the perception of a lack of light. In the Truth, there is Illumination which reveals the true lesson and is the vibration of compassion and love that is in all things. If you but look under the physical surface of such things. Including humans.

Again, if you were to go into your house at night in the darkness, you would stumble over your things in the house clumsily. Yet, you do not turn the darkness switch off. You turn the LIGHT on and the darkness simply disappears on its own. You illuminate the room, and you can see your obstacles, thus being able to avoid them without stumbling. Apply this same example to the Self and your life, and you will quickly understand why it is that people who do the inner work and development are often the happiest as they are illuminated within, hence, do not perceive...thus experience as many challenges in life.

Humans are gifted with a rational mind to make choices, and choose their perception, which guides their reactions, which creates the filter through which they view and ever so efficiently paint their reality. They are forever setting themselves free of emotional clutter, based upon their perceptions. Or holding themselves hostage to them as they have not yet learned, understood, and appreciated the lesson to be integrated. Integrate the lesson of the soul and you rise above (literally vibrationally speaking here) the challenge that once seemed to trouble you.

Rise in consciousness (vibrational frequency), you rise and expand your perception. Automatically. Events no longer seem to bother you and you integrate lessons more easily, naturally, and live in the true more unimpeded flow of life. You are ever creating your reality *through* your own consciousness...the immortal energy within that provides the physical body its life animation.

> *"God" can do no more for you than "God" can do through you. For you are the channel through which the consciousness of "God" works to express the physical reflection of reality you yourself create.*

Again, you create your own reality and how you perceive, and hence, experience it. You choose the perception filter through which you view that reality, and hence, experience it. You do the inner development work or you do not. You experience freedom, peace, joy, and higher vibrational experiences, events, conditions, and so forth, or you do not. If you're paying attention then, at an energy level here, the events of your life are reflecting the inner *being's* state of consciousness, vibrational frequency, and hence, the kind of objects, events, and conditions that present themselves to you as life unfolding each day.

Now, while miracles, magical events, and Divine intervention does indeed occur, it is yourself that creates your life, day by day, week by week, year by year, and sets the overall "tone" of your life path and the direction of it. You set up your accomplishments as you draw forth all things from "God"/Creator/Source/The Universe, etc. to work together in the grandest nature of harmony to display the physically appearing 3-dimensional environment in which a portion of your soul/consciousness is now focused for its learning, evolution and value fulfillment.

When you realize that you yourself are the creator of your life, the painter on the eternal palette of reality, then you realize that you are in full control of changing it if you do not enjoy it as it is. It may take some time to slow the train on the tracks before you can stop it, reverse the direction, and gain ground in the opposite direction, however, it can be done. If one human can do it, ALL humans have the potential, as physical reality is expressed from consciousness and all human consciousness is indeed, shared and connected. Aware of this truth or not.

All objects, events, conditions, and perceptions of them, then, flow through the consciousness of your Self. Therefore, again, your inner *being* is the "filter" through which your 3-dimensional reality is formed for the physical senses to perceive.

At any given moment in time, you are expressing into physical terms of matter the distilled, cumulative vibrational frequency (state of consciousness) and feeling-tones of your inner *being* that appears to you as physical reality. Life as you know it to be and experience it.

Jackson Note: I taught myself to channel Angel messages and messages from my family and loved ones crossed over more than 15 years ago. I learned that having several full-time professional psychic-medium friends who did this for a living was not a coincidence in my being close friends with them. Therefore, I had been channeling Angel messages for years before I became aware that Seth had been shadowing me and guiding me along my path to our mission we are now embarking upon. As I stated in my introduction, I was actually calling upon the "Christ" consciousness when it was <u>Seth</u> that answered and began our daily channeled messages back then. That said, sometimes when I sit for a session with Seth, instead of Seth coming through, Angels will come through and speak to me. I have so many absolutely profound Angel messages from the years that I could write a book on them all by themselves. However, on one particular day when I got still in my mind and body and quietly said in my mind: "I am ready when you are. Are you there?" It was the Angels who answered. As this particular message has to do with the Perception Filter, I wanted to include it here for several reasons. For one, because it's a beautiful perspective on the same subject of perceptions and vibrations that I believe will be helpful for others to understand the process, and understand their own perception filters through which they view, and hence, understand and interact with all life. For another, to show that when Angels come in as a Divine source that offers wisdom to help guide humanity, you go with it and let it flow with love and light.

Good morning, Jackson-Thomas, we are here, and we do hear you. You are well aware by now that we are never "without" you and that there is an eternal connection between "us" all and you at every moment in time. It is the matter of recognition of this, and drawing it to the forefront of your own awareness and attention.

If one focuses too much on the physical world and the challenges, problems, or tasks to do, you are then, not leaving much room for inner guidance to come to you as you are, perhaps, if you were to sit in silence, expand your consciousness to tap into the infinite sources of guidance and resources every *being* of consciousness has at their disposal to use. Eternally, these things are yours and you cannot ever separate yourself from them except mentally when one pinches oneself off with thoughts, emotions, and lower vibrations that are not conducive to the free flow of Divine energy.

This is why it is so important to keep your vibrations as high as possible during your busy days.

This allows a more natural and open flow of communication from the Divine ("God"/Source/Creator/Universe/Angels/*Beings*, etc.) to flow into your awareness so that you may tap into the sources whereby ALL issues, challenges, and needs have answers, clarity, understanding, connections, road maps, directions, guidance, ideas to achieve means, and ways and resources to accomplish and achieve your goals.

We want to make this clear that these sources of guidance noted above - and infinitely more - are eternally available to all *beings*, and this is true of the human-*being* as well. They are available to your soul before your physical birth. They are available after your physical death. They are available as fully DURING your physical life, as they are innate, natural, and inclusive to ALL consciousness which is the very essence of the soul that gives life to the physical body.

> *One must endeavor to make lifestyle*
> *changes that set up a pattern of opening*
> *the rational/intellectual mind to the*
> *awareness of the being within.*

Read that again. You must develop yourself. And you are responsible for making choices with the rational and intellectual part of yourself that set up that pattern of behavior to meditate, reflect, turn within, and TUNE INTO this inner Self that is your connection to "God" by any and all names.

As ALL physical reality is an expression of "God", then there is nothing in physical reality that cannot be resolved within the root assumptions of the reality in which you reside for your physical learning experience. ("Root Assumptions" meaning: the basis for your 3-dimensional world. Such things as Length, Width, and Height provide you 3-dimensional reality. Space and Time are root assumptions that are inherent within your 3-dimensions. Gravity is another root assumption, for example, or the fact that you will not sprout wings and fly like an eagle, as it is not a "root assumption" of the consciousness species that you are and the 3-dimensions in which you are learning.)

Therefore, it is *your* responsibility to make a regular habit of turning within to foster, grow, and strengthen this innate, inseparable connection of All That Is ("God" by all names); then ideas, inspiration, epiphanies, sudden realizations, magical events, seemingly strange coincidences, magical synchronicities, meeting just the right person at just the right time, and blessings, seemingly out of the blue, help you along your path to move forward in life more easily...naturally, as nature does. You *are* nature. You are designed divinely to flow in life as such, without impediments.

It is often the perception of challenges that create reactions, that set up negative patterns of expression, for if you perceive something to be insurmountable and contemplate that...hold it in your attention and awareness, then you will indeed meet the conditions by which you find things to be insurmountable. *It is that the rational/intellectual mind finds them insurmountable, not the Divine mind that is within your soul....connected to ALL answers, clarity, and resolutions.* With which are you focusing through as your Perception Filter, then, to perceive your reality? Rational/Intellectual mind or Divine mind? You have both. You are both. Human-*Being*, Mortal-Immortal, Rational-Divine.

Which do *you* choose to serve (operate *FROM* as your orientation to life) today?

If you perceive an event or condition or any situation in physical reality to be a highly problematic one, then "negative" (lower vibrational thoughts) about the event, condition, or situation will follow. Lower vibrational thoughts produce lower vibrational emotions, as emotions always follow thought. Hence, you are more likely to react to the situation with lower vibrational thoughts and emotions, which does not lead to a conducive, natural flow of Divine guidance, answers, insights, wisdom, and clarity that your soul and consciousness that gives you life IS, and you tend to pinch off that flow of such things from your own awareness.

You do not react to events in your 3-dimensional world as much as you react, then, to your perception OF those events.

Change your vibrations (to higher vibrational frequencies) and you will change your beliefs and perceptions; for your perception filter is created and guided largely by the vibrational frequency that you are in any given moment in time, vibrating to/as. Rising in vibrational frequency then, by regular practice to foster the flow of the Divine within you into the awareness of your own rational/intellectual mind, (awakening to your truth within) will, over time, cumulatively raise your level of perception. This then expands your consciousness, which expands your perceptions and will automatically incorporate into your own awareness a view (perception) of the situation that allows you to become aware of the lesson behind the event or condition and, the way over, around, or through such an event while empowering your Self, and not getting stuck in life.

You open yourself, your rational/intellectual mind, to perceive the answers or guidance to them.

You see, there is no "God"/Source/Angels/*Beings*/Creator/All That Is, that is _outside_ of your human body that is not already _within_ it. It is your recognition and embracement of this truth that opens up, or perhaps pinches off your perception and understanding of this truth, and the massive life-altering implications of that timeless truth.

Now, given the above, what do you _feel_ (not think) you may desire to do moving forward to change your own experiences in life since the answers lie within you as the low but very strong "pull" of energy to take action to set up new patterns that creatively express as new physical outcomes being brought into visibility in your life? You create your own reality. It is time for mankind and humanity to do so intentionally and purposefully in ways that are not only self-fulfilling in the development of the Self, but also maximizing the potential of yourself as a human *being* while benefiting the greater good of all your world around you.

With love and light eternally, send our message along to those you share with, and let them share it with those they love and share with. You are all not just there to raise your own vibrations and develop your potential. You are there to assist those around you and your planet in doing the same. Follow the inner pull of the compass within and it will, indeed, lead you to magical places in your life.

- The Angels

Notes and Quotes

_____

_____

_____

_____

_____

_____

_____

_____

_____

_____

_____

_____

_____

_____

_____

_____

_____

_____

_____

_____

_____

_____

Notes and Quotes

_____

_____

_____

_____

_____

_____

_____

_____

_____

_____

_____

_____

_____

_____

_____

_____

_____

_____

_____

_____

_____

_____

_____

_____

Section 3:

Communication Among Consciousness

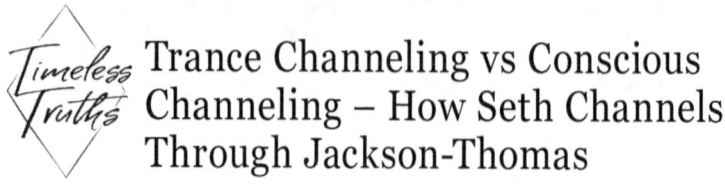

Good afternoon to you Jackson-Thomas, we ARE here with you, as if we could be any "place" else. (Smile)

You, my friend, are now aware that I have had many, many, incarnations on the earth plane, and as such, have had many personalities that have developed in those incarnations. During those lifetime incarnations and physical experiences, they each developed their personalities which, of course, had names associated with the human (and personality within that human). To simply name a few of my own; Seth, Frank, Thomas, Walter, and countless others are personalities that are an inseparable part of the larger entity that spoke to Jane (Ruburt) as "Seth" and who now speaks to you as Seth, Seth2, and more.

Now, of the Seth <u>personality</u> then, I use this personality to communicate with Jackson-Thomas as I did with Jane-Ruburt, speaking from the entity, *through the filter of the personality of Seth* consciousness to, say, Jackson's consciousness; which then translates vibrations, intentions, inflections, purpose, etc. into English words that are spoken and/or written into our book. As I have stated in other sections about myself, I have as a larger entity, many, many personalities that make up an ever-growing larger entity. Through <u>every</u> interaction in both physical and nonphysical reality, of <u>every</u> portion of personalities, I learn and grow in each moment. This is the eternal evolution of consciousness and is, aware of it or not, natural to all consciousness as it learns, grows, and evolves into more, in a constant state of "Becoming".

I can with a mere effortless shift of focus, change the personality through which I speak to you. Although you sense an inflection in the difference at one layer of that communication, you are innately aware that the underlying source is from the same "Seth" entity/conscious collective that speaks to you.

To describe it briefly here, when Jackson and I are setting down for a session, he will put himself into a meditative or altered state of consciousness whereby he shifts the attention from the outer physical world to the inner nonphysical senses and sharpens his clairabilities to be used for our communication. His consciousness, or the portion that I call "Thomas" for the personality that once incarnated with another of my personalities in another lifetime we shared together, expands outward, inward, and in every conceivable direction, yet it also expands outside of time and space itself.

My consciousness, as the larger entity that you know to be Seth, expands also, and focuses my attention and intentions for communication to Jackson, impinging upon his consciousness in a "meeting area" where our consciousnesses expand and remain open to one another. My intended communication then is sent via my intentions, purposes, and desires, that which I desire to articulate, and is picked up and received by Thomas, Jackson's consciousness here...and then translated through his consciousness, into symbols, images, feelings, sensations, and so forth that are understood through the natural innate clairabilities of human consciousness, and then decoded into their appropriate meaningful symbols that are the letters that form words that form sentences that contain within the sentences the nuances of meaning that I desire to convey through Jackson-Thomas here and onto the pages of our book.

When a question is asked by Jackson, that question is then translated with meaning, purposes and intentions, inflections, and so forth, into vibrational frequencies that mix and match within our "meeting area" and are thereby received and immediately understood at many different levels of meaning other than simply English language. The meaning of Jackson's questions or conversation to me then, is received and understood with what you would think of as ALL clairabilities, all at once. Multidimensional coherent communication.

Example:

The main entity or Conscious Collective "Seth" communicates → through the Personality of Seth → through "Thomas" the larger soul and personality consciousness of Jackson, received via his clairabilities, natural to all human consciousness (clairaudience, clairvoyance, claircognizance, etc.), →

deciphered by the mind as the vibrational frequencies reach the brain through the mind-brain connection, and the brain then organizes them into language in a linear context using the filter of the current personality of Jackson-Thomas whose native language is English in this lifetime, which then he streams through this consciousness-mind-brain connection and types onto the page English words that appear as dictated materials for our book.

Without getting too "technical" in nature, this is more or less the process of communication from myself through Jackson-Thomas to dictate all materials for our books and teachings, personal guidance for him, etc. Now, we will describe the clairabilities later in another section; however, I will mention here that all of the clairabilities of human (and other) consciousness, are inseparable and they will ALL be active at any given time.

This means that: My intention to communicate truths and materials through Jackson-Thomas, for sharing with the world then, moves from the "deepest" portion of nonphysical consciousness as the entity or Conscious Collective of entities, through consciousness and through the _being_ (Thomas) portion of the human-*being*, and then outward through the physical human (Jackson) into physical reality that appears as the words on the pages of his notebook, journal, or the typed page on his computer.

Now, we outline this process briefly here, so you understand how it is that we are writing this book. However, _we are also pointing out here that you, the reader, are also quite capable of receiving information for yourselves should you desire to learn to communicate with Divine sources._

We are here my immortal friend, and a good, good morning to you. Now, we love this side of you when you deeply desire and intend the connection between our dimensions - as it truly opens up the channel through which we enter your dimension of reality. Through this channel, not only do I come through, but you are also reaching into depths of dimensions from which the miracles and magic are sourced and originated. That which is outside the normal day-to-day manufacturing of your physical reality.

The more we channel and open the energy corridors that I have spoken of in previous sessions, the wider the channel through which energy comes into and through you and expresses out into the time and space that you are presently focused within. Practice widens the channel through which we communicate. It keeps clear of clutter and debris the channels through which we communicate. Also, the more you are focused into our communications and sessions, the "deeper" and broader the material that you will receive for our books and teaching materials.

It is true to the degree that is pertinent to our communication, that the rational/intellectual mind must be removed from the role of being the filter through which you are perceiving your reality. Where you put the thinking, judging mind at rest so that you are open to receiving the materials from us, unfiltered as much as possible so that it is "loud and clear". Jane would accomplish this by removing her attention from the physical world and reality around her by going into a meditative trance. She would then be open as a "pipe" or "garden hose" would be for the free-flow of dictation coming to her clairaudiently through her natural 6th senses.

For Jane, it was much more of a challenge to receive materials from me and not judge what was coming through, question it, or filter it in such a fashion while it was coming through that it would inhibit the free-flow of the material, or interrupt the process as it was moving along. There were a number of reasons for this. As you know, in the time period of history in which I began communicating with Jane and Rob via the Ouija board and then moving into our sessions later on, psychic activities, extra-sensory perception (ESP), and mediumship/ channeling were at a point of early development. It was not as well known or accepted that the living could indeed communicate with those disembodied, be they loved ones who had passed away or beings of consciousness such as us. She also had a strong religious background that created a very strong rational mind filter that caused her to question such things; and even if they were possible, they were likely taboo as the uneducated in those days thought such communications to be from the devil or evil spirits.

Therefore, Jane had to remove the attention and focus on the physical world and step aside from the judging mind so that free-flowing communication could take place as easily as possible. She also did not believe at the beginning of our communication that reincarnation was real or possible and did indeed think that living many lives was even scandalous.

As you can see by reading our book on the *Seth Materials*, she...the rational/intellect side of Jane was constantly judging, inquiring, and questioning the source of the material that she was receiving from me, questioning who or what I was, from where I was sourced, if I was a part of her subconscious or a separate personality that was simply coming through her consciousness to express the material, and so forth. For some years she questioned privately and as often noted in the introductions of our books from then, the validity that she was actually communicating with a being of consciousness, a personality essence, etc. that was speaking from a dimension outside of time and space for the purposes of authoring books *through* her to insert new ideas and truths into the world and assist and foster the evolution of human and physically oriented consciousness.

At the beginning of communications between Ruburt and me, there was a great need for the rational mind of *Jane* to understand that she *was* actually communicating with an interdimensional being of many personalities and consciousness that could interact within space and time as easily as a shift in the focus of my attention. The culture and society in the 1960s and 1970s were not as spiritually developed as it is now, and the acceptance of this material coming through from a nonphysical being or entity was not as accepted in that time frame and period of history as it is now. Therefore, there was a need on Jane's part...the rational mind, to qualify and prove her experience was real, based upon the scientific methods that she and others then pursued to place qualifications upon our work.

Therefore, it was quite necessary for us, to remove the rational and intellectual mind-filter of Jane, to move it out of the way...slightly to the side if you will, through the meditative trance in which she would relax into, so that the materials we channeled through her consciousness could be expressed verbally, with as little distortion and judgment as possible.

In the time period of history in 2022 that we are now working together for my next succession of books as our *Timeless Truth Series*, spiritualism or the study and development of the inner immortal self/soul and consciousness has come a long way since Jane and I first worked together.

The mass consciousness of humanity has expanded by individuals over time reading our books and many others written on the subject, and through self-reflective exercises to understand one's reality. Therefore, the channeling of a nonphysical being of consciousness today in 2022, is to a large degree, much more commonly accepted and understood than it was "then". Although we are now exposing even more people on the planet to these truths so that they, too, open the awareness of the source of their very existence and all physical reality around them in which they find themselves comfortably ensconced.

Now, you, Jackson are living in the future probable reality where humanity and society have developed along the lines of reading, understanding, and applying the spiritual development truths that Ruburt and I published some 45-50 years ago. As my original books with Ruburt were published and inserted into the world-view, it opened up an infinite array of probable futures for humanity to develop along the lines wherein the timeless truths in those books were a guiding light, if you will, for the spiritual development of millions of people across the planet that would read and in some way be touched by those truths. Not simply MY truths. *Their* truths also.

Today, in 2023 nearly 50 years later after those books were released into physical reality, there are many, many <u>MILLIONS</u> of people across the planet who have read my original books and were inspired to teach and share with others, promoted our materials from those books, and went on to inspire still more people. Tens of thousands who were inspired went a step further and went on to write their own books and teaching materials that also have immeasurably added to the development of the culture and society in which you are now living and present in 2023. From that point in time in which my original books were published and appeared in physical reality, then, we have impacted hundreds of millions of lives that span out from my original books into countless spiritual truth teachings, events, materials, etc. Many of the most famous, well-known, and loved spiritual authors, speakers, and leaders for the last few decades were inspired in part or in whole by truths that I had published through our beloved medium friend Jane Roberts (Ruburt).

Now, your path Jackson, of course, varied from Jane's in some significant ways, yet these ways you chose before your incarnation and have, to a large degree, followed as your life path. Knowingly or not. You began your spiritual awakening early. As a young child, you were raised going to a Catholic Church and from that moment on, you questioned when you were screamed at for being a "miserable sinner" at the young age of 5 years old, for example. You questioned the dogma and indoctrination of the church and religion and as your parents moved to other religions in search of answers and spiritual truths, you found that none of them seemed to fit what you innately felt to be the truth.

As an older child, you had your Near-Death Experience (NDE) event. Which of course was a _Death Experience_ only called a "near-death" as supposedly only Christ could die a physical death and come back from the dead as you did, and millions now have documented across the Earth. That provided you with yet another view of reality that also did not fit the accepted picture. You knew intimately and to the depth of your very soul that there was MUCH more beyond physical life and reality that you knew to be the only reality up until that point of your NDE. Many now around the world have had NDEs or Out Of Body Experiences (OBEs) and have come to the same stark and unavoidable realization that they do indeed exist in nonphysical form beyond physical death.

Now, you have learned over the years, to challenge the rational mind's perceptions in other ways. You are not speaking from a deep trance in which the rational mind and intellect are in the background so much that you are not aware of the environment around you to the degree that Jane was not aware of it around her. You have learned, as a channel, to simply shift the focus of your consciousness to almost literally, step aside from the rational and intellectual filter, and simply open the faucet, if you will, for the material to flow. You learned at the beginning of your development of your clairaudience training, that it was important to simply write what you receive and to write (or type) it as fast as you could possibly record it. This is, in a fashion, a training method whereby you are not allowing the rational mind to regain its focus as the primary filter through which you are perceiving reality and the materials that you are receiving.

If you paused for any length of time, the rational mind could then jump in and attempt to judge the material that was coming to you and through you, and out onto the pages of your written journal, and later onto the pages you typed and are typing now. So the speed of dictation would often act as a training tool to keep the focus of your consciousness where it was to be, rather than to allow it to jump back into the physically focused world of intellect and rational conditions.

At the beginning of our re-connection with each other in *this lifetime* as you know yourself to be Jackson, you too had similar doubts and qualification questions and were truly seeking to understand that you were, indeed, communicating with the "Seth" entity and personality that Jane had communicated with to write our original set of books. It took us many sessions for **you** to understand the depth of our communication and you are still learning of the eternal history and eons of time periods in history, in which you and I, in body and out, by many names in many lifetimes and dimensions of time and history, beyond what is generally known and accepted by science.

You have sought to overcome, then, the rational and intellectual mind in other ways. Not hindered by strong religious beliefs to the degree that Ruburt was as Jane, but in other ways, you have sought to overcome the rational mind's judgments. In your case, it is often focused on the creation of physical reality and understanding the source from which all physical objects are actually objectified into time and space, as 3-dimensional objects, and events, that make up your reality. (Aka manifestation)

The rational and intellectual mind is of course only ever seeing the physical manifestations of that which has <u>ALREADY</u> been manifested and expressed. It is the source of this expression that you have, in this lifetime context, sought to understand for in so doing, you then understand how to manipulate and purposefully, intentionally direct consciousness to overcome the perceptions of the physical world that seem so limited.

In overcoming these challenges in life then, you are able to more readily teach others how to overcome them as well and illuminate the path for many that follow - who will, in one way or another, experience challenges similar for humanity.

Again, this is not the first time, nor the last by any means that you and I have done this and will do this and are doing this. This is what we are. This is what you and I do, as I have done also with Ruburt and with others that are outside of your present view of time and space.

You see now, why it is that overcoming the rational/intellectual mind is so important here to the development of the inner being within.

What we want to relay to our readers is that Jane-Ruburt had this challenge. You, Jackson-Thomas have this challenge. Humanity has this challenge - as all have a rational mind that is used to judge, make decisions about, and successfully navigate the physical reality in which they find themselves now living. It is in overcoming the challenges that you then teach and lead others on the path of "enlightenment" or "ascension", which is simply the deeply integrated understanding as to the nature of yourselves and all that you are eternally immersed in and inseparably a part of. All That Is.

The more you challenge the limitations of the views, perspectives, understandings, and beliefs of the rational/intellectual mind, the more one opens the mind to perceive a far greater reality from which all life and existence are Sourced.

You - the immortal part of you that we have been affectionately calling Thomas - have chosen to, once again, appear on the physical plane in space and time to face these challenges, overcome them to the best possible degree, and lead others into the same progression and evolution that innately is, by all regards, "God" or the Divine working *through you* as we work *through you*.

In reality, ALL human-beings are channels through which the Divine expresses. It is largely a matter of....from which perception and understanding of reality they are currently directing eternally creative energies toward the physical manufacture of your present reality. Is it *FROM* the perspective of the Divine, spiritual, immortal, eternal being of love and light that you are at the core of yourself as a human-being? Or is it from the rational and intellectual perception and viewpoint that is so limited in its point of view and scope of understanding?

Now, you have a meeting to attend today so we will trim this session here so that you may prepare for that and the rest of your day.

Communication Through Consciousness Between The Divine Being And The Human Being

More than just channeling your own Divine guidance for daily living, we are here describing to the best of our ability to articulate, ways in which communication occurs between the human-being and the Divine realm of infinitely alive, creative, intelligent consciousness that many think of as "God"/Source/ The Universe, or what we refer to as <u>All That Is</u>. Now, while I am a portion of that source of consciousness, so also are you a portion of the same, eternally. Think about what that means, and its truth is infinite in the nature of its expressions.

Although you may as a <u>Channel</u> (psychic/intuitive medium) receive words (clairaudiently) from the Divine source/being that are in your native language (for example English), it is that your mind decodes the intentions, inflections, and meanings carried through consciousness to then be constructed by the brain into a linear, coherent message or response.

These are VERY important truths to understand as to how this communication takes place as it is the<u> foundation upon which you begin to understand how you, as a human-being, actually communicate with ALL other forms of physically focused and oriented consciousness that appear to you as animals, plants, Mother Earth and the physical universe around you that you know. This understanding is paramount to a more expanded understanding of how you, the reader, in every moment of your physical life, are "communicating" with all other forms/species/ expressions of consciousness, in your physically appearing environment, to engage the so-called "Laws of Attraction" and bring into physical focus all that becomes your life experiences unfolding before you daily.</u>

You may have heard the saying:

> **The Universe does not speak English.**
> **It "speaks" in vibrational frequencies.**

And it is through this level of "communication" and natural connection to all other consciousness that you actually form the physical reality and life that you know. Learn to understand how the "Universe" ("God", Source, Divine, Creator, All That IS) "communicates" and you will indeed be on your way to a more magical and fruitful relationship with all things around you, to create and attract into your life experience that which you desire to improve and enrich the life that you know.

1. Your prayer to the Divine in written or spoken words of your native language → translates into intentions, meaning, inflections, desire, and purpose. → These are then

2. Communicated through consciousness naturally → "Received" instantaneously by All That Is.

3. Energy out solicits energy returned (response). Intentions, meaning, inflections, desire, purpose, etc. are then intentioned to the individual praying or calling upon the Divine.

If one is open and has learned to develop their clairabilities, they may clairaudiently "hear" messages or words responded back to them and will understand them in terms of their native language. They may also receive communicated responses on multiple levels simultaneously as consciousness is not limited to response over one medium/clairability. For example, if you were to pray and ask, "Where would be a very good place to go camping that I would enjoy this weekend?"

The one praying might, for example, listen closely and tune in for an answer and perhaps receive

◊ English words that say "The lake would be a fun place!" (clairaudience)

◊ An image of camping near the lake shore appears in their mind's eye (clairvoyantly) as they are hearing the words about the lake location

◊ They may hear the splashing of the waves shushing upon the shoreline (clairaudience)

◇ They may feel the open air and freshness of the camping location on the lake shore that would be of fun interest to them (clairsentience)

Now, this is but a simple example of how communication takes place through consciousness when one sends out a request and receives from the Divine guidance, responses, answers, clarity, etc. via your normal and very natural clairabilities. If one has not yet learned to develop and use their natural clairabilities that are inherent within all human consciousness, the "Universe" if you will...the Divine/"God"/Source...may "communicate" with you through physical objects, people, events, seeming coincidences, and happenings. Again, be open to the ways in which this communication can take place, as it can, but need not be, through clairaudient messages - unless, of course, that is your intention and you are relaxed enough to tune within for that purpose and intention. It may come to you as guidance and answers in another form, through another physical object, event, or condition.

For instance, in our example above you are thinking about perhaps going camping somewhere for the upcoming weekend, and throughout your day, as you are pondering this in your mind, your thoughts, though not formal "prayers" are indeed vibrating those thought patterns of energy out into consciousness. A day later someone is having a conversation with you and tells you that they just got back from a wonderful camping trip out at such, and such lake and it was exhilarating!

If you are paying attention then, you have received your "answer" or guidance, if you will, through another human being that acted as a "channel" through which the Divine answered you or responded to your inquiry. This happens constantly for millions and millions of people daily, though they do not realize or are not always aware that seemingly coincidentally, they received the answer or guidance, or solution that they were seeking.

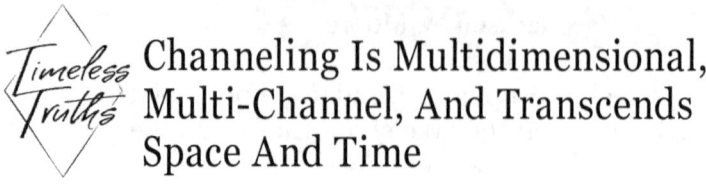

We have mentioned there is no separation of consciousness, as consciousness does not take up space and time. It appears, in what appears to be the phenomenon of space and time, where it expresses into 3-dimensions; however, at the layer beneath the atoms and molecules that make up that solid-appearing reality, it is consciousness that gives the objects physical form and existence.

Now, as there is no separation of consciousness, then there is no separation of the clairabilities of humans and, to a degree, animals and other consciousness. This means that there is no separation between your clairvoyant abilities, your clairaudient abilities, or your claircognizance, etc.

This means then, that consciousness can and does, aware of it or not, communicate at ALL levels, layers, and via the clairabilities, all <u>simultaneously</u>, as they are inseparable. Developing one of these abilities then, to a degree, will assist in the overall development of them ALL. The human (and other) consciousness is quite capable of sending and receiving data, information, feelings, sensations, images, light, truths, and inflections upon certain things. For example: when I stress a word for Jackson to <u>underline</u> or **bold**, I have sent him an "inflection" on that word so that he senses through his clairabilities that inflection and can then bold or underline words I desire to place special contextual attention upon for emphasis and learning of our readers. The "inflection" upon the word, as noted above, is embedded within the word itself. It is inseparable from the word as it is expressed, thus he will "automatically" place the inflection desired on the word when it is expressed into physical words of English as he types them on the page.

In another example: I may be channeling with Jackson-Thomas and say, *"The ocean is a beautiful place to find one's inner vibration tones expanding naturally as you listen to it and watch it crash upon the shoreline."*

As Jane (Ruburt) did also, Jackson is likely to receive this message:

◇ Clairvoyantly – he will see an image of the ocean in his mind's eye, with waves crashing upon the shore

◇ Clairaudiently - simultaneously, he may hear the crashing of the ocean as it washes up onto the rocks in a white frothy splash of water and rolling ocean waves...this being received at the same instant that he is typing the letters he clairaudiently hears in our dictation

◇ Clairsentience – he may "feel" the environment of that particular location, the peace, and the vibration of that particular environment, and sense the peace and higher vibrations there

◇ Claircognizance – he may also **_know_** that this location is a peaceful, serene location that is safe, beautiful, natural in its beauty, and would be a location that expands the vibrations as he doesn't just _receive_ such information. He can experience the information directly to the depth of his soul as it is tuned into at a layer of consciousness that is beyond all 5-human senses, that transcends time, space, and all human physical senses.

Now, in our example here, all of this communication will come to the medium/channel simultaneously when I am sending them the dictation. Again, this occurs all day, every day with everyone; however, most are not aware of the "communication" that is coming to them from their environment, the forest, the ocean, someone speaking to them, or any interaction in 3-dimensional reality. As your consciousness is eternally operating within and outside of that context of reality and is able to send and receive and "communicate" with it all simultaneously.

In another example: those who have read my original set of books may remember that, at times, Jane would comment that when in dictation sessions, she would occasionally receive information on "more than one channel". This occurs with Jackson here, also. Meaning that via consciousness, I can be literally dictating two or more different sentences with all of the above inflections and nuances in them, and they are received and understood by Ruburt or Thomas, the consciousness portion of Jane and Jackson, and can be coherently understood at those levels, even if the hands or physical portions of the human are not able to type or speak both sentences at the same.

The consciousness then, is able to coherently track and communicate at multiple channels, through multiple dimensions of reality, nonphysical and physical, all simultaneously. It is the rational mind/intellect that is typically the narrowly focused funnel through which linear context is applied for the 3-dimensional world, that cannot effectively operate to the same capacity as the consciousness in its unlimited nature.

It can be, to a degree, trained to operate at a more expansive level and receive such multi-channeled information and understand it, though it is not capable of FULLY multi-streaming simultaneously occurring, multidimensional, multi-channeled information on a greater scale as the unlimited consciousness is.

Channeling Can Be From Multiple Sources Or Beings, Simultaneously

We will here begin discussing a bit more information about the channeling of consciousness, such as Jackson-Thomas does with me for the purposes of writing our book here. We want to remind you about consciousness not truly being "singular" in focus and that you cannot ever physically separate the consciousness of one entity from another, as ALL entities of consciousness of multitudinous species, focus, and perceptions all exist simultaneously within All That Is.

So it is that when a human channels, the information may originate from an entity, a soul or personality of someone who has incarnated into human physical form before and lived a human life, if even for a brief few moments, or it may originate from what you call Angels or other beings. In reality, it can originate from "The Universe" or any portion of "God"/All That Is. However, the source for the communications, the knowledge, wisdom, insights, and that which is streamed to and <u>through</u> the human-_being_ that is channeling _can and do originate from many "sources" of consciousness all simultaneously._ While there are no physical boundaries or separations in consciousness, there are indeed _psychic_ ones that involve layers of existence that do not have a context that would make sense to one viewing them from a 3-dimensional world.

Intentions to communicate the meaning behind the words and concepts that are being related through the human-being's natural faculties of clairaudience, clairvoyance, clairsentience, and so forth are all used by Source consciousness to direct the focus of the _intentions of meaning_, into the consciousness of the human-being that is doing the channeling.

For example: it is much like a choir or group of Christmas carolers when they are singing in unison. There are many people or sources that are together forming one stream of information that comes out as a linear, coherent song, yet it has come from each individual contributing energy of the intended song and meanings into that one stream of words that you hear when listening to the carolers' singing.

In a very similar fashion then, our intentions for communication will all join in a stream of vibrational frequencies that are then decoded, if you will, by the human consciousness and formulated into linear symbols that, to you, make up the English language of words, sentences, and paragraphs that are then typed, written, or otherwise recorded as our dictation.

In the nonphysical dimensions, we do not have nor use names as you do on the physical plane.

A portion of us, or soul, may have incarnated into a physical lifetime whereby that physical human body was given a name...as it appeared separate from all other human bodies and, in such a fashion, is given a name for others, who also appear separate, to reference this person.

Truly, I suppose, I have <u>many names</u> - if you were to use each name of each soul or personality that incarnated into a human body to live a physical lifetime, in any dimension of historical time, and in that lifetime as a male or female, had a name by which other humans that were physically separate from me called me for reference in that lifetime. Then in this frame of context, as the entity you call "Seth" that authored all the *Seth books*, I have many names.

In many physical lifetimes with Jackson-Thomas here, I was not called by the name Seth, though I am the same <u>source entity</u> (entities or Conscious Collective if that term makes more sense) from which all of these personalities and souls have originated and been given existence.

The importance here is that you can, as all humans can, call upon whatever <u>higher consciousness</u>, by whatever name you choose, to direct the focus of your calling in prayer or your invitation for the Divine to focus into you and what you are desiring to communicate with us.

Names are used on the physical plane to describe objects within 3-dimensional reality that <u>appear</u> to you to be separated by "space".

However, at their lowest level of existence, we perceive objects in your 3-dimensional plane to be not just physical, solid-appearing objects, but rather vibrations of energy that are formed into atoms and molecules that make up atomic mass. At their lowest level of existence beyond the atoms and molecules that make up physically appearing objects, these objects are actually the consciousness that has intended to express itself in terms of those atoms and molecules, which impinge upon and appear within the 3-dimensions of reality that you know to be your physical world and universe. Now we, as in Divine entities of much higher vibrational frequency ranges that focus into your and other 3-dimensional physically appearing systems of reality, can of course shift the focus of our consciousness to see physically appearing objects as you perceive them. Or we can see through them, beyond them, or perceive them over time instantaneously spanning, say, a millennium.

We can, for example, perceive into your reality and see the coffee table in your living room as you see it, as it appears to be a solid object. Yet, we are not limited as conscious beings, to _only_ that perception; we can, of course, see the living, vibrant atoms, molecules, and so forth that make up the solid appearing coffee table, and still further see/perceive within the atoms to see their individual electron orbits, see and sense the intelligence that is within the "space" you would perceive to be between the electrons and the nucleus, and communicate intelligently with the very consciousness that is the source energy that expresses itself as those atoms and molecules. You see, once again, consciousness is not limited in any fashion and certainly not in any way that you perceive as physical limitations on your 3-dimensional plane.

What I would like to also point out here, once again, is that the very self-awareness that allows you to perceive yourself as a human-being, your consciousness that provides your physical human body its life animation to walk around during your physical life, is also not at all limited. It is critically important that you understand this truth as within it lies the secrets to unlocking and activating your own Divine abilities to create in ways previously perhaps only dreamed of.

Your consciousness, awareness of Self or "I AM" as it is often called, is indeed consciousness with unlimited capabilities and levels of perception that can, to some degree, be tapped into when you rise in personal vibration, expand your perceptions and beliefs to include the nonphysical nature of yourself as a _being_ that has a human body during this (and other) physical lifetime experiences.

You, dear friends, are vastly capable beyond your wildest dreams. You need only learn to tap into the nature of yourselves and bring it to the forefront of your walking waking awareness so that you can begin to direct it, use it, apply it, and source that which you desire from All That Is/Source/The Universe/"God" etc.

We will of course speak about rising in personal vibrations and ways to do so, using tools that are innate and natural to your consciousness, later. However, we are first moving through the multi-faceted, unlimited natural characteristics of consciousness, as it applies not only to you as human-beings, but also to animals, plants, Earth, and all things in your universe.

Consciousness Does Not Have Nor Use Names And Names As Symbols

Now: Your names are *symbols* that describe objects that appear to be separate to those who are also on the same 3-dimensional plane with them, immersed then in a uniquely rich learning environment that is everywhere around you alive with conscious energy. Consciousness is the very "fabric" of each and every physically appearing object and there is not a grain of dust on any planet in your entire known and unknown physical universe that is not, at its lowest level of existence, the very species of consciousness that has in its own way, intended to express itself as a grain of dust into 3-dimensions of reality to partake in this unique expression of All That Is. Even the space that you perceive to be in between physical objects, is indeed very much "alive" and infinitely diverse in creative, intelligent consciousness. Of course, you cannot have "God", Source, The Universe, etc., that is *Omnipresent* if this "being-ness" is not EVERYWHERE present now, can you?

In nonphysical reality, we do not have nor use names for they have no context to us here. Let's use Jackson here as an example. While his soul may have once incarnated as a man who was then named Thomas, truly, this soul, or consciousness, does not have a name. The human expression and physical body had a name in that lifetime, yet it does not retain the name Thomas from one lifetime to another so that other souls, entities, or beings of consciousness can call you by name.

So it is that the same soul has many personalities that may each have had a name for the male or female that the personality is incarnated into for each lifetime. There is then, a psychic separation and individuality to each personality, but not a physical separation. They are all therefore connected to the soul or main entity and the main entity learns and expands through the experiences of each personality.

Again, natural communication methods are all infinite vibrations of consciousness-alive and intelligent forms that are themselves valid and unique; yet connected, immersed in, and eternally a part of all consciousness that humanity throughout the millennia has called "God" by one name or another. In our natural environment in which I have my present reality, communications are more of the nature of what I often term thermal images, which, when presented in the context of your understanding, could be compared to vibrational frequencies that make up these images, though the images themselves do not correspond to what you think of as a 3-dimensional image. They are different in unique ways that are challenging to relate to you, as you tend to base your understanding *from* the 3-dimensional perception of which you are presently most accustomed. You see and understand things from your "Earth-bound" perception/point of view and understanding.

Seth's Message To Jackson On Our Mission, His Intentions Behind Our Mission

*Jackson Note: This message was given to me in a private session with Seth that I wanted to share with our readers as it applies to all of humanity.

Now: Our mission in this lifetime is the same in many ways as many prior lifetimes we have shared together. Both with me in spirit/the nonphysical realm guiding you while you are incarnated in human form, and those lifetimes in which we both were in the human flesh in the same lifetime, teaching together on the physical plane. That mission has always been to bring more consciousness, awareness, love, and light to the people of the planet. In the old days, it was much slower and harder. So think about this, 2,000 years ago, very few people could read or write or have access to textbooks, etc. So our teachings were limited in exposure from one person to another. Even as recent in historical time as my original books were written through Ruburt, incarnated as Jane Roberts, there was no internet and no social media; our global outreach was limited to the books, newspapers, and occasional video recordings.

However, with the new technology, fast methods of the internet, and access to social media that many, many have today in your historical period of our teaching, it is amazing the amount of people across the planet that we can reach in one lifetime, using this technology. You have a technological background and degrees in computer science for a reason. You were not aware then, when you were seeking out these milestones earlier in this lifetime, that it would one day lay the foundational beginnings of the mission we are now fully embarked upon. But then again, you were also not aware that your death experience as a child was indeed a pre-intentioned event that you called into focus in physical reality, again, preparation for the same mission we are now fulfilling.

Our mission then, among many things, is still in this lifetime, as others, to bring love, light, increased conscious awareness, expansion of consciousness of the humans that we reach with our teachings and materials, increased consciousness of the inner Self and one's own power and connection to "God"/All That Is.

Now for you, Jackson - **Do not get caught up in the limitation of thoughts of who you are and your name Jackson as it refers to the human physical body, nor in who we are as the Multidimensional Conscious Collective that the world knows to be "Seth", as this will only serve to limit the pathways and messages that come to you and through you. Both for your own personal guidance in your lifetime and in our mission and for that of our teachings to the world. Your name Jackson does not define you unless you allow it to. My name of the soul you call "Seth", that is a portion of the much, much greater conscious collective of souls and entities of which I am, <u>does not define me either</u>. Nor should <u>any human</u>, including any and all of our readers and those around the world, allow their name to define who or what they are.**

This is vital for understanding the multidimensional soul that you are. If you believe, for example, that you are just "Jackson" or "Tom" or "Mary" or any NAME for example, you are limiting yourself to THAT personality, and closing off, to a degree, your own multidimensional knowledge, wisdom, insights, and abilities that can eternally be shared and communicated among the various personalities of your own souls, as you also have had many names. All must begin to shift their perception and definition of the Self to be an eternally evolving soul with many personality portions of itself, learning, growing, and interacting in and outside of physical reality, eternally.

Again, names are only useful in the context of 3-dimensions in which objects appear to be separated from one another. In reality, at the core existence of ALL humans, you are not at all separable and it is time that humanity comes to this stark and very real truth so that they may begin to draw upon the unlimited nature of themselves as creative beings eternally existing within ALL possible creativity that is of All That Is.

Now, be open to our materials changing from time to time to different ideas and subjects for you and for our book dictation and such. As you may not get all of the information for any given subject at one time. Meaning that, perhaps, I will give you information on xxxx for a few days, then go off topic to zzzz, and then back to xxxx again later. There is great purpose in my approach so just let it flow as it comes to you. We will organize book material as it moves toward production and publication.

My purpose, our purpose, is to share information, tips, and tools for the soul connection, for information on the foundation of success as a soul incarnated on Earth, for how the personal inner power of a person is the creator of their life and world, and for increased understanding in the awakening of consciousness and why it is important to the collective good future that all yearn for on Earth and beyond. All of this information being brought to you is, of course, for your personal life vibration, as it cannot reach the world through you as a Divine channel, without also blessing you, Jackson, in the process. As it comes to you and through you, as you are the Divine channel through which we, the "Seth" Conscious Collective/Entity/Entities/Angels, etc. work, it blesses you as it comes to you and through you to bless the world. Again, it is not just that you are the end-point for the materials and our timeless truths. We do not give them to you so that they enhance your life and that alone. It is that when they pass through you and you teach, speak, write, mentor, guide, and reach the rest of the world, then you (Jackson-Thomas) become the Divine channel which is growing, expanding, and BEING, for all of "us" to also reach humanity, animals, nature, your planet, and the physical universe.

I want it to be very clear to all who we reach, that these messages in our books, and all materials we create, are to improve everyone's life, no matter where they start, right now, and your life will be enhanced by Light, blessings, "God"/All That Is.

Now, as I have stated in our book here, do not get caught up in names. I say this to ALL humans, for you only serve to limit yourself if you do so. Our book, our teachings for thousands upon thousands of years, going back to the ancient times before Christ, during his lifetime when the soul of Jackson was indeed present and teaching and supporting our mission then, and even back to historical time periods in other civilizations before your current version of history takes place - teach the eternal power, creativity, and Divine unique validity of all souls, all consciousness, for all expressions in your dimension and beyond.

Therefore, your own being and existence is far, far beyond the human name you now carry that belongs to the physical flesh avatar that you have expressed as your human self in this lifetime for your physical learning experiences. Our books, our teachings, and our ancient manuscripts from, again, before, during the time of Christ, and my original *"Seth books"* through this *Timeless Truth Series*, and into futures that you largely do not yet perceive, all bring these messages of unity to the Earth, humanity and All That Is.

If you, as the reader, are inspired by reading our book, for example, and learn to channel as Jackson learned to channel and has taught many, many others how to channel Divine Source/"God"/Angels/ Beings of Light and Love, do not, then, be dismayed if the one answering you is not named "Seth" or "Christ" or ANY name; for again, although our human incarnations may have had names for those who have incarnated to the earth plane, we do not retain names, nor use them here, and limiting your channeling to a "name" that seems to be fitting for you, will only serve to limit the messages you receive.

Again, I tell you all: Do not get caught up in names. If the materials that you receive are in love and light, they will indeed strike a chord of vibration within the very soul, your being within your human, and you will feel or even *experience* the words of wisdom coming to you. When you read our book here, when you perhaps learn to channel yourself and use your own clairabilities to gain direct immediate eternal access to ALL wisdom, knowledge, insight, guidance, and so forth, when it vibrates to the core of your being, your soul, your inner Self, then you will Know The Truth, and The Truth Shall Set You Free (in the mind that you were once self-imprisoned within limited vision and understanding).

Though the greater entity/entities/Conscious Collective enjoys speaking through the personality of Seth, you could call me by any of my many, many names I have held in my lives incarnated on the earth plane and I do not care. I have said this before in my books and writings and I will again say it here: Names are not important, but you may call me Seth. You may call me Walter, Frank, or many other names I have held. They do not define me, nor do they define you. My soul energy has been many names in many lifetimes and frequencies, and now I would also be considered Seth2, the "larger" entity that was a portion of myself that Jane-Ruburt spoke with occasionally, as <u>my vibration as the entity has infinitely grown and expanded in magnitude and frequency since "your past" in 1975, in your perception of time.</u> I am willing to come in any form, with any

132

name, and share the love and light with humanity, and many other dimensions in which I interact and teach.

For many, many years I was _known_ by my followers as Immanuel. (Emmanuel depending on translation). You, the soul of Jackson-Thomas, knew me in that lifetime and indeed, supported me and our teachings of truth that have made it through history into the teachings still known today. In that lifetime, and in others such as when I was a Pope, I molded my teachings and messages to fit a more religious path to heighten, bring awareness and expanded consciousness to humanity in those historical periods. Although my _given name_ was not Immanuel, it was indeed what I was _called_ throughout that lifetime and for many years to follow. Though it is not the name of the personality that I choose to speak through now.

In _those_ times, people were seeking unity through religion as it was a newly budding form of truth. Before religions formed into institutional, dogmatic organizations that had set boundaries that defined one from another, religion was intended to establish a foundation for Timeless Truths that would guide humanity for the very purposes of our mission today, my books with Ruburt (Jane) and those of Jackson-Thomas now. Though you do not perceive it of course, I am also dictating "books" in what would appear to be your future, through another, though they are not in the forms you have in your society and culture today, but more electronic in nature and expression.

My point here is that, depending on the historical time period in which we are teaching, or I have been teaching in one form or another, by one name or another, I have always colored my teachings to be representative of the expanding consciousness, understanding, depth, and breadth of humanity _IN that time period._ I must always work within the root assumptions, perceptions, and understandings of the time period of your history in which I am interacting and teaching. My ancient teachings are now being presented in new ways, breathing new life into the ancient ways and meanings, providing a context that was not in "those days" understood, yet now is and will be as it has grown in the consciousness of humanity for thousands of years now.

We seek then, now, in your time period of history, as I did through Ruburt in his/Jane's to bring new light and context to our ancient, but truly timeless teachings of truth. For the same timeless truths that applied then as to the inner power and eternally creative, unlimited, and infinite love and light of all human beings were as true and applicable in ancient times as it is now in 2023, and will be a thousand years from "now". We will in Volume 2 of *The Nature of Consciousness*, speak more about our ancient teachings of timeless truths, how they were intended to transcend time and guide humanity from that point in human history, how some of these truths got off track and the true meaning and context of them distorted, and why it is that now we bring them to humanity in a new light so that the distortions are cleared, and the eternal truths understood. Then will humanity exponentially expand in consciousness and utilize creative means and ways that were only heretofore dreamed of. This is the evolution of humanity. Our work has always been to guide that; and for eternity, it will continue for there is no end to the expansion of consciousness and the creativity that it expresses, in physical terms and otherwise, in your dimension of space and time and others.

As another example here, I might add that although I call Jackson here in our book "Jackson-Thomas" referring to the mortal human "Jackson" and the immortal being "Thomas"... his soul, of course, does not have a name either. His soul of the man we see in this lifetime to be the human Jackson has had many, many names over many, many lifetimes, and incarnations. Both male and female in human terms, just as I have. Therefore, although herein we call his soul/being "Thomas" – it has had, in greater terms, many names. Again, **do not get caught up in your name now in this lifetime, for you are indeed, vastly beyond the identity of the name you have given the physical body in this lifetime**. Opening yourself to that timeless truth will assist you, then, in being open to perceiving those other lifetimes, lessons, and energies that are transparent to the consciousness you know to be you in <u>this</u> lifetime.

Now, Jackson - that will be all for this particular session in this section of our book. Again, more will come in our Volume 2 as we shape that into the evolution of our book and our Timeless Truths. Thank you for the session today. Much love and light to you and all.

Timeless Truths

Now: While the word prayer tends to have a more religious tone to it, it is simply calling upon a higher form of consciousness than that of the portion of yourself that is, at the moment, focused into the physical 3-dimensional world, so as to receive guidance, answers, solutions, healing, protection, and any other need that humanity may identify.

While many think that they are calling upon an "outside source", separate from themselves perhaps, to come from some distant location to help, guide, or assist them, it is really more of a welling-up of this vibrational frequency of a higher consciousness within so that it illuminates the answers, guidance, etc. that you seek or call upon higher consciousness for whatever purpose.

Again, you may think of us - ALL beings of consciousness, entities, Angels, or what have you - as being separate from you, as you are looking through the 5-human sense perception and not through your inner, natural being which realizes that it is never separate from us at all. However, as "God" or the Divine by all names, is indeed Omnipresent; all consciousness that you may think of as being outside of you is also inside of you, for there is "no other place" that it could be, <u>as consciousness does not take up space as you perceive it</u>.

The consciousness of your own soul and larger entity, if it had a size, would be greater than the size of your entire universe. So if you think of your entire universe already within your physical body, this prayer, or calling upon higher consciousness then, draws forth from the dimensions of consciousness that are infinite in nature, the vibrational frequencies, answers, guidance, ideas, inventions, love, light, and all things... and calls them to the forefront of your <u>own</u> awareness...within.

These things may *seem* to come to your aid or attention from outside of yourself, as you are, again, focusing within 3-dimensions in which objects appear to be separated from one another. However, it is only an illusion that it would ever come from "outside" of you. As space is only a phenomenon of appearance, an illusion for your 3-dimensionally focused 5-human senses, so that you may navigate that fascinating reality.

The enormity of these simple truths, when contemplated and understood deeper and deeper, is one of the keys to the evolution of your Selves as souls, as you may draw from this universe within infinitely more than you do so now with abilities that today would seem like science fiction, awaiting discovery, understanding, application, and use.

Let us begin our brief materials about calling upon higher consciousness with some key reminders:

1. Names are used on your 3-dimensional plane to describe physical objects (even human beings) that all _appear_ to be separate from one another. To the human-being, names assist with learning within 3-dimensional reality where objects appear to be separated by space.

2. When you pray, ask, invite Divine consciousness - higher vibrational beings of Light, you may call upon us by whatever name you desire, yet your "answer", or in the case of those that have learned to use their natural clairabilities and channel Divine Source, may come from what you would think of as many sources/areas/ dimensions/beings that all are perceived by you, to be one clairaudient voice coming through to you. Like a choir singing, for example.

3. When you pray or call upon Divine beings, higher vibrations, Source, "God", Angels, etc., there is a call, if you will, that extends out into "The Universe" (Consciousness of All That Is) and a vibrational match to the calling that focuses Divine energy, consciousness, awareness to your calling. When you call upon higher consciousness by any name, it is the meaning and _intentions_ to reach such consciousness, that is indeed received instantly, as you would think of it, by All That Is, and a response is indeed immediate, whether or not you can perceive it, accept it, or sense it. There is a call from you and a match...your intentions to reach higher consciousness and draw forth from this source are "heard"/felt/registered/acknowledged.

Beyond your 3-dimensional plane, your words do not have the meaningful context they do on your plane of existence as you are in the human experience. Again, it is your _intention_ to communicate and the meaning BEHIND and WITHIN the letters, symbols, and words... the emotions that are carried with those intentions, that we receive as a "call" upon us in prayer, for example. Meaning - We do not receive English (or Spanish or any other) language and seek out an English-fluent entity or Divine being of consciousness to hear and answer your prayers or calling. We receive the intentions, emotions, and the meaning that is BEHIND and WITHIN the letters (which are symbols) that are put together to form words that you are using to express the meaning you are trying to convey when you speak or think these words. Your words, then, are simply symbols that you use to convey meaning, intentions, and inflections that all have vibratory ranges that are "received" and understood via consciousness.

This meaning then, is what is "received" – not English words. This gives you an understanding of how your calling, prayer, and seeking of guidance, etc. is received by us in the Divine realm. Yet remember it is also the very same type of process in reverse when we then communicate with human-beings through their consciousness via vibrational frequencies, which are then interpreted and translated into words, in their native language that can be understood, as well as pictures or images that are themselves symbols with meaning that we are conveying to the one we are communicating with and through.

An important point to call out here is that you do _not_ need to write or say your prayer "perfectly" for it to be fully effective. In fact, you may misspell it all you would like. You can write it or speak it in many different languages. It need not be perfect at all, for it is the meaning, emotion, intentions, and inflections that all are conveyed through consciousness, and are received by the Divine as you think of it. We "hear" you and understand you, better than you hear and understand yourselves, as we "hear" and receive your prayers and communications on many levels that are beyond simple languages, words, sentences, etc. It is a multidimensional communication through consciousness and cannot be any other way.

Now, as there is no space that separates consciousness, communication is instantaneous. It is fully, completely, and unquestionably understood as vibrations of infinite frequencies that all carry meaning at many different levels which are understood by all other forms, types, and species of consciousness that have relevance to that particular focus of reality, physical or nonphysical. No human thought has ever been thought that goes "unnoticed" or does not in some way create throughout many dimensions of reality(s). That which you call "God"/Source/The Universe is eternally "listening" as you cannot, again, separate yourself from All Consciousness.

What I want to make clear here is that in prayer or calling upon higher consciousness for any purpose:

> *It is not that you are calling upon an "outside force" to come in and save the day or provide that which you seek. You are calling forth that vibrational frequency, consciousness, being, into your own consciousness/soul and calling it forth to the forefront of your intellectual mind's awareness so that your consciousness expands and you allow yourself to perceive the answers, guidance, wisdom, clarity, solutions, protection, etc. You open yourself to the Divine providing that which you seek through yourself, not from an "outside source" coming to you, but from an inside source coming <u>through</u> you.*

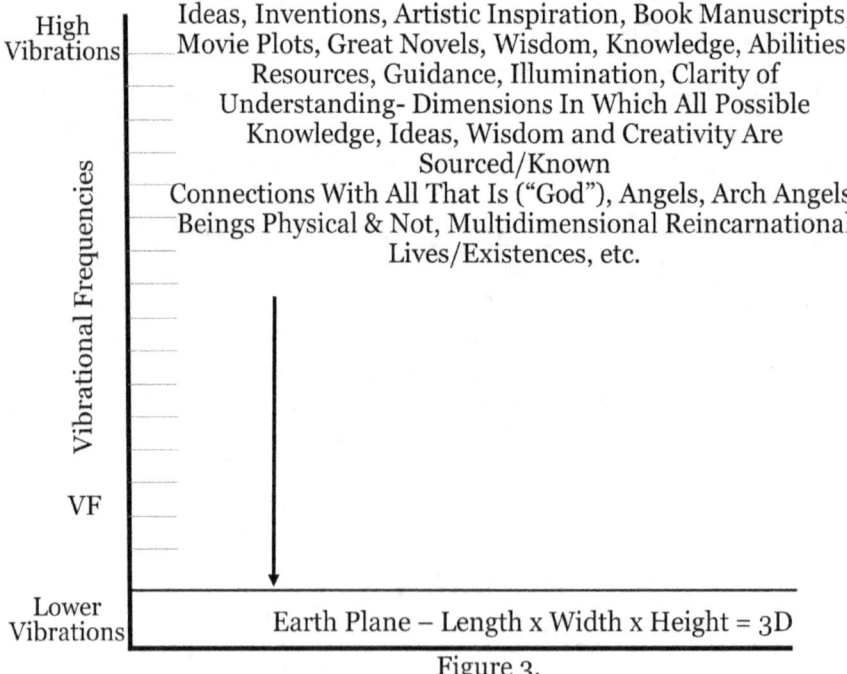

Figure 3.

Challenges Occur Most Frequently At Lower VF

138

Think in terms of consciousness, energy, and vibrational frequency. As the Divine is super high in vibrational frequency then, and you are on the earth plane of lower frequencies of vibration where objects appear as solid, 3-dimensional matter, the Divine does not lower its vibrations to come in and save you or fix what needs to be fixed, to provide the wisdom, guidance, and understanding of clarity that you need to resolve your situation.

You raise your own vibrational frequency to MATCH higher vibrations in which the solutions are already present, eternally awaiting for your opening and expanded consciousness to perceive them.

You are your answers, your guidance, your wisdom, and your supply. It is, rather, your failure to recognize and embrace this truth that seems to hold such things at arm's length from you. Again, you create your own reality. While the mass environment and society around you, does indeed have its own vibrational tones that set the overall psychic environment and "feeling tones" of the experiences in that particular environment, your personal perception of it, and hence your personal experience of it, is your own. Even someone standing next to you for your entire lifetime would experience your reality quite differently, as their perception filters are based upon their own vibrational frequency, states of consciousness, and hence, understanding of the very same things that you would perceive next to them.

Remember then, "God"/Source/Creator/The Universe/All That Is can do no more for you than through you. Again, while miracles and Divine interventions can and do occur, the day-to-day creation and expression of your life path and experiences of it are your own to create, perceive, and experience. If you remember then, that ALL of your life experiences are going to flow through your own consciousness, and your consciousness (state of consciousness) and inner vibrational feeling tones set the filters through which your life is expressed, perceived, and experienced, then you will quickly understand why it is that you want to keep your personal vibrational frequency at higher levels to illuminate the darkness, bring light into your life, and experience the physical life of dreams coming true more effortlessly and peacefully based in the love and light of All That Is.

This is not a one-time, one-and-done fix and all things are better.

This is you creating an entirely shifted orientation in regards to your understanding of the physical and nonphysical world from which you and all physical things are derived and then creating in harmony with all things to experience physical reality in ways you desire, love, and enjoy, that bring value and fulfillment to yourself and benefit the overall society and cultures of which you are a living portion. Therefore, it is creating a new way of life and orientation through regular, practical applications of the wisdom and truths that we are herein describing. Again, in future books, we will indeed detail the tools that you can use to raise your personal vibrations, those of the physical human body for healing and health and those of the inner being and soul to enhance all physical experiences, and precisely how you can do so. However, you must first understand the nature of consciousness of which you are not only a portion of, but also what every single thing in your universe is constructed of and from, is, was, and will be. For eternity. This book is foundational material upon which others will build to grow your power within to be a Divine creator of your world.

Gestalt consciousness simply means a being of consciousness that is more (in many ways) than the sum total of its parts. Here in this section, we will be discussing calling into your own consciousness the vibrations and consciousness of other beings of higher vibrations such as myself or Christ consciousness, etc., so as to add _to_ and expand that which you are.

The forming of gestalt consciousness can occur in many ways, for example: by journaling, mediumship, prayer, and perhaps even when not aware that you are doing so. When one calls upon higher consciousness, say in prayer, you are inviting that higher vibration into your own, thus increasing the vibrational frequency of your own inner self or soul. Therefore, prayer or calling upon or inviting higher beings of consciousness into your own being will raise your own vibrational frequency, expanding the soul and consciousness that you are. Now, if you make this a regular practice, it will, over time, raise your personal vibration.

For example, each time Jackson-Thomas and I sit for a session, he calls upon higher consciousness by whatever name or method. The intentions, again, are received and there is a match in vibrational frequency to those higher vibrations. Therefore, Divine beings...those that do not have names, Angels as you would think of them, multidimensional consciousness such as ourselves here, etc. will then focus into and through the consciousness portion of Jackson, which, for our teaching purposes, we have used the name Thomas. A name given to his soul in another lifetime that we had shared in the ancient past as you perceive linear historical time.

Now, as our consciousness comes to and through his own when we are dictating sessions, it will raise his own personal vibrational frequency so that there is a greatly expanded, gestalt consciousness that is formed and hence, expands the perceptions that are available to Jackson at the rational/intellectual mind level with which he is then able to access and make use of in various ways to improve his life experience and to create our book, of course. The regular practice of this is somewhat similar to going to the gym to build upon your physical health, only we are expanding and improving your spiritual health here. Therefore, the more regularly you do this over time, the more it will raise your personal vibrations, and form a growing gestalt consciousness within yourself. You expand you. You evolve you. Yet all have free will and free choice, so therefore it is a conscious decision to do so and to act upon such activities.

To place this into another context for example here: If your soul was the warm water in a bathtub, and you were to call upon higher consciousness (hot water) and each time you do so, you add a bucket of that higher consciousness of hot water into your soul/bathtub water. You expand you. You grow you. You evolve you. So in our example here, over time by adding more and more buckets of hot water to the original bath water, you expand what it is, adding to it, growing it, and it increases in vibration (temperature).

Now, there are many, many methods and tools to raise your inner vibrations and we will get to that later; however, it is the regular practice of drawing that higher consciousness into your own, that expands you and provides the individual with a far greater perception of reality, knowing of tools to use to direct consciousness and energy to form it into matter as objects, events, conditions, etc.

Now: What I want to make clear in this particular session, again through reinforcement until it is vibrating from within you, the reader, is that channeling beings of nonphysical consciousness is NATURAL for you. Channeling of Angels, entities, beings that perhaps have not incarnated into human form but do indeed guide humans, and even channeling of loved ones who have passed away, is natural to ALL human-beings.

In fact, it is _more natural_ than humans actually talking to one another with their voices, as it is through consciousness that you are constantly "communicating" with all other consciousness, aware of it or not. Waking or dreaming, sleeping, or any other activity, all portions of the human body are "communicating" with and through consciousness with all other forms of consciousness around you expressed into physical objects, events, conditions, etc.

Channeling materials then will often come through the characteristic or trait you call "clairaudience". Clear hearing seems to you to take place in the mind, although it only seems that way as the brain is the sensory perception where you register activity while you are in human form.

Clairaudience, again, is natural, innate, and inseparable eternally from consciousness. Your consciousness. So it is that if one human-being can learn it, all human-beings also have the abilities latent or dormant as potentials undeveloped within yourselves.

If you are alive as a human-being, then you have the ability to learn it and develop it. If you are not alive, well then, you already know of these truths to the core of being. (Smile) Jackson has given classes and personal one-on-one coaching and in his coaching, Jackson has taught others to successfully develop their abilities to hear Divine beings and to receive direct communication from such sources for their own development and learning purposes.

I will again here state, that as attributes or characteristics of human consciousness, the "clairabilities" as we call them, cannot be separated as portions of consciousness. Therefore, developing one of these areas, such as clairaudience, will to some degree, develop the others - Some stronger and some not as much. Some individuals will have an automatic propensity, if you will, or naturally draw toward one or more abilities, and perhaps not as much as others. Although your consciousness has the capabilities among all human-beings, it is also filtered through the "mind" and perceptions of the individual who is receiving the material. Therefore, as an individual's thoughts, beliefs, etc. and other influences do play a role, some may develop a few areas that are very strong and others not as much. Often when one learns to develop one clairability, at the wonderment of having received definitive information that is quite clearly beyond their own thoughts, wisdom, and knowledge, they may focus on the application and use of that clairability; forsaking, if you will, others - tuning them out as they are focused on the one. However, again, if you have discovered one, then all others are also there for your discovery, application, and use.

In channeling and the development of your clairabilities, it is more of an _allowing_, than a forced activity. You do not force your consciousness to develop, as it doesn't work. It is allowed and guided to develop, but any attempts to force development beyond normal "spiritual exercises" and using one's tools, will likely lead to frustration. All inner development is guided and allowed. Never forced, for there is no pushing dominion, even over the Self, that will be successful in the end results.

Bless that which you have developed and know that the rest may come later on. Do everything you do in self-development in the undertones of love and light. Ultimate timeless patience and trustful passivity. Joyful indifference, focusing heavily into every single little success as if it were the greatest ever, generates the electromagnetic laws of attraction to draw forth from all consciousness, other assistive energies, consciousness, guidance, help, etc. While we will not go into a deep dive here, I am sufficiently pointing out that you, the reader, do indeed have within you at this very moment, all abilities awaiting your recognition, awareness, focus of attention, belief, emotion, and directional choices of free will to use your own tools and directed use of consciousness to develop them. _You must believe in you._

Consciousness As The Source For All Possible Inventions, Ideas, Artwork, Books, Movie Scripts, Technological Advances, Etc. That Form Your Civilization

Timeless Truths

Now: Every great artist, painter, creative architect, author, and so forth, are aware that often the ideas, images, and materials they are receiving in their mind, whether it be in their dreams, waking daydream, etc., are coming from "somewhere" outside or beyond their own mind and intellectual thoughts. In other words, it is often very apparent to the perceiver that the materials they are receiving in the form of ideas, inspiration, designs, art, inspired actions to take, and so forth, did not appear to them to come from their own thought. Often, they appear in their awareness in the midst of their daily activities or perhaps in the dream state and are then remembered and reflected upon when they have awakened. There have been many brilliant authors throughout your history that have claimed quite clearly that the manuscripts or songs, great symphonies, movie scripts, etc. nearly "wrote themselves".

Yet, where were these ideas, images, inspired action plans, movie plots, and book storylines before they came into their awareness for them to record, write, or transform into some production of art or expression of them into physical terms? Where did they originate and from where have they come? They did not exist, <u>in physical terms</u>, until the one inspired took some form of action to move the nonphysical ideas into physical reality by taking some form of action upon them.

Great works of accomplishment of any kind do not develop on their own. While the Divine inspiration may come in the form of an idea, dream, daydream, sudden realization, etc....it is only through physical action that you move the nonphysical
→ into physical reality (book, painting, poetry, building, and construction designs, etc.)

Again, we reflect upon the point here that these great things, actions, movements of society, leaders, etc. were all simply ideas;

inspiration that was, what we call, probable reality outcomes that were in the nonphysical realm of consciousness - accessed, tapped into and drawn into the awareness of the individual perceiving them by their vibrational frequency, intentions, beliefs, desires, that _expanded their own consciousness_ in such a fashion that they then were able to perceive these ideas and inspirations that were in the nonphysical consciousness.

The "_being_" portion of them as a human-being, expanded and opened to allow a new potential. A probable reality object or event to come into their perception and field of awareness from the greater realm of All That Is/The Universe/Source, etc. The ideas, designs, inventions, images, inspiration, and storylines for great book series, movies, works of art, etc. all came into the conscious awareness of those who eventually expressed them.

Nikola Tesla, Albert Einstein, and many others are examples known around the world. Other famous receivers of such information from Divine sources would be Christ and Buddha. Now, we assure you that it could not come to the individual human that eventually expressed these ideas if it did not first come to them through their own consciousness. Open to receiving from the greater consciousness of ALL ideas and inspiration.

ALL human thoughts are nonphysical patterns of energy that are indeed instantaneously "heard", felt, registered, and received in consciousness. You might say that "God"/Source/The Universe.... never misses a single thought, for all thought and emotions adds eternally to the greater consciousness of All That Is, and affects the world that you perceive around you, as well as yourself and all other things in that environment.

Therefore, the picture that we are painting here in _our_ book is that the greater consciousness of _All That Is_, was drawn forth from that greater realm of nonphysical ideas and inspiration, into their personal consciousness, as a human-being, and then acted upon...which moves that energy from nonphysical reality into physical reality, the moment they act upon it by recording, drawing, painting, writing, documenting, these ideas, and inspiration.

The realm of All That Is (Consciousness) → Infinite Probable Realities, inventions, creations, paintings, movies, and novels, etc. → is received by the consciousness of the person inspired and forms as the ideas, inventions, plans, manuscripts, movie plot that then unfolds in their mind. When acted upon and recorded, painted, drawn, and expressed into physical terms, or the designs of your greatest building structures, it moves the idea from nonphysical reality into physical reality, forming objects, events, and conditions that then form your world.

This is a path that all physical 3-dimensional reality follows, aware of it or not, intentional or not.

Our medium friend whom I originally authored my books through wrote of the physical universe being an expression of idea-construction. Meaning that it is formed and constructed from ideas that were once in nonphysical terms. Again, from where do the ideas originate? Consciousness.

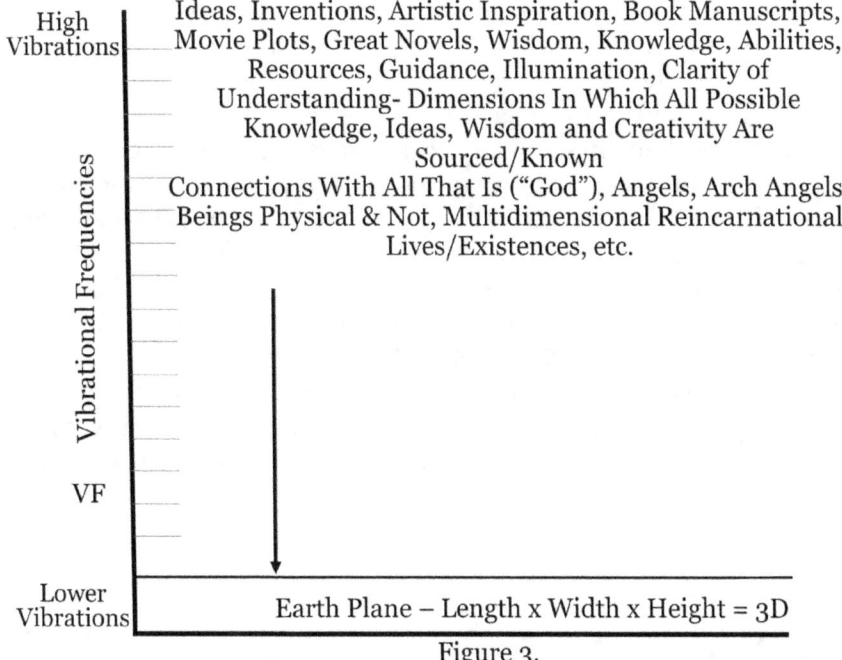

Divine Plane

High Vibrations — Ideas, Inventions, Artistic Inspiration, Book Manuscripts, Movie Plots, Great Novels, Wisdom, Knowledge, Abilities, Resources, Guidance, Illumination, Clarity of Understanding- Dimensions In Which All Possible Knowledge, Ideas, Wisdom and Creativity Are Sourced/Known

Connections With All That Is ("God"), Angels, Arch Angels, Beings Physical & Not, Multidimensional Reincarnational Lives/Existences, etc.

Vibrational Frequencies

VF

Lower Vibrations — Earth Plane – Length x Width x Height = 3D

Figure 3.

Challenges Occur Most Frequently At Lower VF

The individual that has at any point in human history expressed anything into physical terms, received the inspired ideas from nonphysical reality of consciousness, that came to the forefront of their personal conscious awareness and thus became an idea that was acted upon.

Yet, it could not have arrived onto the physical plane if it were not first originated in the nonphysical realm of consciousness. It is not then that an idea or inspiration joins your consciousness as if it were separate from it in the first place. It is that your rational and intellectual mind becomes aware of it, as it was always "there" awaiting your discovery of it.

Your consciousness, then, has grown, expanded, and received an idea or inspiration that grows your consciousness into more than it was - more aware. One may or may not act upon ideas and inspiration that come to them, through the faculty of free will, yet the ideas have come to that person through their conscious awareness.

Now, what we want to point out here is that within the idea, image, or inspiration that comes to an individual are all the potential outcomes of that idea's expression, and the myriad of ways in which it could then become physical. An infinite array of possibilities is always present and, depending on the actions taken, it would then express and become physical in one fashion or another, along one path or another, being successful in your terms or not, or anywhere in between. The thing we want to point out here, then, is that it is not just the idea that comes to one in consciousness, but also the infinite probable reality outcomes that exist within that idea, forming a gestalt idea in consciousness that is more than the sum total of just the idea itself. The ideas then, expand your own consciousness as you become aware of them, becoming more and more as your awareness and contemplation of any idea is held in your attention.

Seeing Through Time And Space Using Clairvoyant Characteristics Inherent To All Human Consciousness.

Good morning, Now: We are as always, "present and accounted for" as there is no other "place" for us to be. (Smile) This morning I simply want to make a few notes about our book progress and state that I am very pleased with how it's coming together. This is a project quite similar to and, at the same time, quite unlike the dictation I have done with Ruburt. There is more challenge in the fact that the dictation was given to you over many sessions; yet, ones that were not successive...not linear in nature as that is one of the very subjects that we are teaching about life and the nature of consciousness. That it is not linear in its true form and nature, and therefore, our book follows the same format you see.

I recognize that for you, Jackson, this is quite a challenge. To take the materials given to you over many months or even the last couple of years, and to add them into our book, organize them, and present them so that they make very good materials for our readers. Yet, it is necessary to teach that consciousness, and truly your physical lives, are not as linear in nature as many believe them to be, and that we also present our book material in the same fashion. You might think of it or relate to it as you would your dreams perhaps. There may be many themes and images presented in your dream state when you sleep at night. Perhaps several dreams from completely different scenarios. However, when you awaken, you remember them in a linear-appearing context as that is how information is translated for your waking, conscious, rational mind to organize them so that it fits into the overall picture and root assumptions of the physical reality in which it finds itself focused.

Again, dreams are not linear, time is not linear, and your lives are not linear, for there truly is no time or space beyond that which you perceive in your physical appearing reality. Now, we state these points of truth in many ways to drive home the truth of the very nature of your existence. When the true nature of your existence is better understood, then your culture and society can begin to explore your existence along other lines of your relationship to all other forms in your physical reality and, to a degree, will be able to more successfully "navigate" time and space in ways that were not before possible - as the minds of mankind excluded them from possible inclusion.

Meaning that there are ways, paths, and answers about more successful ways in which one can live, interact with, and navigate your physical appearing reality; however, an enhanced and expanded understanding of the nonphysical nature from which ALL things physical are created and expressed into the world of matter is necessary for these new ways to "appear" and become perceivable.

Some of the greatest achievements of your so-called science that today, in your terms, are accepted as ways to see, interact with, and relate to things around you, were only one hundred years ago...completely unthought of and hence, not utilized at all. The accumulation of all ideas to come together for every component to build a spacecraft that could successfully reach the moon or Mars did not exist fully in the mind of mankind in the historic year of 1800, for example. There were some in those periods of history who dreamt of such things, and you can see, if one looks enough, examples of such prophetic dreams and images carved into stone temples and monuments that have lasted thousands of years - such as those in pyramid forms around the Earth.

There are quite literally models of airplanes, stone-chiseled images of helicopters, rocket ships, and flying craft that are many thousands of years old. In these instances, it was that the individuals, sometimes called visionaries, glimpsed the visions and images of such spacecraft either in their sleeping dream state or waking daydream state. Now what they are seeing then, via their natural clairvoyance abilities, are future probable reality objects such as these airplanes and helicopters that are in the infinite realm of consciousness, available to humans throughout all time, and they are perceiving them perhaps thousands of years prior to the technology being invented and the airplanes, for example, being built.

It was these dreams, then, that drew forth into the minds of mankind the ideas for the physical construction of the technology that would, in time, accumulate enough technology so as to construct the physical airplanes that ancient people saw in their dreams and drew upon stone walls for example. These dreams would impinge upon time and space and set up the events necessary for the eventual physical construction of the airplanes that they saw in their dreams. At _that_ time in history then, the ideas were <u>always present </u>and available and by the contemplation of them, the ideas sought out their own ways of expression. It was a probable future or probable reality that they were able to see, via their clairvoyant abilities of their consciousness.

These ancient people then were, of course, in the dream state (or while daydreaming), actually clairvoyantly seeing through their own consciousness other dimensions of physical reality, beings, and spacecraft that do exist in other dimensions outside of the one they then perceived to be their own. <u>They are seeing through time</u> to a dimension of time in which the airplanes exist and are flying around. These dreams then, would become contemplated and grow within the consciousness of mankind, being contemplated over time by many, which adds energy to the reality becoming physical, and would eventually lead to airplanes being built.

Like an oak tree sprouting from the seed, the accumulation of energy had to grow out in the "Universe" (consciousness) over time before it would mature into what it is today. The seed of the oak tree perhaps would be like the seed idea of the spacecraft drawn on the walls of such temples and stone structures thousands of years ago; yet, this seed does not grow in the soil of the Earth. It grows in the conscious awareness of mankind to mature into ripe ideas that come forth as inventions and technology that today forms the world and societies around you.

Those dreams then in "ancient times" lead to the creation of the famous golden Quimbaya artifacts, or more specifically, the Quimbaya jets. A collection of golden figures from Columbia that are shaped precisely like modern-day airplanes, as well as the images carved upon many ancient stone structures around the world that also portray very, very accurate depictions of modern-day airplanes.

What I want to call out here is that these dreams in the minds of men and women of those ancient times were the "Divine spark" from which thousands upon thousands of probabilities or probable future events would then be set into motion. The ideas then accumulated other ideas which would lead to thousands more dreams in the minds of mankind, which would eventually lead to the physical production of wires, electronics, metallurgical creation of aerodynamic forms, mechanics, and all components necessary for the fulfillment of the modern-day airplane taking its physical place in human history as a precursor to space exploration and serving humanity in its evolutionary development.

We are mentioning these things as they show examples throughout time and history as you perceive it, that mankind has indeed had glimpses of the future. A future in _their_ terms in that time period did not even occur or happen yet physically.

Yet again, how does one perceive a "future" event that has not even occurred, through the natural communication characteristic of clairvoyance, inherent in all human consciousness, if the _event has not yet even formed and happened_? How, does one experience Deja' vu of knowing they have been somewhere or done a certain thing, known someone they've just met before it ever occurred, and now have the strong sense that it has already happened before? How, does one see "past life" events and happenings in their dream states, visions during meditation, daydreams, or what have you?

The past and the future then, are not linear...but alternate and perhaps what you may think of as "parallel" and occurring simultaneously with the moments you are now experiencing while in the focus within physical life as you now know it.

Notes and Quotes

Notes and Quotes

_____

_____

_____

_____

_____

_____

_____

_____

_____

_____

_____

_____

_____

_____

_____

_____

_____

_____

_____

_____

_____

Section 4:

<u>Consciousness And</u>
<u>Belief Systems</u>

Frequency Of Vibration
And Overcoming The "Darkness"
In Your Life

Now: All energy, as with consciousness, is "alive" and vibrant and has a vibration to it. The rate at which something vibrates is considered its frequency of vibration. In science, frequencies are measured over time where a particular frequency will vibrate a certain number of times over a period of time such as one second.

Physical matter is composed of atoms and molecules which have infinite rates of vibration; however, their ranges of frequency are slower than that of nonphysical energy. Let's take water, for example. If you were to observe the vibrational rate of frequency of frozen water, it would be very slow appearing then as ice. Warming up a bit would excite the vibrational rate of the atoms and so forth so that it became liquid, and still further it would become steam and evaporate into humidity and so on. At the highest rate of vibrational frequency then, water becomes "nonphysical".

Divine frequencies then, are nonphysical that are, to an infinite degree, much higher in vibrations and frequency ranges than the slower vibrations of solid-appearing objects of your earth plane. Therefore, it stands to reason that the higher someone is in their personal vibrational frequency, the closer a match they are to the Divine frequencies or Source, Angels, beings, and entities of Light (Truth).

On the earth plane, while living your physical life, you experience challenges. Challenges are indeed an impetus for you to seek ways to resolve them through naturally creative means. In the Divine realm of consciousness, a being or entity can "manifest" a psychic reality with what you might think of as an intentional thought focus that would occur instantaneously. On the earth plane where vibrations are much slower, materializations of physical matter in the form of objects, events, and conditions, must unfold over time, as you are in the space and time constructs of 3-dimensional reality.

Now, to put it plainly, the higher you are in vibrational frequency, the less challenges appear before you and the more life simply flows easily and effortlessly. You direct your life harmoniously with all things around you, yet you do not "control" it in a forceful manner. Synchronicities become commonplace and it seems that what you need simply flows to you and appears without much effort.

Jackson W. Moore

However, if one's personal rate of vibrational frequency is lower, great challenges can, and indeed do, appear in your life experience. These great challenge periods in one's life are often referred to as "darkness" or simply, the ***illusion* of lack of Light**, understanding, clarity, resolution, etc. To be clear, great challenges, or darkness, then, are a very clear sign that your personal rate of vibration has dipped, and this is your "natural sign" that you must use your tools and techniques to raise your vibration.

At every moment of your physical life, you are attracting into your field of perception, the essence of the cumulative, distilled, vibrational frequency that you yourself are currently vibrating to as your present state of consciousness.

Your present state of consciousness is not what it is because of your world. On the contrary, your world is what it appears to be because of your present state of consciousness.

Divine Plane

High Vibrations — Wisdom, Knowledge, Abilities, Resources, Guidance, Illumination, Clarity of Understanding- Connections With All That Is ("God"), Angels, Arch Angels, Beings Physical & Not, Multidimensional Reincarnational Lives/Existences, Peace, Love, Joy, Laughter, Intuitive Hunches, Clairvoyance, Clairaudience, Claircognizance, (All Clairabilities) Telepathy, Freedom
INFINITE POTENTIAL, ENERGY RESOURCES ETERNALLY AVAILABLE TO YOU NOW
No Space/No Time

Vibrational Frequencies

VF — Perceived "Darkness", Appearances of "Evil", Appearances Of Lack, Disconnection, Depression, Rage, Anger, Hate, Frustration, Fear, Doubt, Insecurities, Hesitation, Procrastination, Jealousy, Resentment, Anxiety, Insecurities, Hopelessness, Challenges

Lower Vibrations — 3-D = Appearance Of Space/Time

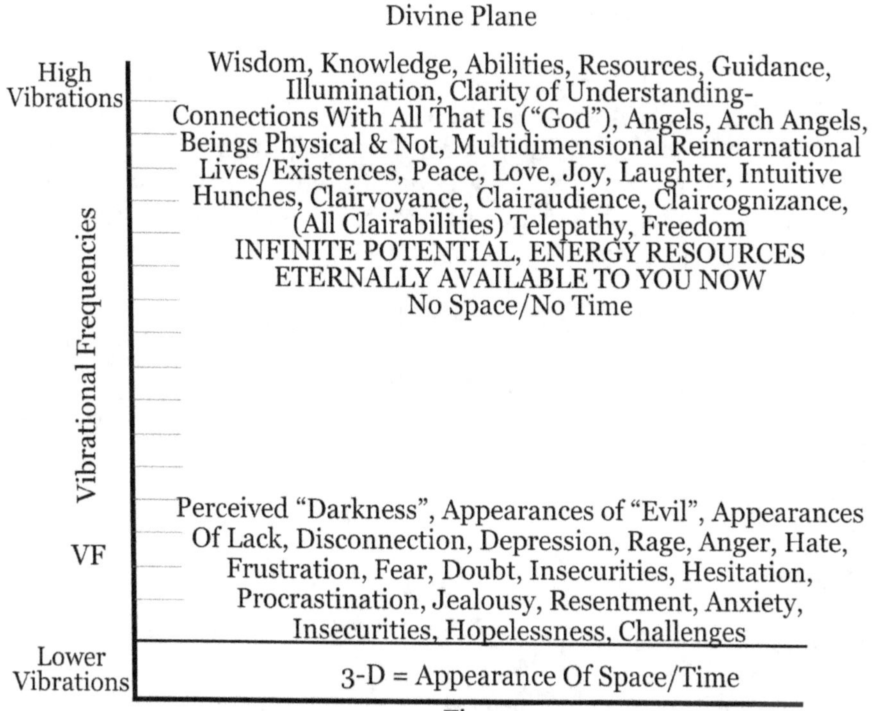

Figure 4.

Now, in the present context of spiritual teachings around the world in the time period we are writing this book, Divine <u>Light</u> is referred to meaning the illumination of "God" by any and all names. The Light then is the Truth. The Truth is the Light.

As the soul and consciousness are Divine in nature, and a portion of your greater soul is presently focused within your flesh looking outward into physical reality, "YOU" then, are the Light of the Divine. Your own light. Your own power. It is only perhaps your true understanding of the massive implications of this and depth of it, that perhaps prevent you from perceiving the immense creative power that you, each as individuals, have as Divine creators of your world.

<u>YOU *ARE the Light*</u>. The *being* portion of you as a <u>human-being</u>. You cannot say that you are not, for you would not exist as a human-being without the being or consciousness within you that provides your body life animation. The immortal portion that most think of as the "soul". ***YOU must turn on your own illumination within***. No other human-being on Earth can turn on your *inner illumination*. This is a personal journey of expanding and evolving in consciousness, as consciousness. Again, you illuminate your truths from within. You light your own path from within. You are your own power within. You find your own answers, solutions, resolutions, ideas, inventions, and creativity within.

Again, in the Light (Truth) there can be no "darkness" (lack of illumination) and the Truth (all answers, solutions, guidance, health, healing, means, ways, paths, etc.) is revealed. It is illuminated and comes into your present conscious awareness so that you may make use of it.

Now, "I AM" is your awareness of your Self as a unique individual soul of consciousness. When you describe yourself, you would say "I AM" this or that. It is self-awareness, of your Self. The inner Self.

I AM the Light of the world.

I AM the Truth.

I AM the way.

I AM the illumination.

I AM the solution made visible now.

Or

I AM the Light of the world – ALL illumination of all knowledge, wisdom, insights, answers, etc.

I AM the Truth – the core truth of something's existence, physical or nonphysical.

I AM the way – the path to success, healing, health, wealth, advancement, life's purpose, value fulfillment, etc.

I AM the illumination – Clear visibility and understanding of the truth of all things and *The Nature Of Consciousness.*

I AM the solution made visible now - ALL solutions to mankind's problems, challenges, or issues. If it exists in physical reality and seems to be a challenge, it was created from consciousness, therefore, it must have a corresponding answer, solution, or resolution, even if it has not yet come to your present state of awareness. This is how ALL discoveries on the physical plane begin. In consciousness.

When you say these statements above, you are stating <u>affirmations of truth</u> (A-Firm-Truth) as such that your immortal <u>being</u> within is quite literally all of these things, and, as you believe and vibrate to BEING these truths, so, too, will they correspondingly appear to you as the conditions that make up your physical reality around you. Again, you create your own reality and limited beliefs are truly the boundaries within which you create, see, perceive, and live your life in physical existence.

When you are BEING your truth, light, etc.....then it is vibrating in the core of your being and, as such, it is your point of attraction in life. Now, I will go into much greater detail on this subject in a future book on how to use one's Divine creative tools to manifest and materialize your physical reality, however, I will briefly state here that when it comes to the "law of attraction" I will tell you that you may think you draw objects, events, and conditions to yourself, the physical human you see in the mirror.

In reality, <u>you are drawing them to the inner being or consciousness that is focused within that physical body of flesh</u>, and your physical body is what perceives them in the physical world. They are "magnetized" then and attracted to the inner being, which then, of course, seems like something is manifesting to you.

It is manifesting to your being, not to your human. It is just that you think you are the human, when in truth, you are the being within the human, as the human.

"And I, if I be lifted up (in consciousness and vibrational frequency), shall draw all men (things) unto me" - The law of attraction as described by the Christ consciousness.

Meaning here that when manifesting your reality (conscious, intentional, purposeful creation), as you rise in consciousness and vibrational frequency, you will draw all things ("men") to you, via the natural laws of electromagnetic properties in energy and matter.

These affirmations of truth of yourself as a being, are, of course, ***states of consciousness*** that you choose to BE, or not to be. You are not saying, thinking, or affirming any of these "I AM" statements to <u>make them true</u>. They ARE your truth, and you are affirming them, silently, written, or aloud, to grow it within your awareness, to train your rational and intellectual mind, that <u>you are indeed these attributes of the Divine</u>. Again - they are natural, innate, and inherent within the very consciousness that provides a human body its awareness of Self and its life animation to walk the Earth. You cannot, as a human-being, ever state in truth that you are not these attributes for they are inescapable, inexorable – Omnipotent, Omniscient, Omnipresent - within your being as a human-being.

Therefore, ALL human creatures to ever walk the Earth, have these attributes and natural characteristics of "God"/Source/All that IS within them. You must first become aware that you have them within you, then seek to actively develop them to maximize your understanding and proficiency in using such unlimited resources, and then practice your intentional directive use of personal focus and energy to create outcomes using the tools that are inherent to you as a being of consciousness.

> *How else do you think the so-called law of attraction would attract any and all things to your physical experience if you were not already connected to them, at the layer of consciousness?*

Then by the focus of your attention, your personal vibration, and beliefs and expectations, you draw them unto you as your life experience unfolding before you.

Now, Jackson - Many years ago you were deep in meditation, and we gave you a very vivid vision in which you were told by the Angel of Light that appeared in your vision how to make the darkness in your life at that time come to an end. It was stated to you clearly in that vision:

**"He who knows and *IS* the Light,
shall make the darkness end."**

You were jolted out of meditation by the shear thundering voice that seemed so loud as if it actually shook your house on its foundation, and you ran to the window to look outside to see if other neighbors had heard it as well. Finding, of course, that they were going about their business like nothing was heard by them at all. This was when you began understanding that though it was intensely loud to your perception, it had come to you through clairaudience and was VERY loud to you, personally. Not by the ears of your body nor the neighbors was it heard.

When you come to KNOW the Light of the Divine, the illumination within, you become the Light as you live it in practice daily, in recognition of that which you truly are. A Being of Light, within the physical flesh you see in the mirror, giving it Self-awareness and life animation to beat the heart, walk the Earth, and use your creative energy in fruitful and productive ways that not only benefit you, but also the greater humanity in your time period that you know, personally and *en masse* as a portion of your culture, country, etc., to raise and expand the collective consciousness of not only humanity, but also nature, the Earth, and the universe of which you are indeed an eternally intimately connected portion.

And no, I do not wish to make that last portion "grammatically" correct by breaking it down as we are here learning to live outside the context and box of which was once our "norm"...such as the rules of grammar and what is "proper". It's rather natural for me to operate "outside the box" or the universe even, as it is. (Smile)

When you were illumined from within as such, by the use of all your natural creative tools and by following the processes of BEING the Divine Light, by acting the part, thinking, feeling, and vibrating to that...*the darkness in that period of your life that had lasted years, finally ended*.

This, my friend, is why we write of your experiences and make use of your life challenges and experiences that you have overcome so that others around the world may recognize the patterns that once held you back. That once upon a time, you had found yourself in the darkness of being lost in life and not knowing which direction to turn or how, exactly, to make it end so that you could begin experiencing a much more joyful, fruitful, abundant experience in life. Intuitively, however, you embraced the signs of "darkness" as your directional indicator to turn within for those profound answers that would one day, lead you to me in this lifetime and the mission we now continue.

You see, as we always teach...one comes to the earth plane not just as a student. Every human-being is a student, yet also, to one degree or another, a teacher. Again:

**As you teach, so shall you learn...and
as you learn, so shall you also teach.**

As a being of consciousness, you all learn your chosen directive use of creative energy that is eternally yours to direct, and how your thoughts, the focus of attention, choices, feelings, emotions, and actions help form the very environment you see around you... your societies, cultures and the overall "feeling tones" of those societies and cultures as you all form, personally and *en masse*, your physical reality.

Remember, you raise your own vibrational frequency to allow yourself to perceive the Light (Truth) that was eternally present, yet *seemingly* hidden from your view. Learn to recognize this "darkness" and challenges in your own lives, as a Divine Sign that you are at that moment, being guided by a higher source (your larger self, your entity, Divine beings, etc.) to turn within and raise your vibration to open your conscious awareness to the solutions you seek to overcome said challenges and darkness.

Eternal Connection To All Objects Through Consciousness And The States Of Consciousness That Attract Or Repel Things From Your Experience.

Now: When you are attempting to gain something of importance or value to you and bring it into your life experience, be it improved health, wealth, or living conditions, you SEE them as separate from yourself due to the fact that you perceive physical reality in 3-dimensions. However, if you were to shift your perception to look beneath the atoms and molecules and atomic structures that form the physical objects of your universe, you would see that they are, at their lowest level of existence, consciousness.

At that level, there is no <u>physical</u> separation between them, as there is no separation or space in consciousness. Therefore, the consciousness that is within the atoms and molecules in one physical object is also in the other physical object that appears to you to be in a location across the room or across the Earth. And all things are infinite portions of what humanity has forever thought of as "God"/Source/All That Is by any and all names.

The implications here being that your human body is not disconnected from any other physical object in your universe, nor is there a physical separation from the health, wealth, prosperity, conditions of success, love, peace, and all things of the physical world that you desire to bring into your physical life, personally. It is more that your belief that you are separated from it, that creates the conditions where that appearance is reflected out into the physical world as atomic mass and solid-appearing objects that <u>seem</u> to be out of your reach per se.

The all-important truth to catch here is that though the objects, conditions, etc. appear to be separate from you, they are not. They are eternally, inseparably connected TO you, and no matter what you do in life, you can <u>*NEVER*</u> in all eternity, <u>disconnect</u> yourselves from that which you so desire.

You (the immortal consciousness portion of you) is consciousness. The life force that provides your physical flesh life. That object or condition in your life you desire to draw into your field of perception is also consciousness. Therefore, <u>at the level of consciousness</u>, you are indeed connected to them, and it is through your thoughts, beliefs, emotions, and the use of your natural creative tools that you can draw them to you or repel them from you by the vibrational frequencies and states of consciousness that you so entertain, which become your inner <u>Feeling Tones</u> - the guardrails and guidelines of sorts, within which you are creating and experiencing physical life.

How does this change things, creatively speaking, in <u>your</u> life...the reader here reading our book?

You are a human-BEING. What are you <u>BEING</u> right now? Healthy or not? Wealthy or not? Successful or not? Loving or not?

Now, these are all states of consciousness, which of course have infinite vibrational frequency tones that are inherent in the consciousness of such objects and conditions. So it is a matter of what you are BEING at any given time that determines if various things are attracted to your inner being and appear for your human self to enjoy, or if they are paused or held at a distance because you believe them to be unobtainable or impossible for you to achieve.

To attract the honeybee, a flower simply enjoys <u>BEING</u> a flower.

That vibration automatically, via consciousness, attracts the necessary things in the physical environment to bring fruition to not only its own propagation and the seeds that will grow when pollinated but also benefits the greater environment by providing the honeybee nectar for the hive and its natural environment in which it thrives as a part of nature also. While the honeybee appears to be separate from the flower, at the level or layer of consciousness that gives both physical expression and existence in the 3-dimensional world; there is a natural connection between them, and the vibrations of one seek out the vibrations of the other. As nature tends to do, even human nature if you allow it unimpeded, nature seeks what nature offers and nature finds what nature provides.

There is an intelligence behind the connection between the honeybee and the flower. There is an intelligence between the human-being and the health-being or wealth-being or success-being. It is a matter of what you are <u>BEING</u> then.

> *At every moment of your physical life, you are attracting into your field of perception, the essence of the cumulative, distilled, vibrational frequency that* <u>*you yourself*</u> *are currently vibrating to, as your present state of consciousness. Your* <u>*Being*</u>*.*

Now, there are natural tools by which and through which you can use natural processes to set up the patterns of energy to draw thickness into objects, events, and conditions within the realm and dimensions of consciousness that then express as the physical representations of them. And we will indeed detail these later on. However, for now, we are deepening the understanding that you have of the consciousness within your flesh and around you, and how you are inseparable from these things that appear separate; so that you can THEN, learn the specific tools, methods, and techniques to direct your own consciousness to co-create in harmony with All That Is, to draw such things into the future probabilities that you will then, catch up to in time and space as they appear before you. Physically.

Again, you cannot most efficiently and effectively, or consistently use your consciousness in such productive ways, until you truly understand that which you are capable of, naturally and with little physical effort. Your consciousness, and your clairabilities, are indeed some of the tools you use for Divine creation. Aka: manufacture of physical reality.

ALL human-beings have contained within their consciousness very natural, creative tools. If you do not first understand and accept that you do indeed have them, if you deny this _truth_, you will very effectively create that reality where it _seems_ that you do not have the creative tools and wherewithal to materialize that physical experience you so desire. You will, as we have stated before, create _your_ personal experience of physical reality (your life) within the boundaries of your limited belief structures that you've self-created.

Once you expand upon old limited perceptions and beliefs to include the natural portion of you as a being of which we speak of here in our book, then to the degree you accept them, understand them, utilize and apply them, "BE" them, and act as you already have them, will be to a very parallel degree that you are able then to practice using them, directing them, and achieving magical events, objects, conditions, and healings (physical, emotional or spiritual, etc.) that you desire to experience in your lives. _You_ must first personally open your own door to these magical activities in your life by expanding your beliefs to acknowledge, accept, and integrate that which we speak of in our works as your tools and gifts. Natural to consciousness and, of course, your personal and mass society consciousness.

Now let's give some examples here that are common among the many of the world. You are experiencing perhaps an illness, a condition, or a

165

sickness, and perhaps one that science or doctors believe may be serious or incurable. Now, you would not, or could not, experience the condition if you did not first believe in its ability to affect you in the first place. You do not catch a virus even if it seems to the world to be a pandemic kind of virus unless you first believe that you can, or fear you will, catch it. If you are on the fence about if you would or would not, deep down within, you may fear that you will, and hence, you may be subject to or "open" to that experience.

If on the other hand, you absolutely believe that you are a Divine being, that is wearing this beautiful garment of human flesh, for your learning experience, and that no matter what the ailment, your inner being glows so brightly and strongly from within, out through your flesh like a light bulb glowing, that no serious virus or major condition can set up its home in your body; for it simply cannot exist in your particular, personal vibration where it is not within your belief system - then you will also create such a condition of natural immunity. The vibration of the virus, ailment, or condition simply cannot exist (for any long period of time) in your system and if it did come to be in contact with you, would not have serious effects, or would quickly fade as it passed through your natural body's cleansing and repairing system. So, if you have this condition or illness, is the opposite healthy outcome separate from you? It may appear to be, however, it is not. It may appear that someone else healed from the illness or condition and maybe you have not yet.

However, all healing of flesh of course, for ANY condition, occurs from the inside, out. Your blood may form white blood cell clots to clot a cut on your finger and then the healing begins as new cells are created to replace damaged cells. The new cells and healing does not come from _outside_ of your body. It comes from _within_. And what, exactly, is it that tells these healing cells to create new cells at the very sight of damage, to release and let go of the old, damaged cells, and replace them instead with the new cells that close the cut, repair the damage, clean and replace damaged or cancerous cells, etc? What tells them to do this naturally? Consciousness - Health Consciousness more specifically.

A belief in the natural being within you having the capability that no matter what the _physical appearance_ may seem, you personally believe more in the immortal being within you, inseparable from All That Is, to draw forth all necessary instructions and materials to remove old, damaged cells and replace them with new ones.

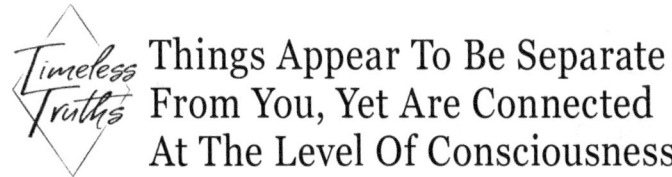
Now: Good afternoon and it is good once again to get back to our dictation, especially with such frequency. What I would like to do is to pick up on the subject matter that we left off on yesterday. That is, the material on the perception that physical objects are separate from you, yet in reality, are not separate at all.

When you see things around you in the physical world that you love and enjoy, you may think to yourself that this object, thing, person, or animal, _brings_ you joy and peace, for example. However, as we are learning in our lessons on the nature of consciousness, things are not separate from you at all - at the level of consciousness. Therefore, if we but shift our way of thinking, our perception, here, to think _from_ the perspective of truth of all things being a form of consciousness and energy, then we see a more realistic view that these things are already a portion of you. Again, as we have stated before, mankind is not apart from _nature_, but rather a part OF nature.

So it is that these things, objects, health, wealth, etc. that you seek that seem to be outside of yourself, are truly already connected and inseparable from the very consciousness that gives you self-identity, awareness of self, and life on the physical plane.

Therefore, as they are not outside of yourself, they do not really bring anything "to you". They simply awake a vibration of what is already _within you_, at the level of consciousness, and in so doing, awaken your awareness to the joy already within you.

You see, it is a vibration and a match. You match your inner vibration with that which you believe is separate from you, say flowers...and the joy wells up _within_ you. The happiness for having anything in physical reality does not come from outside of you, towards you, until it reaches your core of the human self. It wells up what is already within you as the vibration. That vibration then matches the vibration of the object that we are saying, in our example here, flowers that bring you joy, and you feel the flow of that energy from within to without. The joy rises to the surface of your awareness.

Now, this applies to all things in your life and we could go on and on forever to list them.

Now, if we take our example here and we move it to the majestic mountains or ocean or perhaps bright red and orange sunsets over the lands and oceans - these things, you say, bring you joy when you gaze upon them. However, as we are learning, the joy and love for them are already within you. Seeing them awakens the vibration within you that then brings those vibrations to the surface, to the forefront of your awareness, and hence, you experience the joy. Again, the joy of them is within you. It is allowed to surface to your awareness as you match the vibration of that object that you gaze upon, that you understand to bring you joy. We are stating here, multiple examples of how objects that appear physically separate from you are not, at the level of consciousness, separate from you at all and that the energy of the things you see around you that brings you joy, does not come from outside, inward to <u>bring</u> you joy, but rather awakens the vibration of that joy already present within you. There is an important distinction here to remember.

To believe otherwise, that something outside of yourself brings joy from the outside, would be to purport that something, anything, is separate from you and, thus, that you perhaps do not already have that which you love, cherish, and enjoy. "God", the Divine...All That Is, is indeed omnipresent, is it not? Which means there is no "place" in physical reality it is not present in its entirety. Including within the very Self you know to be you. Again - consciousness does not take up "space" as you perceive it; therefore, the entire universe as you think of it, could then, at the level of consciousness, exist within a pin-head size grain of dust or smaller...as it does not consume space, since it is not 3-dimensional in nature.

You could say that all things in your universe, including the planets and space between them, all stars of your heavens, are also within you for at the most basic level of their physical existence, at the level of consciousness, they do indeed exist within your soul, being or consciousness. You are not separate from the tools, health, wealth, answers, means, ways, solutions, inventions, and artistic creations of every conceivable manner. It is already, eternally, inseparably a part of you. You simply must train your mind to seek it within and as you vibrate to it, you raise it to the surface of your awareness for you to utilize in your life.

Where do you think all great books, novels, movie series, ideas, inventions, and all things that humanity has over time, have come "from"? The source of them. Outside of the human-being from a distant galaxy? Not so. They came UP from within them as they allowed the vibration of that which sought expression through them, to rise to the forefront so that they could perceive it in the mind's eye, or through any faculty of the 6th senses, and simply create those world-famous books, movie scripts, paintings, inventions, blueprints, and all things to move and evolve your species on the planet.

Yet in all eternity, not one of them came from "outside" of that human that brought it forth. They came from All That Is - Consciousness of All That Is and ever was or will be; for again, time and history do not exist as you maybe believe they do. They only appear to as a phenomenon and root assumption of your 3-dimensional reality for the purposes of navigation of those 3-dimensions while you are learning in the physical environment.

Now, implications arise from these truths that can greatly impact the creative successes and advancements of you as individuals, and as cultures and societies on Earth right now. If you but ponder what this truly means - that you are not at all separate from all things you might seek, physically. You only believe yourself to be, based upon the physical appearance that objects on your 3-dimensional plane appear to be separate for navigational purposes and learning. Yet to the degree that you truly begin to understand that these things in your environment are not separate from you, at the level of which you both exist, then you open your own awareness of the truth that you can indeed draw them into physical expression within your experience. All things are possible to those who believe.

Jackson's Lesson From The Angels In Consciousness And Awareness Of Self

Jackson Note: Years before I became aware that Seth had been guiding me through this life from before I was born into the human man with the name Jackson, I had, as my story goes, learned to channel Angels and loved ones who had passed away and developed my psychic abilities that I had been acutely aware of since my death experience (NDE) as a child. It was during one of those sessions that my Angels took the opportunity to teach me about our immortal awareness of Self. Our identification of Self. My Self. This was truly a turning point in the understanding of consciousness and of course an influenced event by Seth for future work that is now unfolding as we teach others the same. During this particular session with my Angels, after a bit of material, they asked me about my NDE event in a series of questions and answers, playfully driving a point into my awareness.

At that time, I was doing all my channeling writing with a pen in notebook journals, rather than typing on a laptop as I do most of the time now; so I wrote their questions and followed by writing my answers down the page. As fast as they asked them, I answered them.

Angels: Where are you when your accident happened that day?

Jackson: I am in the barn on the farm where I grew up in upstate New York.

Angels: What are you doing then?

Jackson: I am playing with a friend of mine that lives down the road. He is helping me build a hay fort inside the barn with leftover hay bales so we can hide from all the girls because we don't want them to find us.

Angels: Did your friend see you when the accident happened?

Jackson: I am outside the hay fort, and he is inside with the door bale in place so that it looks like a giant stack of hay, but when you move the door bale, it's hollow inside and we've set up our camp in there. So he does not see what I am doing outside of the fort in the barn.

I am trying to re-tie bailing twine to rebuild a broken swing that once hung down from the ceiling beam at the top of the barn.

Angels: Now, you've had your accident. What are you doing now?

Jackson: I am dead, and my body falls limp.

Angles: Where are you now?

Jackson: I am floating in a dark but warm, loving-like space but without stars. I see a bright, brilliant white circle of light in the distance, and I seem to be moving closer to it.

Angels: Are you walking or how are you moving?

Jackson: I am floating. I look down toward my feet to see what is holding me suspended and I see that my body is like the shape of a human but is a bright, white light shaped like a hologram, filled with billions of sparkling lights like every color of the light spectrum. I am see-through but filled with bright sparkles of light. There is no fear...just massive love everywhere and I can see people and beings in the glow of the light near the edges...

*Many more questions and answers and then they asked:

Angels: This all-encompassing voice booming all around you told that "You must go back now for your work is not yet done." Then, where are you?

Jackson: I am floating, at the top of the barn near the ceiling and I watch my dead body fall to the barn floor about 30 feet below. Now I am floating over top of my dead body. It's not moving or breathing and there is no heartbeat. I think it is cold... and I hear myself out loud, as if my voice comes from everywhere around me, and I am asking myself if I will continue to live this life or move onto another.

*More questions and answers and then they asked:

Angels: Where are you now?

Jackson: I am back inside my body now and it jolted like I was hit by lightning. My heart started beating and my body took a huge gasp of air, and I am screaming in my mind, but no voice is coming out of my throat as there is no oxygenated blood to my vocal chords yet....and I can't see. Everything is black as there's no oxygenated blood to my eyes yet, but I am screaming because I'm scared now. I can't move yet as there is no oxygenated blood to my muscles, and I feel what feels like searing hot blood move from my heart, outward into my veins and out to my extremities and my muscles start spasmodically contracting and retracting. I think I am dying as I saw and spoke to Angels and had conversations with them and with beings and with my grandparents who have been dead for some years now...

Angels: Where are you after you recover for a moment?

Jackson: I am running up to the house to tell my mother...and so I can ask her what happened to me; how did I see Angels and my dead grandparents and other beings and talk to them and who was the voice that spoke to me from all over, where was I and how did I watch my body fall to the barn floor and how was I outside of my body, looking AT it, and floating over my friend playing obliviously, and then outside the barn and...lots of questions..... (What I wrote in my answer to them that appeared on the notebook pages before me.)

**They continued to ask me a few more questions and then, as they paused, they showed me clairvoyantly as a picture in my mind, that also correlated with my answers written down the page, all of my answers pushed together. This is in essence what they showed me very clearly:

I AM in the barn on the farm where I grew up in upstate New York...

I AM playing with a friend of mine...

I AM outside the hay fort, and he is inside...

I AM doing outside of the fort in the barn...

I AM dead, and my body falls limp...

I AM floating in a dark but warm, loving-like space...

I AM floating...

I AM floating over top of my dead body...

I AM asking myself if I will continue to live this life...

I AM back inside my body now and it jolted...

I AM screaming because I'm scared now...

I AM dying as I saw and spoke to Angels and...

I AM running up to the house to tell my mother...

That's when it became clear as day that in every single answer, I referred to myself as "I AM". When I was alive before the accident, I referred to myself as "I AM". When I was physically and clinically dead with no breath and no heartbeat, I referred to myself as "I AM". When I was in "heaven" or at least my rendition of it, I referred to myself as "I AM" and after my heart jumped back to life and I took my first breath again and then ran to the house, I referred to myself as "I AM".

Clearly this "I AM" is my identification of myself. The immortal being that was within my body that we call a soul, or in other words, my consciousness that gives my physical body life. This "I AM" then, my consciousness, is what was floating at the top of the barn roof, watching as my body fell all the way to the floor. Floating over the top of my body, then moving inside the hay fort and floating over my friend who was playing, then outside the barn, and eventually back over my body again to grow closer until my point of view shifted from outside looking AT, to inside and everything being dark where I was momentarily unable to move.

The point that my Angels were making was that, physically alive or physically dead, I still existed as the consciousness of "I AM", my consciousness, awareness of myself. It was also very clear that my consciousness could focus "into heaven" or nonphysical reality and it could also focus back into 3-dimensional reality where I could see all things around me, I could hear sounds, I could clearly think and reason, I could move from place to place, sense the environment, feel the sun and the air as I went "through" the barn walls, etc.

The Angels rather put it right in front of my face for me to see, and I was the one who wrote it in response to their questions. Yet it was glaringly apparent that their point was well taken and understood that this "I AM" is our awareness of our Self. Our consciousness. I was fully aware of myself, thinking, talking to myself seemingly "out loud", reasoning while floating above and STARING at my dead, crumpled up, lifeless body.

It was the most amazing experience to be fully cognizant and lucidly aware and staring at my physical, lifeless body. I could see that, without the soul/my consciousness focused _from within_ my physical body, my body was absolutely as lifeless as a living room couch. You could've poked it with a sharp stick, and it would not have twitched one muscle. It was my soul/my consciousness... connected to ALL consciousness that is immortal, that gives my body life animation and, without being focused from within, the body was just an avatar without animation. I clearly understood from that day on, that there was WAY more to life than I ever knew of or had ever heard of anyone speak of except my mother.

There are hundreds of thousands if not millions of people around the world who have experienced the point of view from their consciousness being outside the body, either from death (NDE) or from an Out-of-Body Experience (OBE), Astral Travel, etc. This is not a book detailing my experience; however, I share a brief snippet of the story here to explain to the readers how I was shown the glaringly obvious right in front of my nose, or within my entire body, should I say.

It would be decades later before I found out that "I", my soul consciousness, and the Seth soul and larger entity behind that soul, and others of great wisdom, had planned that NDE event to occur so that from a very young age, I would question physical reality and spend my entire lifetime learning about what had happened, why, how, who, what, and every nuance I could possibly learn about consciousness.

To help me, my mother, who had actually read a copy of _Seth Speaks_, helped me understand my event and the highly psychic events and occurrences that would then fill my following years with wonder.

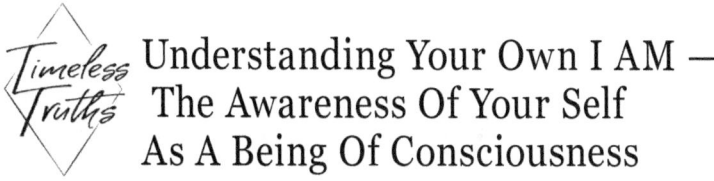

Understanding Your Own I AM —
The Awareness Of Your Self
As A Being Of Consciousness

This is what our book is all about of course. Shifting the very position, standpoint, and perspective of the reader, and yourself of course, FROM the human self that seems separated and thus limited as to its capabilities to create and succeed, TO the immortal Self of consciousness, your own awareness of Being/existing that is called by the various names that we teach (I AM, Christ, Lord, "God", etc).

ALL HUMANITY to walk the Earth are NOT the physical flesh body alone. You are the Self that is within the physical flesh body, having your physical experience on Earth. You are the immortal Being of consciousness, connected intimately and eternally, to all other species and their expressive, objective forms (objects/physical reality) through the immortal soul/being that you are. Eternally.

Now, it is the recognition of this truth as to the nature of your Self, your own being within, that opens the door to learn more, expand more, and begin to shift your _physical_ experiences, as you shift the inner direction of your eternally creative Self and how it is used to create your physical reality. Again, you cannot most effectively and fruitfully use that which you do not as yet know that you <u>are</u> as the natural Self.

You would do well, then, if you draft up your own statements of TRUTH about yourself that begin to open your mind to the true potentials that you are, and how they are quite unlimited in nature. Statements such as:

"I AM the immortal Being within this flesh. Faceless and formless, yet I take on form as I express my inner Self through the human form that is my body.

I AM naturally a gestalt consciousness within and I AM not at all separate from all other consciousness. I can direct my attention, beliefs, and creative energy to draw forth the objects, events, and conditions of my life intentionally, purposefully, and joyfully.

I AM the WAY, I AM the TRUTH, and I AM THE LIFE of this physical body.

I AM, the awareness of Being within me, is already connected to and a part of ALL physical objects, animals, plants, oceans, and all forms of consciousness expressed into physical matter. This is how I can easily draw them to me via the laws of attraction inherent in all energy.

The focus of my attention, thoughts, emotions, and beliefs all direct the inner being of consciousness that I AM eternally connected to ALL consciousness to attract into my physical life that which I am focused on, regardless as to my perception if it's "good" or "not good", wanted or not."

As an exercise, you can develop your own inner being statements of truth, and write them as if it was literally your soul/being within that is speaking these things and not the human of flesh. Write them from the orientation and perspective of the inner being and you will start to open up the mind as to its truth in nature so that your rational and intellectual mind becomes aware of your truths. (Awakened to them.)

Now, these of course are simply some beginning statements of truth that the inner self makes and one could create these endlessly to suit their personal needs, to overcome limiting beliefs, understanding that **_the physical brain does not have to know the way_**, for something to be achieved, healing to occur, paths to be opened and success to be experienced.

Your rational and intellectual mind is _learning to trust the inner being_ and begin to act _from_ the perception, standpoint, and beliefs of this inner being that you are, in order for you to shift your _physical_ experiences in ways you desire. As the saying goes "As within, so without."

As we have stated, consciousness cannot EVER be separated and thus, that which gives you your awareness of Self, provides your physical body its cellular structures and functions, provides the beat of the heart, and the body its life animation. This means that you are not at all separate from;

◊ Answers you seek

◊ Divine guidance

◊ Clarity

◊ Path to take for best success

⋄ Solutions to problems, challenges and that which confronts you

⋄ Means, money, wealth

⋄ Improved healing, health, and physical function

⋄ Inventions and technological innovations

⋄ Artistic expressions of any and all kinds

⋄ The means by which to create objects, events, and conditions anew in your life

If you believe in limitations, then you will certainly meet with them in your life experience.

Conversely, if you believe that there is a way, a path, a solution, etc.... and that even though your brain and intellect may not "yet" have the awareness of it, you _know_ that your inner being _does have access to that information_, then you yourself open the doors for that potential to arise within you, attract such answers, solutions, and guidance to you that comes to your awareness in a dream, waking state, a sudden moment of realization.

You create your own reality. To a large degree then, your beliefs in limitations are quite literally the sides of the "box" within which you yourself create a more limited physical life experience. Expand your beliefs and perception of Self and you will then begin more and more to expand your physical experiences that then must follow.

You cannot escape YOU. And that inner "YOU"...your "I AM" awareness by any name you wish to call it, IS... an intimately connected and eternal portion of "God" by any and all names humanity has ever called it. You are a part of "the Creator" itself; though this creator is not a single being or human-like consciousness, but rather infinitely beyond what you could fathom to imagine.

Within your mind may be the questions.

Within your Self will be the answers.

You _cannot_.... I repeat this and I want this made clear, _you cannot_ separate your Self from the answers, means, solutions, healing/health, success, wealth, peace, joy, love, and all things you may desire. Your rational mind may create what we call the **Rational Mind Veil**, that you are challenged with, that then becomes the filter of perception through which you view, understand, and hence, interact with your reality. Think of it like a thick cloud that may surround your physical body like an aura-cloud, that then impedes or blocks the free-flow of energy in and through your Self, from expressing around you as the life you desire and love so dearly.

The Rational Mind Veil is something that in the future we will speak more of, for it is a very real, self-created filter through which the natural, creative flow of Divine energy and higher vibrations are impeded. **It is self-created. It is self-eliminated.** All lower vibrational human emotions create it, which leads to limited perceptions, and hence, challenges in your physical life experience. It is indeed a tool by and through which you can recognize your own "guidance" on which directions you need to take with your personal vibrational frequency to BE where you desire to experience the flow of higher vibrational experiences.

However, dear ones, this is how you grow. A self-created challenge of perhaps a physical nature, to serve you as the impetus for you to turn within, to seek from the eternal wisdom that is already a portion of your Self, and bring that wisdom to the forefront of your conscious awareness, to "school" and teach the rational mind/intellect so that it shifts in time, its perception of what you really are that then, allows these natural resources to flow forth into your awareness and then, into your field of visibility.

You awaken yourself.

Again, if you personally do not believe this to be possible, then I assure you, to you it will seem impossible. To those, however, that believe it is possible, and even absolutely their truth...their nature as a Being of Consciousness, then to those individuals, it will well-up within you and you will in time, and with consistent practice, expand this inner Self so that it is able to perceive an infinitely rich, vast source of knowledge, wisdom, and insights to achieve your goals and dreams.

The incredible emotional richness, variety, and splendor of your physical experience is the material, physical reflection of your inner feeling tones. **It pervades the events in your life, the overall inner direction, and the quality of _perception_.** It fills up and illuminates the individual aspects of your life, and largely determines the pervasive subjective climate in which you dwell.

This is a very important sentence and point to understand. Your inner rate of vibration, your personal, cumulative frequency at any given time is your inner feeling tone, and this...is what sets the overall "tone" of the events and happenings in your life. The inner feeling tone, your personal rate of frequency vibration, also helps determine the perception you have of objective, physical reality. It is rather a filter, if you will, through which you perceive and interact with reality.

The higher the inner feeling tone, the higher the inner frequency vibration, and the greater your perception of physical reality shifts so that you then PERCEIVE a much better, improved, smoother, and more enjoyable physical reality. You perceive events that are more pleasing and less of those that are not. When you perceive those that are not pleasing, you simply let them fade away, knowing that your focus of attention is what feeds them the energy of life to exist in consciousness.

If they do not exist in your mind and are not held in consciousness by your attention to them, then they cease to affect you at all. Hence, problems - challenges - fade away on their own. This is a massively important key concept to understand and explains precisely how the core of the laws of attraction via electromagnetic attraction works, based upon your inner feeling tones.

Good morning, Jackson-Thomas. We are here, and we do hear your calling to us. We are pleased to see that you are gaining momentum in our works and in the choices of free will to fulfill more and more of our mission's potential. You know as well that the more we channel, the more we work with you and through you, the wider that channel gets for more "God" energy to flow into and through you. It is not just words that come into your consciousness and through you onto the page, it is the vibrational energies of "God"/ Source/All That Is that are flowing into and through you; and with that comes the opening of pathways, channels, and corridors through which more Divine energy may reach you. As we have explained before, our channeling sessions, then, raise your vibrational frequency of your own consciousness/soul/being and expand it immeasurably, allowing an enhanced experience in your physical life as well.

We are enjoying your re-focused efforts into our book, and we are pleased with the progress. It does take quite a bit of physical effort to gather the materials, put them into our manuscript draft, organize them, and then we can add to them, clean them up, and format all of it so that it is in a more presentable form to be printed/published.

You are correct in that all things are beginning now to move forward. The Universe if you will, the greater mass energy around you and within which you also have your being focused, is shifting energies and focus, even as the new "delta variant" drama plays itself out. As you see most people are truly moving past the fear factor that once caused a very, big shift in the earth plane energy and the fields of related channels through which Divine energy moves into expression. The greater mass society upset the apple cart and rocked the boat, and it was the waves that you yourself have had to contend with as the greater ocean of consciousness around you was in more chaos. Now it subsides as all storms must. Your cultures and societies are largely ignoring the fear that some are trying to induce on purpose for the people of the world. As the fear is released and life gets back to normal, so too, does the flow of energy within that realm get back to free-flowing instead of blocked energy. And you have yourself survived the "Global Pandemic" without so much as a sniffle, even when traveling into hospitals that were exposed to greater numbers of virus-infected people. Again, it is your belief in the Divine protection of your natural being within that has, in fact, kept you healthy and vibrating to that health that you believe is innately yours to begin with.

You see, reality is created from the inside out. From the Divine being within you outward into your physically appearing environment. That reality will not succumb to a virus of any manner from the outside, attacking you and your body, unless you first believe it is possible within. If your belief system sets up the conditions and state of consciousness where you believe more in an external virus of any kind (cold, flu, or covid-#, whatever bug of the day, etc.) having the ability to attack you from the outside, then you will, of course, create the conditions in which this probable reality may express itself into your experience.

If on the other hand, you believe that you are a Divine being of "God" Light and Love and that the inner being within you knows only pure health of the highest vibration, and that you emit that from the core of your being, like a light bulb, radiating outward so that it acts as a protective energy layer to protect you from such things external, well then, you will also meet with those conditions.

If you truly believe you are immune to such things naturally, then such viruses, sickness, or illness cannot readily take hold in your particular body or system. You may be exposed to it, and indeed you have been fully exposed to the supposed C-19 virus many times over as of now. However, it could not take root in your physical body as you truly believe you are immune to it, without a doubt – BECAUSE YOU UNDERSTAND that you are a Divine Being that is having a physical experience as a human-being, and you personally believe that all is well and under control.

Now, as a teacher on the earth plane, often you must experience the challenges of humanity so that you understand them firsthand at the level of the intellect and rational mind. Therefore, your soul may choose to experience a virus, simply so that you understand with compassion what it is like and are able to guide others to overcome the experience. However, as a general rule, this is why you, Jackson-Thomas, seem to be exceedingly healthy throughout your life, as you hold this inner belief that keeps you from getting every bug that comes along. You simply vibrate at a higher level of frequency whereby the "bug of the day" be it a cold or flu or what have you, simply cannot take hold in your body as it is out of alignment with the inner Self, which is reflected AS the outer physical self. To put it another way, let's say a cold virus can only exist between temperatures A to C. If you personally then are at a temperature (frequency of vibration) that is say M, N or X, Y, Z...then you are outside of the temperature in which the virus could exist.

Take this temperature example and equate that to vibrational frequency and you will understand that you can indeed be more protected naturally as your vibrational frequency is higher/faster.

Fear, of course, is of the <u>rational mind of mankind</u>. Obviously, beings of consciousness, such as your inner Self, your soul, etc., do not fear anything for we are beyond such experiences. If you were then to literally shift your perception to viewing all reality around you from the INNER being, Self, well then, you also would not be fearful of anything. Not even mortal death. You would, of course, avoid mortal death as it would cut short your physical life; however, you would not fear it at all, as the inner Self of consciousness does not fear. That is a lower vibrational, earth plane emotion based upon limited knowledge and perceptions of understanding that create that experience for you to overcome.

Fear is often as the popular saying goes:
<u>F</u>antasized <u>E</u>xperiences <u>A</u>ppearing <u>R</u>eal.

It is the <u>rational mind</u> that fears something which it may not truly understand. As I have stated before, when you live <u>from</u> the point of view and perception that you are "just human", then you alienate yourself from the rich, infinitely supportive, loving, and all-resourceful sources that your inner being and soul are eternally connected to and have access from which to draw upon; and therefore, the rational mind or ego-self can feel like it does not have the answers, support, or wisdom to accomplish something, etc.

The rational mind then, when not monitored by awareness of your TRUE self as the inner being and infinitely resourceful self, can feel alone in the vast physical universe and world in which it seems your human body is separate from these resources, wisdom, knowledge, etc. This is the underlying cause of fear, doubt, hesitation, lack of motivation, lack of inspiration, procrastination, and many of the lower vibrational emotions that are caused by perceiving your reality FROM the physical "I'm only human" point of view and perception.

Now this said, you live in fear, or perhaps you live by a belief that you are an impervious Divine being that is within that flesh, and you simply take necessary precautions to wash your hands and such as you would for any bacteria, virus environment during cold or flu season, etc.

Your natural physical body's protection, then, is also directly affected by the vibrational

frequency, or state of consciousness in which you are presently existing. Make no mistake, if you are in lower vibrational states of consciousness, you will indeed experience lower vibrational states of expressions. Physical experiences, perceptions, thoughts, and emotions all exist as lessons at these lower vibrational states of consciousness.

That is to say that if you are completely tired, drained exhausted, upset, angry, depressed, etc..... you are then very much indeed vibrating to the state of consciousness that is associated with the 3-dimensional rational mind thoughts and emotions that stem from those thoughts, and hence, your cumulative vibration would be of a lower vibrational frequency. This may open your physical body to the similar experiences of illness or disease. If there is dis-ease or uneasy conflict within, then you may see that manifested in your external environment including within the physical self.

Conversely, if you are using your natural tools, taking time to stop and sniff the roses, getting adequate rest for the physical self to self-clean, self-heal, self-protect, and letting worries go, while fostering the inner belief in your natural protection, participating in activities that bring you joy, even if it's a few brief moments of walking barefoot in the grass or sand of the ocean shore, watching the clouds while feeling free - all of these activities then create the state of consciousness in which you are vibrating to much lighter, higher frequencies, which are, of course, more in alignment with Divine, nonphysical energies - frequencies. This automatically activates inner protections as a vibrational consciousness that emit outward through the physical self, and even extending into the physical environment in which you then find yourself. You see, even in the midst of a supposed "Global Pandemic" you can walk into hospitals with sick patients, colds, flu, Covid-19 you name it, and simply are not at all phased by any of it. Almost as if an invisible force field (such as your personal Aura) is surrounding you and protecting you no matter where you walk.

Again, your thoughts, your actions, and your beliefs, all direct the inner being to create the state of consciousness within which you are then creating your experiences of physical reality. Shift the state of consciousness in which you are dominantly focused and you will shift your human psyche. Shift your human psyche and the inner Self and you will shift the experiences of the physical self. As all outer physical reality is first created within before it expresses externally into the world of physical matter.

Now: Good afternoon, Jackson-Thomas, our Divine channel through which we create and express onto the earth plane!

We will discuss here for this session, the selectivity of consciousness in its focus. On the earth plane, of course, the soul/entity of consciousness is narrowed down so that a small portion of the soul is focused from within the human flesh body, looking outward to perceive your physical environment in which you are taking part in your learning experience. The larger portion of you is still far "beyond" the physical body and, of course, connected through many dimensions as you extend in what you might think of as "outward" from the physical 3-dimensional system. These are psychic dimensions in consciousness, of course, not physical dimensions. As I have mentioned before, the energy of the entire soul or larger Self that you are as a being of consciousness is not capable of narrowing its entire self down so as to focus all of itself in and through the human body, for it is much too powerful for that.

Most may not be aware of this, however, you do indeed perceive quite readily both from inside the body looking outward using your physical senses; however, you also simultaneously perceive the greater reality in which your consciousness is connected, an active portion of and interacting with, what is far beyond the scope of your focus within 3-dimensional reality. People may not be aware of the fact that though they are focused on reading a book, their energy, feelings, and emotions are emitting outward, in your terms now, from you in all directions and impacting and affecting the physical world and environment around you. Plants, animals, the weather, the Earth, and your physical universe is not hidden from your thoughts and emotions. So while you may not be aware of it, the greater portion of you as a being of consciousness is at all times connected with all else, interacting and creating reality *en masse*. Mass consciousness.

However, what we want to discuss here is that you are also quite able to focus your consciousness into a particular "direction" or vibratory environment that may or may not appear as physical. For example, in the dream state, either at night or when you are daydreaming, your consciousness is more focused into a dimension that is nonphysical and outside of time and space. It is as "real" and valid as the 3-dimensional physical objective world, yet you are at that moment focusing that portion of you in another "direction" if you will. So rather than focusing your consciousness on the 3-dimensions of objective reality around you that seem so solid in appearance and texture, you are focusing inward during the dreams, daydreaming, or visualization activities.

Think of it like this. You are at a very large gathering of many people. A party, concert, or other event in which there are hundreds of people all talking at the same time all around you. Loud noises, music playing, or what have you going on. The conversations of a hundred people can be heard mixed in with all of this as well, making the sounds quite overwhelming to some.

Yet if a friend or significant person were to speak to you from say 20 or 30 feet away, over all the noise of others speaking intelligent conversations and music, noise, etc., you are able to clearly focus only on what that person is saying to you so that you can understand them. In our example here, during the concert, your friend yells out to you among the many and asks if you would like a snack from the snack stand as they are going there to get a snack themselves. In this example then, you are able narrow the focus of your consciousness so that all of your attention and physical senses are focused in that direction, on that person speaking to you, so that you drown out all other sounds and, through your selective focus of listening, are able to understand exactly what they are asking or saying to you over the crowd.

You might perhaps even unknowingly be reading body language, facial expressions, hand signals, and other physical forms of communication, yet you are able to distill all of them into the very meaning that this person is trying to convey to you. You are then, selectively focusing your attention, awareness, and consciousness to a degree, in that person's direction.

Again, as we have described in other portions of our books and works, the narrowed focus is particularly useful when navigating and operating in your physical environment, given that the human mind and bodily mechanisms can only utilize so much data at one time to effectively operate in such a fashion so as to be coordinated in the physical environment.

Now, multiply our example here by hundreds of thousands of people speaking to you simultaneously and imagine being able to track each and every conversation coherently, and communicate coherently back to each person, and you would begin to understand a very, very extremely limited idea of how your greater consciousness is in its natural state when focused from outside the physical body.

Consciousness then, your consciousness specifically in this subject material we are talking about here, is able to focus itself into a particular "direction" or dimensions in nonphysical reality and create and experience all sorts of fascinating experiences. What you may not realize is that, at any given time, your greater entity from which you are derived as a soul in this lifetime is also focusing into other Reincarnational lifetime simultaneously with the one that you know. Other probable selves, then, of your own soul are incarnated into other lifetimes, and your own consciousness is, at a higher level or beyond the physical reality you know as this lifetime, also focusing a portion of itself in another lifetime within time and space. Again, selective focus of the consciousness into physically appearing dimensions that, to you, represent different time periods of historical time.

Now, you specifically, Jackson, remember well when you died as a child playing in the barn where you grew up and you "went to heaven", as is the popular terminology. Your consciousness, for that experience, was focused _into_ nonphysical reality that humans enter for a familiar greeting arena when you transition focus from within the body to outside the body after physical death. You may, as in your case, see, speak to, and coherently communicate with the souls (consciousness) of loved ones long passed away, Angels, beings of light, etc. These are, in fact, real, and you are perceiving them correctly. However, as you also noted after your experience was nearing its end, you were told that "you must go back to the earth plane as your work was not yet done."

The very next instant you remember floating at the top of your barn roof, staring at your lifeless body, and then seeing and hearing the rope break, your body fall to the floor and impact, etc. While we are not describing the specifics of that event, we are showing here that you, Jackson, personally remember exactly what it was like shifting from one instant focusing _into_ "heaven" (nonphysical reality), and the very next instant you are focused _into_ physical reality where your _current_ lifetime is taking place within space and time, and this then provided you the experience that led you to eventually reconnect with me in this particular lifetime as you have now in many, many lifetimes.

Our point here is that you shifted instantly the focus of your consciousness into the dimension of reality in which your larger self desired to focus into for that moment. Just as you can focus on someone speaking to you in a large and noisy crowd. Now, in describing the event, one who has had a Near-Death Experience (died physically) may say that they "went to heaven" or even some who create a self-created experience of hell (which of course does not exist). The truth is that you... didn't GO anywhere as there is nowhere (no space and time) to go TO. You...simply shifted the focus of your consciousness.

Outside of the body when it left the focus from within the body, and then you shifted the focus of your consciousness back into the direction of 3-dimensional reality to see your lifeless body and the environment in which that body known as the man named Jackson was living previously/prior to your accident. Using you as an example, as we so often love to do, we can paint the picture of the shifting of consciousness in its selective focus into "directions", if you will, of realities that are physical in context and those that are not.

In a way of speaking, this is, of course, what I do when I connect with you, Ruburt, or any conscious being. I simply shift my focus into that being's perception in physical realities or not. As we have noted in our prior materials, blogs on our website, etc., time and space do not exist as you perceive it while you are in the human body (incarnated).

Briefly, time and space are necessary constructs for you to perceive a physical reality in which your objects are separated by space and perceived to use time to get from one to another, etc. However, outside of physical reality, the portion of reality in which the greater self is rooted, originated, eternally connected, etc... time does not exist. From my perspective, speaking to Ruburt in 1969 or to you in 2021 is simply an intention of focus as to where I place a portion of my focus in what you perceive to be time. As I have said, all time is "simultaneous"; therefore, to me, there is no future, nor past, and to the portion of you that is not focused within the body, this is also precisely the case.

Now, there are many, many creative implications of the truth that there is no actual time and how that impacts your physical life and environment as you know it, and we will get into those in future works; however, for now, we are simply pointing out another trait and ability of the nature of consciousness. Your consciousness.

From my perspective and from the dimension that I would refer to as my dimension of consciousness in which I place the core of my existence, I can focus into hundreds of thousands of directions and dimensions and have connections with hundreds of thousands of beings, within the human body or not, in your dimension of time and others, all simultaneously. Much like cherry picking at the fruit stand or tree, I can select which I desire connections with and "enhance" them in ways that bring a more fruitful and "colorful" experience to that being.

To you, Jackson, we can wrap up this session for now; however, we will later pick up on and develop this subject into more material about the selective capacity of consciousness focusing. The applicability of importance here for our readers is that this selective focus of their consciousness is something that can be used as a tool to focus into the nonphysical for creative visualization purposes, manifestation, seeking information, ideas, solutions, etc. as well as focusing the consciousness into other dimensions of knowledge and wisdom of your (and other) species.

This is much like you calling upon the wisdom and knowledge of past gold miners and the nature of the Earth to "speak to you" in terms of what you are looking for, seeking to learn, know, and gain knowledge and understanding about. We will talk about focusing the consciousness into and through a bee or butterfly, a bird or animal, or even into a tree or the Earth. As you are well aware, some of your loved ones who have crossed over into nonphysical reality (passed away physically), are then able to merge their consciousness into the consciousness of a butterfly or a bird, and "communicate" through physical animate objects with loved ones still living. They can "fly" or steer a butterfly. Perhaps after loved ones have passed and they loved butterflies, all of a sudden a butterfly may fly right up to a loved one in the family and land on them or near them, or fly alongside them as they walk along in the park. A bluebird, blue jay, cardinal or other bird may show up at the window, day after day seemingly to come and say hello. Again, this is a selective focus of consciousness at work here, and human consciousness working in harmony and love with other natural consciousness to reach out to loved ones and let them know they are there, around them in ways they may not have previously thought possible. However, they are indeed using the selective focus of their consciousness to communicate via consciousness.

This selective focus of consciousness also applies to healing, Reiki, and sending positive healing energies, love, light, and communication to other individuals. Which also leads us into the communication among consciousness at all times anyway, even when you are not aware of it.

More on... Telepathy and vibes of a room, people, group, place, etc. So there is much more material here for our book to yet be developed. For now, have a wonderful evening with your son, and enjoy your time with him. He is indeed special and going through his own challenges to learn his value and place in this world. It will come... in time, as all things do to you there.

Now: When Jackson-Thomas had his NDE as a child, he was, when out of the body, completely and lucidly aware. Aware of himself as a conscious being and then, when he returned from his focus into "heaven" after his experiences there, he floated at the top of the barn near the ceiling and looked down upon his dead and lifeless body. At that point, as "he" looked down from the viewpoint of hovering near the ceiling, he was as lucidly aware of his environment and surroundings as you are right now reading this book. He could hear, feel, sense, smell, and see everything around him in the 3-dimensional world. At that time one of the questions he asked himself was: "That's my human body. I wonder if it will continue to live in this lifetime?"

What I want to point out here, using Jackson as an example as we love to do, is that the soul or being of consciousness was acutely aware, at that moment, that the soul HAD a physical body that lay on the barn floor, crumpled in the hay. He was NOT the physical body itself, nor was he the thoughts asking the question if it would continue to live in that physical body for this lifetime where he is known as Jackson. "He" was the being of consciousness that was experiencing the thoughts and questions, as well as perceiving them multidimensionally as all do when they have a so-called "Near-Death" Experience or an Out-of-Body Experience (OBE).

So, we are pointing out here that "he" (his "I AM") was fully, lucidly aware, thinking and reasoning while OUTSIDE his body. He was aware of _Being_, before his consciousness re-entered his physical body to continue this physical lifetime. It was at that point he was aware of being-human. That he was a human-being.

Again, you are first and foremost, eternally, a conscious being. You are aware of being...before you are born, and after your physical death. **You do not lose your awareness or sense of self after death.** You only have the opportunity to expand it infinitely into many more realms and dimensions than the 3-dimensions from which you have just returned. Older individuals reading this may find great comfort in the truth that no matter how "good or bad" you've been in your lifetime, you do indeed transition your consciousness back into the natural state whereby you are lucidly aware of yourself in consciousness. You return to your natural state and perceptions. Now, I have detailed some of the experiences that occur after the physical death and the truth that you may enter an infinite nonphysical stage or drama whereby you are acclimated to your new environmental view until you remember, of course, that is the dimension of "home" that you have returned to. We will not go through the after-death experiences here, or the time of choosing, reflection upon one's life, and lessons learned during the physical lifetime. However, we do want to call out in this book here that you do exist as lucidly aware of yourself and your environment (and even more so) after your physical death. Again, the eternal validity of the soul, as described in *Seth Speaks*.

It has been said many times that you are a *spiritual being, having a human experience*. This is quite true, for being is what you eternally are. The sooner you open your mind to that truth, the sooner you will yourself be able to tap into areas of knowledge, wisdom, and direct knowing that you once only thought were myths.

Now, direct knowing, occurs at a level of consciousness that is beyond the rational, intellectual mind. For example, after a loved one passes away from the physical world, that loved one may be felt as a real presence of energy by a family member within a few moments, a day, a week, a month, or even years later. They may suddenly sense that the loved one is near them, or watching over them, or in the room with them, etc. They may sense the loved one in the distance. Meaning some will feel as if mom or dad or their husband, wife or child passed on is in the same room with them, or even standing right beside them and even have a strong sense of love or that there is a loving message to their presence. Perhaps that they are simply saying without words: "I am here...I am well and I love you." Often then, without realizing it, for those that have sensed loved ones like this, they can sense the "distance" at which the soul of that individual intrudes upon physical reality and is, in physical terms now, across the room, or right next to them. They can sense the direction and distance between their core being, and that of the loved one. This sensing then is accomplished, of course, through your consciousness.

When this occurs, there are many around the world who will tell you that they truly *KNOW* that their loved one was there in the room or nearby or present within close proximity. And no matter how crazy people may call them, they are not moved from their knowing as it is a DIRECT KNOWING. Direct knowing from the consciousness of the one passed on directly into and through the consciousness of the one still living. In fact, the feelings and sensations may be so strong and so clear that it is as if the feelings and sensations are their own, as they are experienced at a layer of their own consciousness and, therefore, sensed deeply within the core of their being. So it is that your consciousness is then sensing theirs and, at a layer beyond human language, communicating love and light to one another beyond death.

You are piercing the veil. Perceiving beyond time and space via your consciousness. Now, for those of you who may be experiencing this right now with a loved one that has crossed over/died their physical death and is coming to visit you lovingly, the next time you sense them strongly in the room with you, quiet the mind for a moment and ask in your mind quietly: "Mom, is that you I feel?" (or whatever name/title you would call your loved one). If you are listening with a quiet mind, you may very well hear, quietly but quite clearly (through clairaudience, natural to your consciousness) they may answer you with a simple "Yes", or they may begin speaking an entire storybook to you about their experiences or that they are okay and made it safely to "heaven", etc.

This communication and knowing then, telepathy and direct knowing through the medium of consciousness occurs both ways, of course. As one can sense a loved one while still living their physical existence, the loved ones passed on can also sense you in the same and, in many ways, sense even more from you, as they no longer have the rational, intellectual mind that often serves as the veil through which one's clear perceptions are often clouded. The loved one then, through consciousness, can indeed tune into you, just as you can tune into them. Forever. So it is that they are not "gone". They are simply no longer physical, and a call to their name will indeed solicit their attention in nonphysical reality as they then focus their consciousness in your direction and tune into you at many layers via consciousness.

In our example here of the loved one passed on, one may simply be on the physical plane going about their normal day-to-day activities, driving or perhaps in the shower, gardening or what have you, when all of a sudden, that loved one comes to mind. PAY ATTENTION TO THIS!

You may think of them briefly and perhaps see an image of them in your mind's eye. (Clairvoyance.) More often than not, they "appear" in your field of awareness because your consciousness already senses them, or the fact that they too may be focused on you at that moment. Your brain and intellectual mind may, or may not...in your busy day, catch the fact that the loved one came to mind. In the cases when you do notice, you might at times be surprised to find that there is nearby you, a remnant of their belongings in your home near you, or you are wearing their sweater or hat, or perhaps doing something you once did together, etc.

Now, again, I will tell you that while you can sense them, they also can sense you. Meaning that if you are thinking of them, contemplating good memories or what have you, they will indeed become acutely aware of this, and it is almost as if it's a call to them. It is a vibrational frequency, if you will, that in the most complex of patterns and ways, that make up the personality and the consciousness of that loved one that creates a unique vibration that can never be copied or imitated, that is almost like a direct-call to them. Through consciousness. Again, as you are contacting them through the direct-knowing, telepathy, and your clairabilities as you do from living person to living person.

Now remember - there is no time nor space in consciousness. Therefore, again, they are not "gone" from you physically. As there is no "where" or place for them to go...physically. So it is that when you call to them and think of them vividly, and especially so when the emotions of love are present (the basis for all soul's existence as you are all a portion of the love of All That Is), they will focus on you/into your present human self. Now, they may be out "exploring the universe". They can indeed, explore all planets and stars of your physical universe; however, they can visit and explore infinite dimensions of reality that are beyond that. That said, as there is no time and space, even from the "farthest reaches" their consciousness is able to "find you" and tune into you, instantaneously.

There are infinite benefits for humanity when, in time, you come to a more in-depth and expanded understanding of the phenomena of time and space, and the implications that come forth when you embrace that there is no time and space, and what that means to life, IN time and space in terms of creativity and experience.

I remind you again that here, at this layer of communication, at the level of consciousness, you are not using English or any other human language, though you may be thinking thoughts of such. It is your natural vibrational energy, your personal aura, and your own unique, unmistakable, and eternally valid "you" in consciousness that they too can tune into.

Here are a few more fascinating truths for you. Jackson-Thomas has personal experience here and can relate to my example. I believe there will be many of our readers who will *also identify* with precisely these kinds of examples of connections among the living and the dead, through consciousness...and the communication phenomenon that takes place, initiated from the physically dead to the physically living to let them know they are still "there" with them, comfort them, and communicate the underlying love that is eternal.

Now, when Jackson's father passed away a few years back, physically coming to the end of his lifetime, shortly thereafter, Jackson and his siblings started experiencing communication where his father's soul was communicating with them by blinking their lights, causing TVs to turn on by themselves in the middle of the night and all sorts of electronic fun. So excited was his father that he was in his "home" dimension in consciousness, and that he could now do magical things that he now remembered how to do, that he sought to let Jackson and his siblings know he was there. To let them know he was very well and excited about meeting the family members there who were there to greet him upon his arrival "home"...nonphysical reality.

A week after his physical passing, Jackson was in a hotel room while traveling to the funeral in Montana where his father lived at the time. At approximately 3 am in the morning while sleeping, the TV in his hotel room turned itself on, and was blaring "white noise" with the volume turned up to maximum volume 100%, and the screen simply "white snow" or static or what have you. Shocked at the massive intrusion of sound and the TV coming on by itself at 3 am, while the remote control was out in the main room of the hotel on the coffee table, Jackson, of course, knew it was his father who had indeed turned the TV on and set the volume to 100% to communicate to him quite clearly that he was aware Jackson was on the way to the funeral, was saying "hello" and that everything was fine, he had made it to "heaven" (transitioned his focus from outside the body), and was looking in on him as he slept in the hotel room.

A few days later his sister Sherry was on the phone with Jackson one evening and telling him that her lights were blinking at her home, *on command*, where when she would ask: "Dad...if that's you, can you please blink the light twice." And the light over the sink would blink twice, then not blink for another 5 minutes. Then she would ask again, "Dad...if that's you, can you please blink the light twice." And the light over the sink would blink three times. Within seconds the light blinked 3 times and then stopped.

Fascinated by this, Sherry called Jackson excitedly to tell him about it, only to discover that _the very same thing was happening at his house, right then while she was on the phone with him and it was simultaneously occurring at her house more than 1,000 miles apart._

For weeks, these phenomena happened to them with lights blinking on command, TVs turning on, and the radio turning on by itself with a song playing that was a favorite song of their father. Their cell phones would ring and it would show that the number calling was 07734, however, when they would answer, there would be no one there. Now, if you look at your phone with these numbers on them, in a digital font that was on older cell phones and pagers, this number, upside down spells "hELLO".

Meaning, that their loved one was actually communicating with them by affecting the electronics in their phones. A call from "heaven" you might say. Millions of these events occur every day around the Earth and, if you are paying attention after a loved one passes away physically, often you will receive such physical signs that they are okay, and still with you. Often objects in the home will move on their own and perhaps the keys to the car were found on the floor, or somewhere other than where they were left. A picture of the loved one perhaps may fall over or come off the wall where hung. They are not "haunting" you. They are conveying love to you in the only way that they can, by affecting physical reality through the directed use of their own consciousness, which affects physical matter through consciousness to communicate with those that are still living. If you are open to such things and acknowledge them, talk to them, invite them to come by and say hello, you can open the door for loved ones to communicate in such a way that it's obvious that it's them responding to you.

Now, if something of this nature bothers you, and you ask them not to give you signs or are afraid, then they may well comply and leave you alone; however, to many spiritual people, this type of phenomenon is indeed fascinating as they enjoy the expanded experience of consciousness at work, naturally. I give you these examples of Jackson's experience because millions of our readers will indeed identify with the fact that these kinds of events have also happened to

Jackson W. Moore

them. Personal experiences they know themselves to be true, as they have lived through them.

Now, the all-important question here was how could Jackson's father be blinking the lights in California and in Oklahoma at the same time or, _be in two places at once?_

The answer goes back to our traits and characteristics about consciousness and the phenomenon that are root assumptions of your 3-dimensional environment. That is, consciousness eternally exists outside of space and time. Meaning it is everywhere at once (**_omnipresent_**). Again, there truly is no time and space.

You only _perceive_ consciousness of energy slowed down and accumulated into atomic mass that appears as 3-dimensional objects such as your universe. However, from your native point of view in nonphysical reality, there is no distance between physical locations as space is only a phenomenon of **_perception_** when in the human form peeking outward from the body.

As I have mentioned before, the "mobility" of consciousness is not limited by any physical factor such as space or the perception of linear time. Consciousness can "move" back and forth from the farthest reaches of your universe with a mere shift in focus, and it can look upon the dinosaurs or the future as easily as it can look upon your time period in history today, as you perceive it.

I will say again, Consciousness, your consciousness, and all consciousness, eternally exists outside of space and time. Its expressions can appear in space and time; however, at the lowest level that is the fabric and intelligence behind the atoms that form atomic mass, and thus, solid-appearing objects, consciousness exists outside of time and space.

You _can_, then, sense the loved ones passed on, and they can indeed sense you. They "hear" you clairaudiently and receive your telepathic messages through consciousness, direct to the core of their being, just as you may be able to sense a loved one passed on at the core of your being when they are "near" (in _your terms_ of space I am speaking). Many will identify with this as it is truly a common occurrence that demonstrates the natural communication of consciousness to consciousness and "life" (full awareness and existence) beyond physical death.

195

Good morning our immortal friend and Divine channel through which we bless the world. Now, as there is great energy in the air around you with the storms that now come through your area, there is great cleansing and renewing of life that comes following those storms. In the same manner, there are great storms, you might say, in the Universe or in the consciousness of humanity at the moment and, therefore, in like manner, there is a great cleansing and renewing of life energy following these "storms", also.

There are, in some ways, appearances of destruction when the storms of the Earth pass through. In the older days, they would say that the gods were angry or that they had done something as a tribe or group to upset these gods. When, at times, they misinterpreted then, as many do now, that it is not a destructive force that seeks to destroy, but rather to sweep clean, refresh and renew the lands. Animals and man alike are affected by the storms around you, and more so by the storms _within_ you.

Now, you have been reading a little of my early material with Ruburt and Joseph and that has, and will, help you learn more, become more aware, and, of course, will help you broaden your understanding of the truths that we now teach to many. The more you practice each day, the more we channel, I again remind you, that the more and more you will find yourself easily viewing, and interacting with reality from the higher perspective and standpoint of the natural self. One of your challenges at the moment is to find the time in your daily schedule to sit still, go within, and focus with us so that we can get the materials out through you, and record them in a physical manner to use in our teachings.

Once you find the time, as you see...it just flows easily and effortlessly as it can and should. It is not "hard work" to sit and channel. The hard part for humans is the sitting. Taking the time from your daily schedules, sitting still, and listening with intention to hear, feel, see, and sense us. You have found that even as your schedule gets busy, busy, busy on the DOING plane of the physical Earth, that you MUST, by free will choice, decide when it is that you yourself are going to sit still long enough to be able to get dictated materials through you. With Ruburt (Jane), writing was her full-time vocation. This is not the case with you and your work as the Executive Vice President over Sales, Marketing, and Engineering with a Healthcare IT company takes you across the world traveling up to 100% at times, working long hours, and focused on very physical tasks, strategic (rational/ intellectual mind) thinking, planning and so forth. Your job is very focused on physical tasks on the physical plane. That said, all things on the physical plane, then, are lower vibrational frequencies to a degree, as they are consciousness expressed through Electromagnetic Energy Units (EEUs) into atoms and molecules, slowed down in vibrations so as to accumulate into atomic mass and thus producing physically appearing reality.

Now, as you have discovered, the busier you are focusing on physical plane activities, the more you must also take the time to "let go and let flow" if you are to allow, then, the Divine to work freely through you...through your consciousness, to manifest into your life that which you are attempting to create at any given time. Creative goals in life. The key here being *"allowed to work freely through you, through your consciousness"*. Meaning, unimpeded by thoughts, perceptions, and emotions of limitations, lack, or things being missing from your life experience. You do not FORCE Divine energy. Ever. That, of course, doesn't work. You ALLOW Divine energy to flow through nonresistance, trustful passivity, indifference as to outcome, beliefs, trust, etc.

Then you must shift yourself from doing to not doing and go within to use the creative side of your being so that you can create the conditions that align themselves as the reality you desire unfolding before you.

Now, the "doing" portion of physical activity on the earth plane can and does make progress and achievement because you are still using the metaphysical means for creation...although they are in ways being "pushed" out into physical reality more than simply allowed. There is resistance from the physical plane for them to appear and often this is what you would call "the hard way". They can be great learning lessons in life. So, you can and do create this way....more physically oriented and forceful, yet, you are still using all of the natural creative methods and ways by imagining that which you desire to do or achieve or accomplish and then setting about physical actions to create that achievement.

However, I assure you that you do not create anything physical without it first being within your consciousness or thoughts. Even the most successful, physical achievements, begin as ideas of what it is that the human desires to achieve as their end-goal or physical creation. They are still thinking about it, contemplating it, envisioning it in their mind's eye, and taking actions to get there. Usually, this will bring them on a path of great trial and error....and finding out many more ways that something does _not work_ before they discover that which does.

However, some of the most creative geniuses over time, have simply tapped into the inner being, and with the intention to create, and the imagination, simply contemplated the goals as already achieved and thus experienced great moments of inspiration, ideas, solutions, inventions, resolutions, mathematical equations, stories, novel material, movie scripts, musical masterpieces, paintings, and what have you. They do not express into physical reality without having contemplated the goals in the first place. Then you can open the inner channel for them to flow into the outer physical reality more easily, effortlessly, and in peace and harmony with all of the physical environment and consciousness in which you are presently ensconced.

In all cases of great successful achievement on the physical plane, it was not the human brain and rational mind that created the path, the tasks, the road map, and, hence, achievements. It is that the human brain or conscious, rational/intellectual mind, became suddenly aware of the road, the path, the map, and the action items that it was being guided to pursue as possible actions...that then the human had to make free-will choices to take action upon which then brought about the end results that appear as their achievements becoming physical reality.

Let's stress this point. The rational/intellectual mind cannot by itself determine the most efficient, effective, consistent path to creative achievement and DOES NOT KNOW THE WAY, in the beginning, of precisely _how_ something will be accomplished. YOUR RATIONAL/INTELLECTUAL MIND IS NOT SUPPOSED TO KNOW THE WAY, THE PATH, AND THE TRUTH OF HOW TO ACHIEVE ALL THINGS POSSIBLE.

The rational mind is to be trained to take inspiration, guidance, and direction from the inner self, which it can then act upon to accomplish its goals and desires. The author of any great book does not see the entire manuscript in complete print all at once, accomplished, in the rational mind. They may see the cover of the book, the goal that they intend with the book's production, even many of the chapter titles, etc. However, the book _reveals itself_, word by word, paragraph by paragraph, page by page, and chapter by chapter as the author receives the words in awareness of the rational/intellectual mind that comes streaming in from seemingly nowhere. Of course, this seemingly nowhere is the inner self which is intimately connected with All That Is and, hence, all sources of inspiration, knowing, ideas, inventions, wisdom, guidance, etc.

You must train your rational mind to understand that it does not need to know the whole way. It must ALLOW the entire way to appear as you move forward using your creative tools. Now, certain successful people may indeed receive large blocks of information, data, formulas, ideas, whole chapters if you will, and very large amounts (physically speaking) of materials that come to their awareness in an "ah-ha" type of epiphany moment. They are called by some to be "downloads" or "downloads from the Universe". Ruburt received them and noted them in some of our books and materials. Jackson receives them often, and so do many of you our readers if you are tuned into paying attention to that creative inspiration appearing in your awareness out of seemingly nowhere.

This is because consciousness, the source from which the material has come, is not linear. Your rational mind may decipher the material as you do your dreams, in a linear manner that can be understood in a frame of context within your 3-dimensional reality that seems to have linear progression; however, the material has come from a dimension in which time is eternal and does not exist. Where all ideas, inspiration, and all such creativity exist eternally NOW, for all of history, for all of eternity.

Therefore, as your natural senses, your clairabilities as we call them, can communicate in terms that are not linear, you can receive large amounts of creative data, chapters of books, movie scripts, screenplays, paintings, poems, or any creative expression, in what seems to be <u>a large block of data given to you all at once</u>. I am certain that many of our creative readers across the world will identify with this and that it has at times occurred to them.

Your consciousness perceives it, then, through your natural senses of clairvoyance and/or clairsentience or perhaps telepathy and/or clairaudience, etc. You sense it as a large block of data/ information, etc. as you are sensing it in your natural self, your native state and orientation, in which the block of information is given to you "all at once" and not in a linear fashion.

Now, your physical self and physical brain, which is used in part to organize things in your physical reality, still resides within the 3-dimensional plane of seeming time and space, so when you record such information, you still must record it within the context of the time and space in which you are presently focused and living your physical life. This means you must read it aloud, or you write it, type it, draw it, or create it physically, in a linear fashion...because you have agreed at a higher level to operate within the constructs of the root assumptions of time and space.

We are providing here some insights on the creative process, outside of simply the instruction of how to use all your natural tools to create/manifest the life you desire. We are framing and presenting a viewpoint of the creative process, from another angle, if you will, so that you the reader are more able to view the truths of creation from many angles which paint the overall larger picture, if you will, so that the depth of your understanding reaches the core of your being within, and you more and more become accustomed to sensing that guidance and direction, inspiration, and source of knowledge within yourselves.

The creations ultimately may <u>appear</u> in time and space, but this is only when they have already become physically manifest. Any physical manifestation or object of your 3-dimensional universe is CREATED in nonphysical, non-linear reality. It is EXPRESSED into linear time and space within 3-dimensions that your physical senses recognize and organize as intelligent data about your environment.

Just as your own consciousness can "look into" time and space of the 3-dimensional plane, for example, when your consciousness leaves the physical body in an Out-of-Body Experience or after physical death when "you" float above your physical body... you can also shift your perception and focus of consciousness outside time and space into the nonphysical dimensions or other dimensions that are similar to 3-dimensional existences.

Again - there are no limitations of consciousness or of the Self and there are no separations of consciousness and the dimensions in which it is possible to explore.

Before we wrap up this morning's session, let me state this phrase that I have been holding in your attention, Jackson-Thomas, for days now:

In ALL CASES of physical achievements of success where individuals created great things of themselves or within their life to contribute to the world, <u>the individual did not identify themselves</u> with the *CURRENT* HUMAN PHYSICAL SELF that they, at the early stages, saw in the mirror.

They innately *KNEW*, deep within their being, that they were more than what they saw in the mirror and that "something" was burning within them that they just *had* to get out and express into physical, material matter.

That is, they identified themselves more as the future self (say as *being* wealthy, healthy, successful, etc.) than they did with the current self. Their focus and imagination of that future state as being who they really are, drew forth the opportunities and open doors, means, and ways to achieve that, as they took small steps in that direction.

They had a vision of what they desired to be in the future. They contemplated that vision and imagined it. They used, knowingly or not, metaphysical creative tools to create the path before them, <u>seeing the end goals clearly in their minds, and feeling the "pull" of them to draw them forward</u>. They trusted the path and took what steps they could and when more of the path appeared, took more steps.

It's like driving at night when you can only see 300 feet of road before you and everything else is lost in the darkness. Yet you keep driving along that path in faith that the next 300 feet, and the next, will appear as you slowly continue your forward progress, all the while having the destination in mind of where you desire to end up, even if that destination is no-where and open to just unfolding.

These are some of the stumbling blocks to creative expression that over the millennia, humankind has sought to overcome. You overcome them by understanding their PURPOSE for existing and that is often the same answer in guidance from the Divine/Source/The Universe, All That Is. To turn within to seek the source from which all guidance, wisdom, insights, inspiration, ideas, and pathways lead to successful creative expressions.

With that...we will break for this morning and call this session a great success! Now, you may prepare for more of your magical adventurous day before you. Thank you for the time this morning to sit still and channel more material for our book. As you see... more of the roadway and path for our progress is appearing before you with each time you shift your focus within and receive the guidance and materials to move our mission forward.

And a final note for the reader, we will later on in your future from the writing of this book, detail many, many tools that you can use for co-creating your reality, what they are, how they direct consciousness and affect energy, and more specific step by step methods and paths through which you may apply your tools toward creative ends and means. Manifestation as many in your period of history call it. We call it "Divine creation", as all creation is, of course, Divine.

Soul Memory

We are here Jackson... Now, we can make this short and sweet for the moment so that you can make your dinner and attend to some of the activities you have planned for the evening. However, you are onto something when we talk about "Soul Memory" in that consciousness not only has "memory", it has access to those events and memories of its lifetimes and at multiple levels of awareness. Meaning that nothing, no thought, no emotion, no event, no-thing in any way, shape, or form that emits from the human-being or, any other creature for that matter, goes "unnoticed" or is not imprinted in one way or another in consciousness. As consciousness is what many think of as "God"/Source/The Universe, etc.... you cannot hide the slightest thought, intention, or feeling from "God"/All That Is. It occurs within consciousness, as consciousness.

So, what we want to talk about briefly, is that...you are correct in your teachings last evening and today in that your "soul" is pure consciousness that <u>exists outside of space and time</u>. Therefore, the events of yesterday, 50 years ago, and 50 years from now are all simultaneously available to the larger portion of yourselves as human-*beings*. So it becomes obvious, then, that you are conscious and aware of these memories of all thoughts, actions, events, and intentions from other lifetimes before you even began this journey in your current incarnation, immersed and ensconced in time and space for this lifetime, and you will have immediate access to them after your physically focused lifetime once again. Not only do you, at the level of consciousness, have access to all of THIS lifetime after your physical death, but you also have immediate access on other levels of awareness to all other lifetimes that you have incarnated into the human form, also.

Your brain may not remember these lifetimes as it only knows the life events and such from this particular incarnation, as it was given physical existence in this and only this incarnation. However, your soul/consciousness does have "memory" of all these lifetimes of yours, including, again, all thoughts, events, emotions, intentions, goals, hopes, dreams, and so forth. They are "impressions" within your own consciousness/soul that grow the soul as a being of consciousness, and a portion of All That Is, and they add immeasurably to your own expansion and evolution, but also to the expansion and evolution of the entity from which you have been given existence as a soul, and to the greater consciousness of All That Is.

As I have stated before, there are NO limitations of consciousness. There are no boundaries or separations of Self (or what you may think of as Selves, or Probable Selves, given that you have had many lifetimes). In the physical state, you may appear separate from these other lifetimes.

In the nonphysical state of consciousness, you are not separate at all. The lessons learned in one lifetime, are, as all things are, available to the individual you know to be yourself now, yet your brain and conscious mind associated with the brain and physical body are not typically aware of this unless you have remembered some of your "past lives". Only when you expand your consciousness, either in the dream state, by daydreaming, and/or through other use of tools to raise your vibration and expand the Self, will you from time-to-time gain access to such knowledge or memories.

Every human that has ever "remembered" a "past life" does not remember the memory from an area of the brain. Rather an area of the brain in THIS lifetime becomes acutely aware of the memory that is in the consciousness of the higher/greater Self that is you, and that comes to the present moment awareness of the brain of the individual then who sees, feels, senses, hears, or in other clairability ways gain access to memories from other lifetimes.

Now, I will mention here when we are talking about the non-limitations of consciousness, that most think you can only remember "past lives" that have already occurred in the framework of historical time as you think of it. Again, as linear time does not exist as you perceive it, those that do remember other lifetime incarnations tend do remember those that are set, like a movie you'd watch on TV or at the theater, in an earlier time in history...because you have a belief in linear time. Most believe, then, that you cannot remember the future if the future has not yet occurred in terms of physical reality.

When in reality, the future is as the past...an infinite set of probabilities from which you will selectively narrow them into one moment of the Present that seems to change as it unfolds in time. You only remember the past that you brought into focus and all other past events that are parallel or probable to that particular one you know, are filtered out so that the physical senses do not perceive them, giving a neatly packaged memory of the past that you do remember.

In reality, however, you can also access FUTURE lifetimes and, in fact, Jackson has done this both in waking daydreams and in the dream state at night, where the memory of a future lifetime comes to the awareness in that dream-like state. Again...you are seeing at these times, actual probable realities, that ARE occurring physically in a dimension that is ever as real and "solid" as your own, simply in a time context that you cannot perceive in your present state of focus....but your consciousness is not limited to the present state and environment in which you are focused for this lifetime.

Are you starting to see the massive implications of understanding this material? Some of you have already had these past life memories, future life memories, and so forth that are eternally a portion of your individual consciousness, and, of course, inseparable from all consciousness so you will know what we are talking about here when we describe these things. However, again, as your consciousness is not limited, you can, with effort and practice, over time, tap into these other dimensions in which you are living alternate lifetimes and existences, both as men and women in those lifetimes.

Bearing in mind that your soul is not physical. It does not have a sex, in terms of male or female. It is indeed a portion of both, though some souls do prefer patterns of incarnating as a male or female to play various roles that move the race and the evolution of Self forward. All souls that choose to incarnate into human form will, at one time or another, choose both sexes as it is natural for consciousness to be "balanced" in terms of energies. Therefore, you may have a dream in which you were a male in another lifetime, though you are female now. Or the reverse, where you are a male now and were a female in another lifetime...yet, in that memory that comes to your awareness, you KNOW that it is indeed you that you become aware of "there" even though the face and physical body do not match your current one.

For an example now: Jackson has had dreams whereby he was, say, a woman or another man in another lifetime, and in that lifetime was looking into a mirror and the reflection of the human looking back at him in the mirror looked differently than he does now as Jackson. He noted, then, in the dream that, "Hey that is me, but I look differently." This is the current, conscious mind, interpreting the dream image that is presented through consciousness from another lifetime in which that lifetime "bleeds through" into this lifetime's awareness in the dream state when the rational/intellectual mind is not blocking or filtering that kind of data out of its field of perception. Upon awakening, however, Jackson might remember the dream and, although the human man or woman in that mirror was indeed quite different in physical appearance, it was the same soul as the one now in the human form as Jackson and it did indeed recognize in the dream state that this person in the mirror was another version of Self.

Not having a physical sex, then, in terms of male or female, the soul will then recognize itself in various characters and forms. Now, again, you do...at the layer of consciousness, have access to this information and data, to a degree, in this current lifetime. Yet, one must practice going within to reach into and through consciousness and the psychic connections between your Self, and other existences to bring the knowledge and awareness of them into this current lifetime.

Now, you actually do this often anyway, unintentionally; however, the inner Self is active with other portions of itself outside of the time and space context that you perceive to be Earth and your universe around you now. There are constant interactions and "communication" between selves and lifetimes.

It is possible then to actually connect with another lifetime Self and draw knowledge or wisdom from that Self into your current lifetime.... though the knowledge, ideas, or wisdom may appear to you (again...in time) days later when it comes to mind simply randomly. It was triggered in your dream say...however, it took "time" before it would appear in your awareness of your current self whereby the brain would notice it, take note of it, and perhaps reflect upon it. The event of tapping into that lifetime self and the knowledge, wisdom, and lessons it has learned is instantaneous. It is only that your HUMAN senses operate in time and space, thus, it takes "time" before it comes to your awareness in what may be days or weeks after you have the dream whereby you received the connected answers, wisdom or guidance.

For this evening... we will trim our session short so you may make dinner but we will continue our discussion about reincarnation, soul memories and the truth about consciousness not having limitations. We are opening minds here to the reality of their own immortal, unlimited existence beyond the physical brain's memories of this lifetime and the tools, knowledge, wisdom, and resources you have available to you, as you can learn to draw from them (and often do without your being aware of it.). Now... have a good evening and we will chatter again tomorrow, my friend. Thank you again for sitting still for a few minutes so we can get more material for our international bestselling book that blesses millions. (Smile) That is a good _intention_ for us to bring into focus!!!

We are here Jackson-Thomas. Now: good morning to you and thank you once again for the time commitment to our mission and for channeling us as you raise your own vibrations and experiences. We will continue with the awareness of consciousness and the memories of "other lifetimes". I prefer that term over calling them "past lives", for truly they are no more in the past than your present moment in this lifetime is in the past. As I have mentioned, then, it is quite possible for people to remember "future" lifetimes, also; yet, most do not do so because they do not believe it to be possible. As we have also stated many times, your personal beliefs of the rational and intellectual mind largely act as the guidelines or the box within which you personally create, perceive, and experience physical reality. Life as you know it to be. Therefore, for those that do not believe it is possible to see or tap into future lifetime moments and glimpses, to them it will seem impossible indeed. To those, however, who understand the simultaneous nature of time, or at least are open to the concepts of it, then to them, it will be an open door through which they can explore via their own adventures in consciousness.

Now, as there is truly no time and space at the layer of consciousness which gives physical reality its expression, there is no separation between objects at this level of awareness in consciousness, and hence, there are no time separations. Which means that all of these potential outcomes, or probable outcomes as we call them, exist simultaneously with one another.

This is why many clairvoyant individuals can see the future, quite literally, as Jackson-Thomas does, and thousands of others do BEFORE it actually ever occurs to you as your physical events unfolding. Precisely because their consciousness is literally viewing them as potential or probable realities before they have come into physical time and space to be perceived. While there are infinite, probable realities, they are likely to see the most likely ones to come into physical expression, based upon the current energies, patterns, beliefs, and all influences that are to come into play for the expression of that outcome to become physically perceivable.

As many a good psychic medium, clairvoyant, intuitive person knows, many times these foreseen future events do indeed come into expression and "happen" in physical terms. Sometimes they do not as something intervenes and alters the probable outcome for another to be selected to come into fruition and be perceived physically. As we have stated before, the future is highly flexible, plastic-like, and not at all set in concrete or stone, if you will. It is altered by your own thoughts, feelings, emotions, beliefs, and so on, as with others in your environment, also; as again, you are not disconnected from all things, and they will, in one way or another, have an effect upon you, also.

Now, what I want to bring to your awareness here is that...given these truths above stated, all events that have occurred and been experienced by a soul ...in every lifetime, regardless of the time period in which it appears to have occurred, (historically speaking here) is occurring simultaneously, and <u>you only perceive the one life that this incarnation of your greater self is focused upon and within.</u>

For an example: the soul of Jackson, here, was incarnated into a human male with a physical brain in the physical body. Part of the task of the physical brain and mind is to organize the data that comes in from the physical senses of this physical body and 3-dimensional world. Therefore, because the physical brain <u>was created in THIS physical lifetime only</u>; it, then, has natural <u>access to THIS physical lifetime's data and memories only</u>. It, then, is focused into the physical life of Jackson.

In the physical lifetime of Thomas, that body has a brain whose task is to organize physical data from THAT physical lifetime and environment. It, then, naturally only has visibility to <u>that</u> current lifetime as the male named Thomas.

However, the greater soul of consciousness that is incarnated into both of these human bodies, Jackson in this lifetime and Thomas in that one, is one and the same <u>soul</u>, or different portions of the greater Self, and connected via consciousness, of course. There may be two different names for personalities of that soul, however, just as I have had many names, and Jackson has had many names, so, too, have you all had many names.

The soul or entity of Jackson has access to data and memories of both of these physical lifetimes. In either lifetime, then, as Jackson the physical man or as Thomas the physical man, the inner Self could access (and does through dreams, daydreams, ideas, inspirations, etc.) data from the _other_ physical lifetime incarnation. Now, you will do this with all of your reincarnational personalities in the same regard noted above.

Which draws the obvious truth that there is no separation of consciousness.

The physical APPEARANCES of the consciousness expressed into atoms and molecules do appear to be separate on the 3-dimensional plane, yet, at its core of existence, as with your own, it is not separate from anything...ever.

Therefore, your higher Self/soul/consciousness and, of course, Source/"God"/The Universe, The Creator, Allah, by any and all names is not separate from all lifetime and experiences of all consciousness either.

You, the greater Self, have eternal memories and perceptions of each and every event, thought, feeling, emotion, and interaction with all other forms and expressions of consciousness, both physical and nonphysical, of every lifetime instance, incarnation, and beyond, all simultaneously and eternally.

You may or may not be aware of it, yet, you do, indeed, access some of these memories, bits, portions, and pieces of them during your dream states, both sleeping and in daydreams; for again, the consciousness is fully aware and operational far beyond the limited focus that the intellect allows it to perceive most of the time when focused into your current reality.

Now, a short summary of the implications here:

◇ You have access to past and future lives, the events, lessons and wisdom, knowledge, and so on, in your current existence, and you can, with practice, patience, and more practice, draw this forth into your current lifetime to use such things. You may not have a dream of yourself speaking to yourself saying, "I am you from another lifetime and I want to give you great information to help you accomplish or avoid XYZ." However, the information can come to you as ideas, inspiration, hunches to act or not act, guidance, etc. It IS there... you simply do not, most of the time, recognize the source from which things have come to your current awareness, beyond space and time and the lifetime you currently know.

◊ There is no separation of consciousness, lifetimes, or experiences. You will not carry, as many believe, karma from one lifetime to another whereby you are paying for "the sins of the past". You will carry lessons of understanding and integration and, if you have not learned and overcome the lesson in another lifetime, your higher Self/soul, etc. will indeed draw the lesson back into this lifetime for you to, once again, face and overcome. It is the lesson your higher Self seeks to overcome...to evolve the consciousness and soul/entity that you are and are eternally growing. You cannot avoid your Self. Even in other lifetimes, as they are eternally connected to the one you now know.

Creatively speaking, in this lifetime that you know, your resources are eternally available to you, vastly beyond what many have any level of awareness of. Again, you cannot make use of the eternal tools you yourself possess if you yourself do not at first believe that they are possible. You create your own reality, and you do so within the belief structures that you yourself hold about yourself and all reality. Hence, the journey to rise in vibration and expand in consciousness expands the perception and widens immensely the filter through which you view, perceive, understand, and interact with all physical reality.

The bold line above here stated is one of our obvious goals of this book and our work, my work as a teaching entity and that of "God" by any and all names that itself seeks to grow, evolve, become, etc., of which you are inseparable. You cannot avoid that which you are by nature. You can avoid your own expansion, growth, and evolution by denying it or ignoring it; yet, you will learn the lessons of such actions and, in one lifetime or another, move beyond them, for again, your own evolution as consciousness is unavoidable...as this is what consciousness eternally does and IS.

There is no avoiding that which you <u>are</u>.
There is only avoiding that
which you can be.

I will also point out that throughout your entire lifetime, in this one you know and are presently aware of and those you are not as yet presently aware of, all of these things...wisdom, knowledge, experiences, lessons and insights, intuitive abilities and so forth, are eternally available to you...<u>now</u>. You must seek them, you must believe in them, and you must open the perception of Self to the awareness of them. No one does this for you for it is indeed a journey of Self. We are giving you the awareness of them through our descriptions of the truths of your very existence. It is up to you, through free will and choices, daily...to pursue understanding, integration, and development of Self. An entirely shifted, expanded, and immensely more satisfying experience of reality awaits you...when you are ready to become aware of that which is eternally present. (Omnipresent)

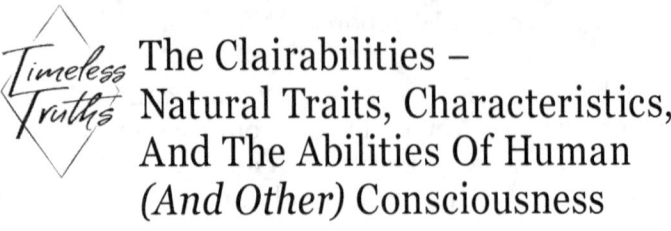

The Clairabilities –
Natural Traits, Characteristics,
And The Abilities Of Human
(And Other) Consciousness

Now: You may think that you need eyes to see, ears to hear, a nose to smell, or fingers to move even the smallest of physical objects. <u>You do not</u>. While your 5-human physical senses are registered with your various organs of the human body, you can indeed see, hear, smell, and perceive your 3-dimensional world, and vastly beyond that, with your consciousness. If you could not, no one would ever remember a dream, have a hunch, or gut feeling of intuition, and indeed, we (nonphysical beings and entities) would not be able to perceive your physical world at all.

As virtually any human who has ever experienced an Out-of-Body Experience (OBE) or died and "ascended to heaven" (transitioned the focus of your consciousness into nonphysical reality) or even had a Near-Death Experience (NDE), it is often reported that the person who had this experienced was clearly able to view their own lifeless body (or living body in the case of an OBE) from the outside, looking AT the physical body and environment.

Again, there are millions of instances around the world, over centuries where individuals have experienced events like this, and they will confirm this is truth. There have been many, many reports of individuals who died on an operating table during surgery or childbirth, only to float over the top of their body, loved ones, and doctors as they perhaps had conversations in other rooms while that person was clinically and physically dead, only to have the conversation lucidly recalled and told after their consciousness fully returned to the body. (You, then, have risen from the dead. Literally.) In one instance, a child died during surgery and briefly floated over his own body, then floated outside the room to listen to his family having conversations in the waiting room, and eventually shifted the focus back through the body to jump-start the physical system again. During that death experience, one of the doctors who was observing the surgery from behind the glass viewing area for physicians in this learning hospital was taking notes on a clipboard notebook and dropped his favorite writing pen. The doctor could not find the pen on the floor or anywhere.

The next day, this very doctor was checking in on the boy who had died during surgery and was "out-of-body", when the boy asked him; "Did you find your favorite pen that you dropped yesterday in the room behind the glass?" The doctor replied; "No, I never did. How did you know I lost my writing pen?"

The boy replied, "Because I saw you drop it when I was floating over my body. The nurse next to you accidentally kicked it with her foot as she moved out of your way to look for it and it went under the cabinet across the room by the door."

Astonished, the doctor proceeded to the observation room and indeed, found his favorite writing pen under the edge of the cabinet by the door in the room - exactly where the boy had told him he would find it.

Again, there are millions of examples like this that have happened over centuries of time. All of them point, quite clearly then, to the truth that you can, indeed, see, hear, smell, and so forth via consciousness and the human body is not the only way you can capture such data about your environment. It is simply the only one most are aware of while incarnated into the human form. They believe they are "only human" and, therefore, only focus on the fact that they can sense physical data via their physical senses. When it is the consciousness within them that actually gives their physical senses existence within the 3-dimensional space-time phenomenon of appearance. The universe as you know it.

As we have outlined, then, in other sections of this book, your **clairabilities**, as we call them:

◊ Clairvoyance

◊ Clairaudience

◊ Clairsentience

◊ Claircognizance

◊ Etc.

All are eternally present within the very consciousness that gives you awareness that you are alive and a human-being. They are eternal traits and characteristics of your particular species of consciousness, and hence, eternally available to you. It is you who must seek to develop them to allow your own rational/intellectual brain and mind to perceive them, develop them, and use them fruitfully and skillfully.

You, all human-beings, co-create your physical world and life as you know it to be already...in harmony with all other species of consciousness that express itself outward into physical form. The key marker and milestone in your evolution is to do so intentionally, fruitfully, and within the core foundation of the Light and Love that your inner Self is already. Not fighting to create a beautiful reality, but rather understanding your eternal place within nature and how you can draw all things forth to immensely and immeasurably enhance the world that you know.

The following are examples of areas in your personal life where you can develop your skills in these areas. Note that ALL of the following are innate, natural traits, characteristics, and capabilities of human consciousness. Therefore, if you are alive and reading this book...you have them latent and dormant within you and it's simply a matter of learning to develop them into fuller potential. [If you are not alive and you are reading this book, well then you are already aware that you have the abilities. (Smile)]

Telepathy – The ability to send/receive data or information via consciousness which may involve a number of clairabilities simultaneously. It is communication through consciousness and, although you may receive thoughts of another, feelings of fear if someone is in danger, etc., the thoughts will often have emotions associated with them, inflections (is it "good" energy or "not good", etc.- AKA- "vibes" or vibrations associated with them). **An example that might strike a chord with many of our readers:** You are in the grocery store and seeking to find perhaps a box of granola. You find the aisle that it's located within and approach the selection of kinds of granola to choose from. As you are standing there contemplating your granola choices, you suddenly become aware that there are now 3 other individuals who are actually looking for the very same granola that you are, when there was no one looking for it a moment ago. Telepathically then, while contemplating your granola, you have transmitted your thoughts out through consciousness and, indeed, others within your general area, unknowingly through telepathy, saw (clairvoyantly) granola in their mind's eye or perhaps caught the whisper of it in the conscious mind, etc. In any case, they did indeed receive your thoughts and come to seek exactly what you were seeking when moments ago, there was no one looking for granola. Case in point on telepathy.

Clairvoyance – Clear seeing in the mind's eye, images in your mind, flashes, "movie-like" scenes, etc. Images are outside of time and space and, although you may think of them in your mind, they are actually in your consciousness, and noticed by the mind as your 5-human physical senses focus on the contemplation of them. Visualization, imagination, and dream recall are all examples of clairvoyance.

Clairaudience – Clear hearing in the mind. Mediums and Channels use this skill often. Information can come from ANY Divine source, or the consciousness of any human, animal, plant, mountain, etc. It may or may not be in language; it could simply be sounds or clairaudiently available tones such as vibrational frequencies of any origin. Even off-planet beings can communicate this way (obviously at the layer of consciousness).

Claircognizance – Clear Knowing or Direct-Knowing. Knowledge "communicated" (available) through consciousness. As this knowledge is sent and received DIRECTLY through consciousness, no thought or contemplation is required for you to KNOW beyond any doubt whatsoever that something is true or you heard something, felt, or sensed something, have insight about any particular subject, etc. As this type of data is received directly via consciousness, the rational/intellectual mind is often completely bypassed and, although something may not make rational sense at all, you KNOW it is true and nothing could change your mind as it vibrates in the core of your being. Love is a very good example that can be known at this level. Not just human-to-human love, but human-to-animal, animal-to-human love, and likewise a "love" from the trees among you or the Earth can, if one pays attention, be known via this ability.

Clairsentience – Clear feeling. This can be sensations that involve emotions, inflections (a sense of direction or very subtle "pull" in a particular direction), and that you can literally feel something as if it were physically real, yet, you are sensing it through this clairability.

Clairkinesthesia – Clear touching. Can be sensed in a way that is similar to telekinesis in that an intuitive may feel a "spirit" or personality that is nonphysical such as a loved one, come and place their hand on their shoulder, as if they were consoling them in times of great sorrow or something similar.

Clairgustance – Clear tasting. Some psychic, intuitive individuals can, at times, taste something via consciousness. For example, a psychic intuitive and medium may be doing a reading for a client and they taste chocolate all of a sudden (they may smell it, also) and the loved one in spirit is relaying to them that they loved to eat chocolate when they were in physical body.

Clairolfactory – Clear smelling. For example, a psychic medium doing a reading for a client and they all of a sudden smell pipe or cigar smoke very strongly. It is not physically present; however, they are smelling it via this clairability, and it triggers that sense of smell recognition to transmit meaning via consciousness.

Telekinesis – The ability to move physical objects intentionally via consciousness, intention, and will. Regardless of nay-sayers, this IS indeed a very real latent/dormant ability within human consciousness. Jackson has himself moved objects across a table numerous times, and other objects in his lifetime. Many people around the world have tapped into this "gift" that is present within all. If one human-being has it present within their being/consciousness, then it is, of course, inherent within the entire species, though it may be dormant or latent in some. Now, previously in this book in our section on The Eternal Connection Between The Living And The Dead- Via Consciousness, we described some very common experiences that do occur across the planet in all of human history, whereby when a loved one, friend, or someone close passes away/has their physical death, very soon after loved ones in the family may experience their house lights blinking on and off, objects moving, keys being moved from where they normally are, pictures moved or tipped over, cell phones ringing and no one is there, TVs turning on, etc.

These are all common examples of Telekinesis in action. It is not accomplished by the human body, but rather by the consciousness of the immortal being within the human body. Therefore, it is not a requirement, then, to have a human body with which to move physical objects on the earth plane, as it can be done in the living physical state with your own consciousness, or before/after a physical life existence when loved ones come and show you that they are indeed still with you, full of love and vigor, and provide you with a physical sign that "life" does exist

216

beyond physical death. As with any ability of the consciousness, with time and much practice, one can indeed learn to succeed in its development and use. In your future, in the next century from now, this ability will be MUCH more prevalent and common in use by humanity, as will many other natural abilities, traits, and characteristics of consciousness. As your species evolves, expands and incorporates these into the rational/intellectual mind's awareness so that you can expand and develop them for use.

◊ Some of the things accomplished with your clairabilities:

◊ Communication with humans across the planet

◊ Communication with your pet, horse, dog, cat, a dolphin, chimpanzee, or other animal

◊ Communication with trees, flowers, and plants (Example: many talk to and communicate with their house plants)

◊ Communication with Mother Earth, the mountains, sea, clouds, wind, etc.

◊ Communication with off-planet, extraterrestrial beings

◊ Communication with off-planet loved ones crossed over/ passed on

◊ Communication with off-planet beings of Consciousness, Angels, etc.

◊ Remote viewing using consciousness

◊ Remote healing via consciousness (Reiki, healing humans, healing animals, healing physical or emotional trauma, etc.)

◊ Training animals and correcting animal's behavioral problems, increasing animal joy and happiness, and performance of sports-focused animals

◊ The list goes on and maybe you can think of some, also!?

Now, when we say "communication"....remember to open your mind and not be boxed into the scientific definition of "communication", for this can encompass an infinite array of data that is indeed discernible and intelligible, yet, may not be in straight English or Spanish, etc. sentences! We are speaking of NATURAL communication...via your clairabilities, not human language. Many spiritual folks will tell you that they sense the "vibe" (vibration) of something (a person, place, business, house, animal, etc.). They are absolutely truthful that they can indeed sense these vibrations and, though you may not read one's mind per se, you can indeed very quickly "know" information about these things or environments when you use your inner abilities. Also, and importantly, you do NOT need physical contact to receive very clear information from them either. Intuitives will identify with this, as well as empaths, which are various angles of the same thing of sorts. Sensing through your clairabilities of consciousness.

An animal may "tell you" that he or she is not feeling well, and you may very clearly receive that message, yet, it does not come to you as say, an English sentence that you receive clairaudiently. So we want to encourage you to expand your ideas of "communication" as any discernible and intelligible way or method of transmitting intentions of meaning via consciousness. In Volume 2 of *The Nature of Consciousness*, we will describe in much greater detail the animal consciousness and how humans and animals can, and do indeed, communicate, help, heal, and promote well-being to one another in a symbiotic relationship that is both physical and nonphysical. Again, in your future, in time... mankind will be able to "read the minds" of animals in terms of sensing the overall mood, health issues, if they are happy or sad, and have a much deeper, meaningful, and robust connection with one another that expands both the animal's consciousness and that of the human to unlock abilities in both that will create harmony among mankind and the animal kingdom in ways today not widely known of.

Each of these above are examples of areas that any reader, could research, learn about, practice, and develop into a meaningful, useful tool through which you can enhance greatly the physical life and experiences you have in it.

Now: Good evening. Dictation for our book. Today's essay will be "Seeing and Sensing <u>through</u> Consciousness"-

This is how many psychics over the years have worked with police detectives to find missing persons, as their consciousness can literally work *through* the consciousness of the individual or individuals present in a given location perhaps, and the psychic perceiver can indeed, see not only outward *through the eyes of the individuals present*, however, as consciousness is, of course, not limited to the physical body, therefore, it can also look around at the surrounding settings to see a house, street, woods, setting, etc.

Many psychic intuitives around the world will tell you that often they can perceive all sorts of data through consciousness.

◇ Visual context of another physical location

◇ Smells such as heavy fuel smell, cigar or pipe smoke, campfire smoke, perfumes, etc.

◇ Sounds such as traffic, train whistle, or barking dogs

◇ Temperatures, light, and darkness if something is at night or daytime, etc.

We point out here the many ways that consciousness can be (and often is) used to perceive physical reality that is outside the geographical or physical location of the perceiver. Remote viewing is made possible, of course, as an individual uses <u>clairvoyant</u> skills to see, in the mind's eye, other environments of a physical nature.

Now, you could do this to perceive other dimensions (and do so in your dreams virtually every night), and you can perceive many traits and characteristics of the dimensions and environments in which you may "visit". Again, you are not <u>physically</u> going anywhere. Your consciousness, however, exists outside of space and time....it works *within* space in time and your physical expressions of consciousness (material objects) appear in space and time, however, the root of their existence in physical form exists eternally outside of that context. Just as the core of your own existence eternally exists outside of space and time.

What you do not realize is that, throughout all moments of your day, your consciousness is perceiving all sorts of data that is outside of the very space-time environment where your physical body is presently. You can perceive it across the planet from another country, as easily as if it were right next to you, for, in larger terms, it is right next to you.

Perception at the level of consciousness then is instantaneous, though the rational/intellectual mind may present it to your clairvoyant senses in a linear manner so that the context of it can be understood and articulated by the intellectual mind.

To the same degree, one can see (clairvoyantly) through the consciousness of another being or even species of consciousness. There are among you now, in 2022/2023, both men and women who have developed the ability to SEE and perceive through the consciousness of animals. They can, indeed, tap into the consciousness of an animal at home or afar and actually see the physical environment that the animal is in. For example, they can tell you by "looking through a dog's eyes" what pictures are on the wall next to the dog. They can describe to you, by looking through the consciousness of a horse, what the barn stall looks like to the very smallest detail.

This is a prime example of the evolution of human consciousness and the capabilities and potentials that all have within their own consciousness, awaiting discovery and activation. For these certain individuals who can see and sense through other physical animals, they are what you might call the spark to illuminate the potential within the human-being, called forth by the greater consciousness of All That Is for the purposes of evolutionary development and display of potentials. Lights in the dark, some might say, as they light the path for others to learn and follow. Inspiring them to ignite the spark within themselves and, hence, nudge them toward their development and evolution, also.

Consciousness can perceive other data, also. Perhaps the sense of smell, where they can smell something that is quite literally around another person that they are tuning into. They may think of grandma and suddenly smell chocolate chip cookies and see an image or a memory of her baking cookies in the kitchen, many thousands of miles away. Are they crazy? Not at all. In fact, they are using their clairabilities to a greater range than most as they are paying attention to them. Perhaps even experimenting with them and developing them.

Which does not require any PHYSICAL activity at all, but rather the *intention* to do so, and the quieting of the mind to allow the focus of the conscious attention of the inner self.

We share all of these with you to give you everyday examples of how people all over the world, if even for a brief moment here and there throughout their day, tune into and *through consciousness* to perceive outside of the immediate environment in which they are physically sitting. Daydreaming is a good example, also.

Driving down the road or perhaps in the shower, grandma baking cookies may come to mind or what have you. You are sensing, when the mind is not busily focused, physical characteristics events, objects, and conditions that are completely beyond the physical environment in which you yourself are sitting. This is accomplished through consciousness.

The brain may record memories of such things and present them in motion pictures in the mind as you remember them, however, they do not exist or occur in a linear fashion. They simply appear to be linear due to the root assumption of the phenomenon of time as it appears within a 3-dimensional plane of context.

Now, I have mentioned before that, if a certain portion of myself desires, I can relax and take a psychic vacation and perhaps merge my consciousness (which does not take up space, mind you) into the consciousness of an ancient redwood tree and perceive the forest around this tree, perceiving as it perceives, for a century of your time. This might be a psychic vacation that I could embark upon for relaxation in what you perceive as the nature of the forest.

Ruburt, as Jane, at times could perceive life from the perception and point of view of a honeybee or a flower and view the world from the miniature perception of that form. You do not invade nor in any way move any other consciousness, for that would take physical space to do so. You simply shift the focus of perception of consciousness to perceive in harmony with other species of consciousness.

This tends to occur more frequently and naturally in the higher states of vibration. As your own consciousness expands, not only do you see and sense through your own consciousness, but you also sense through the medium, if you will, of consciousness; a vast, infinite data bank of information infinite in nature. Virtually anything could come into your awareness as your awareness expands to incorporate the larger field of reality from which you now can cherry-pick data that is significant to you, and focus upon those things to journey in your own conscious awareness.

Along the path of the evolution of humanity, the more humans that develop the *BEING* portion of themselves as human-beings, the more these types of experiences will become commonplace. And the development of just one individual does indeed have an impactful effect on others, other probable or reincarnational selves, as well as your entity and All That Is. And so, evolution can be increased as more and more individuals develop their inner self.

At this stage of development and evolution of the Self...you quite clearly and starkly become aware that you are, truly, not at all separate from the bee, the flower, or the other human-being, regardless of the physical forms you each may present outwardly. It is here that love and light and compassion of the most profound nature pervade your awareness of all things. It may be a different "species" of consciousness, yet communication takes place at levels that do not involve images, symbols, or language as you know it.

When you "see" or perceive through another's eyes, you have rather "walked a mile in their shoes". Compassion for your fellow man and women around you becomes heartfelt as your own when your consciousness expands to understand, at the soul level, their journey is not at all unlike your own. It may have taken a physical path that is seemingly different in objective reality, however, the destination of unlocking the immortal potentials of the creative beings that you are, is the same. One cannot weaponize oneself fruitfully, in that regard. Peace becomes natural. Not the lack of it.

You realize the eternal truth that, not only are humans connected and inseparable from one another, but that you are also connected and inseparable from all other physically appearing phenomena that make up your universe and beyond. You are even connected, then, through consciousness, to off-planet beings, universes, and dimensions of which your current rational/ intellectual mind does not have any awareness of, for they exist outside the context of the physical environment in which your brain and rational/intellectual mind is focused - in different ranges of frequencies that are not perceptible by your specifically tuned 5-human senses.

Precisely, so that you may navigate your current environment with skill and poise and not confuse them with multiple dimensions or lifetimes. This is sometimes the case of some who have been called "insane"...or those that are near the end of their physical life when the "veil" between the physical and nonphysical thins to _their_ perception and they can see loved ones, pets, and Angel beings that may present themselves to prepare and assist the loved one getting ready to transition their focus out of physical reality in the human form. (Death.)

Near the timing of the physical death of a loved one, for example, when they are seeing other loved ones that have been dead for some time, or pets, Angels, or beings of light, etc., they are using MORE of their clairvoyant abilities of the consciousness than they are their physical eyes, though their physical eyes may be open and focusing, say, in the corner of the room or on a chair in which a loved one's physically-appearing human image (as an apparition) might be seen by them.

Again, your 5-human senses only detect the 3-dimensional environment in which you are presently focusing your consciousness, through the flesh. It is the soul, or consciousness within you, that is able to perceive infinite dimensions of realities, both physical in context and those that are not, those that are in your own universe and those that are not. It is, then, able to sense infinite data and information about the nonphysical reality from which all physical reality is given form.

These are merely a few infinite examples of the capabilities of the consciousness...that yes, you guessed it...the consciousness that you are. That which gives you your own awareness of Self (I AM). Note here that the Divine (English) representation of self-awareness and that which is told in some texts to be the name of "God" (I AM) is in *PRESENT tense*.

It is not "I was" or "I will be" or perhaps "I may be one day"....It is I AM. The one you know to be Christ spoke of this immortal self-awareness that he called "God" or "The Father" within himself and is now known to millions as the Christ Consciousness that is within ALL humans as the "I AM" within all.

Now, I want to call out that we are articulating examples here of how consciousness can and does see, feel, sense, and otherwise *perceive* reality through its eternal and inseparable connection to all other objects in physical reality. This is IMPORTANT because it is a key to understanding your own innate Divine power of creative energy and how you can use that to create your reality, intentionally and purposefully, in ways you love and enjoy.

If you take this timeless truth and pair it with the "I AM", you begin to understand the importance of the *"I AM"* affirmation of truth that you are **already** that which you are **conscious** of **being**.

If you are conscious of being healthy...your body will be generally quite healthy. If you are conscious of *BEING* poor or misfortunate, then you are indeed creating that which you are conscious of BEING. Poor or unfortunate. We will detail much more of that subject later on.

The important applicability here on the creation of your life and experience on the physical plane is that you are already connected to and inseparable from the health, wealth, success, ideas, solutions, resolutions, help, guidance, assistance, and so forth that you may desire in your life experience; yet you must first become consciously aware of these truths, and dwell within the state of consciousness in which it is *already* yours. You do not receive or attract that which you want. That is the wrong vibration and "the Universe" communicates via vibrational frequencies in consciousness. You receive, attract or experience what you are vibrating to. What you are at any given moment _being_.

Wanting something - an object, event, or condition in your life - is the incorrect vibrational frequency. Loving something as if you already have it is the way that like or similar objects, events, and conditions are drawn to you...through your connection to them via consciousness.

> "What things soever ye desire, when ye
> pray, _believe that ye have received them_
> _(already), and ye shall have them._"
> Mark 11:24 kjv

Not that you <u>might</u> have them or <u>may</u> have them someday...but that <u>you do already have them</u>. Physically PRESENT (Now Moment). **I AM is PRESENT TENSE.** The eternal <u>Now Moment</u>.

Therefore, the understanding of HOW consciousness is eternally able to perceive, see, and sense through other consciousness, around the Earth or universe, is <u>directly applicable</u> to understanding your own creative potential and the virtually limitless ways in which you can creatively draw upon All That Is to accomplish and achieve that which is desired.

For those who are interested in learning more about their own reincarnational lifetimes:

The window through which you may perceive other lifetimes is through consciousness, for it is through consciousness that you <u>now</u> are connected to them in other periods and dimensions of historical time. You, then, expanding your own consciousness now, will open your awareness to other lifetimes and, in so doing, feel the love and compassion and lessons learned in those lifetimes so that you may make use of them in this one. Improving on, improves them all, to a degree. Not only will you see your own but others as well as the veil between them thins. You will still have private thoughts, of course; however, you will be more in tune with all objects and your physical environment in which you are present.

To help convey a lesson in seeing and sensing through consciousness, take for example, the following:

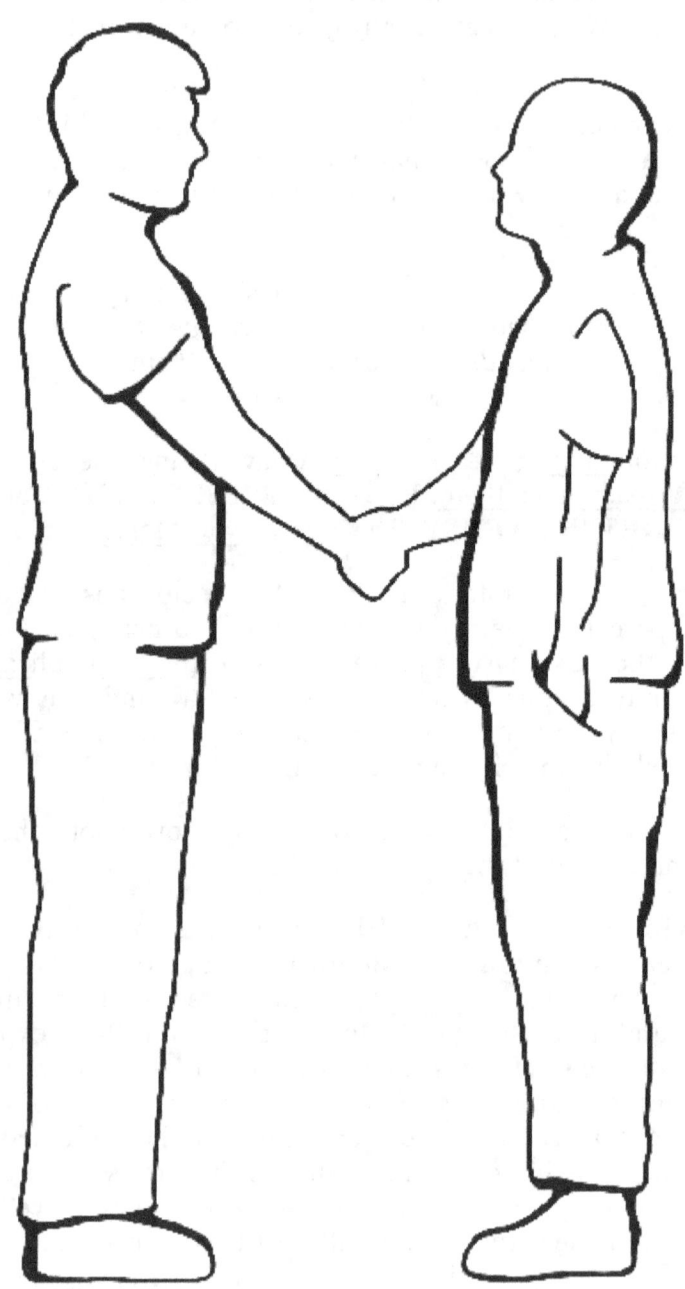

5- Human Senses Only

Figure 5.

Now: When you meet another person (or animal, etc.) and you are using only your 5-human sense filter through which you perceive reality, you are limited then to only the data and information about the subject you are meeting, approaching, shaking hands with, or petting, etc. that the 5-human senses can detect.

In greeting another person, for example, you may see the type of clothes they are wearing. Perhaps this can give you an indication as to their wealth or social status, if they are wearing fine linens, you might say, or dressed in common street casual clothing. Based upon your personal beliefs, you may project an idea about the individual, based upon your visual assessment into your mind's eye, and perceive them as either say, rich or poor (financially). Using another sense, you might smell the scent of cologne or perfume and make a mental assessment that they are perhaps wearing some expensive, pleasant-smelling perfume, or what have you. Conversely, of course, if they are dressed in dirty clothing and smell rather unpleasant, giving you the impression that they have not bathed in a number of days, you might again make an assessment of the individual based upon these physical 5-human sense data available to you as you shake their hand.

Given a soft or a firm hand grip, you may make another assessment as to their character based upon their firmness of handshake, for our example here.

At any rate, you can only learn so much about an individual from physical 5-human sense data, however, I should point out the obvious, your physical senses can indeed be quite deceiving. Meaning that a rich man or woman may dress in casual clothing just as any poor individual could. A wealthy man or woman, who is very successful in business, may or may not smell pleasant, according to your personal ideas about smells. And a soft handshake may not be weakness, but rather compassionate kindness, shown in a physical sense that you have perhaps mistaken.

Our point here is that your 5-human _physical senses_ are limited in their nature of understanding the truth as to the individual or animal to which you are in close proximity, ie. shaking hands with (or petting or training, as with dogs and horses, etc.). Your physical senses then, only show you, at best, a very limited, and often unclear representation of physical reality. If you rely upon them solely then, you are limiting yourself to a very narrow experience of life.

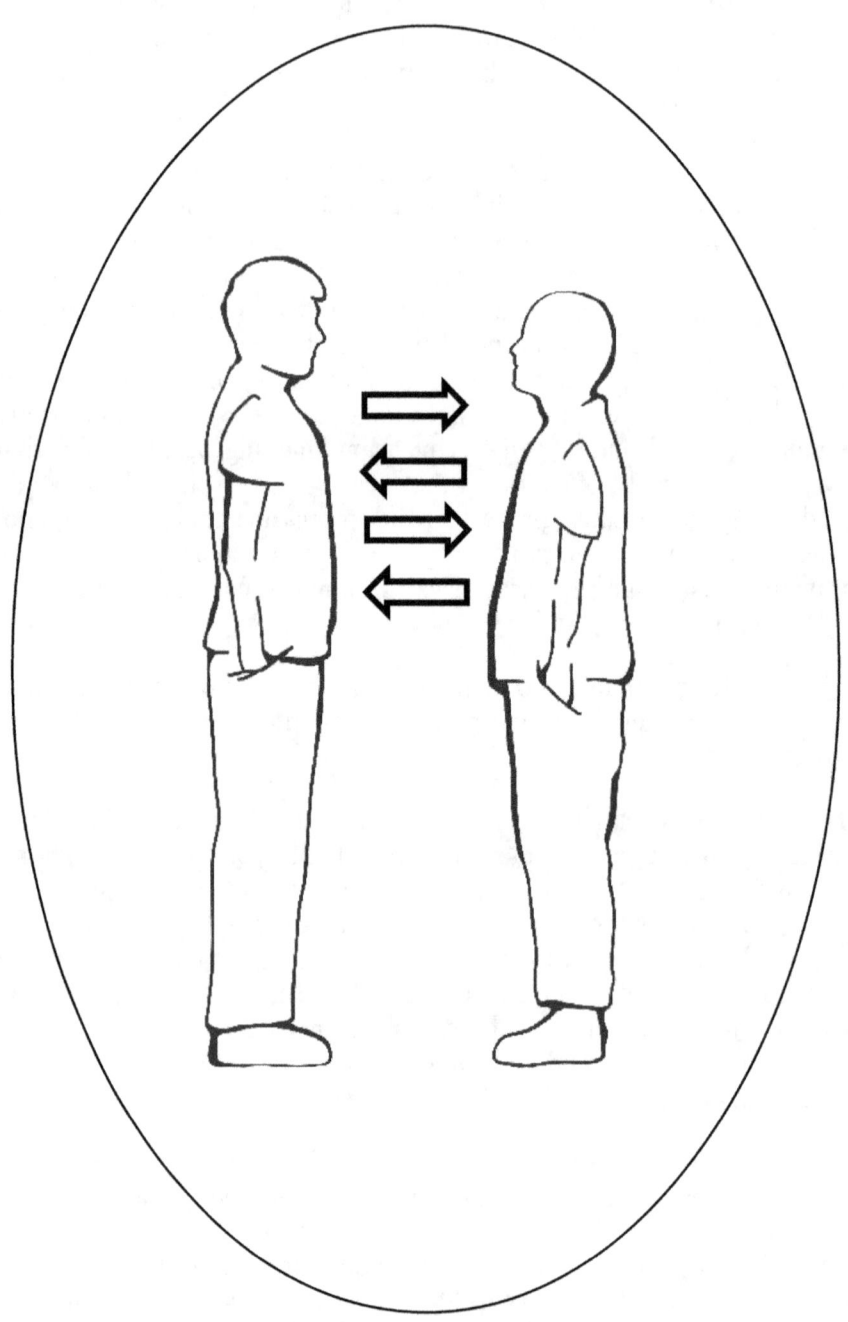

<u>Using Your Consciousness</u>
Figure 6.

In our example shown in Figure 6, we can see two individuals who are approaching one another with the intention to meet, speak, and perhaps shake hands. However, in this figure, our persons are high in vibrational frequency in their personal aura and inner being, and they are well-skilled at using their clirabilities to perceive a larger picture of reality around them.

In this case then, and this is important to make note of, the individuals in this image would sense and KNOW all kinds of data and information about the individual <u>LONG BEFORE they ever approached them or were in close proximity to them!</u> Meaning that perhaps, from across the room they would feel a "slight pull" of energy in the direction of that person they are destined to meet. They may also see an image of shaking that person's hand or a successful meeting or transaction, conversation, or something beneficial to the purpose of their desire to meet them and speak with them. They may see it flash, even if for a second, before their mind's eye (clairvoyantly). They will very much sense this other person's:

◇ Vibrational Frequency

◇ Demeanor

◇ Anger, joy, happiness, mood, etc.

◇ General vibrational status of intentions (What you might think of as the other person being "good" or "bad", based upon the cumulative distilled vibrations that they are emitting, even if at the moment you are meeting them, they are acting a whole new way. A prime example of this would be: if you meet someone and, although they put on a good "show" and say kind things, you sense very strongly that they are deceiving you as you are "reading", understanding, and knowing their vibrational frequency AT the layer of consciousness which you sense in your own soul/consciousness/being, and therefore, KNOW that something is not right, or that they are not as genuine and honest as they portray themselves to be.)

◇ You may sense that you've met this person before, in this lifetime or another. In this dimension of physical experience or another.

While we will get further into the details of animal consciousness in Volume 2 of *The Nature Of Consciousness*, I will use animals as an example here, simply for an illustration, as MANY of our readers will identify with this themselves through their own experiences with their pets.

That is, when a person comes to your home or door, or you meet someone while walking your dog, and your dog, who is normally loving, kind, and playful, immediately reacts aggressively to an individual before they ever come through your door or into the room or near you at the park.

The dog now, has used its consciousness – and does not have a 5-human sense filter, or rational/intellectual thinking mind that interferes with its perceptions of the person who is approaching you. Therefore, through using its own consciousness, it immediately will sense the vibrational "feeling tones" and general demeanor, intentions, vibrations of the thoughts being emitted from the individual, and all sorts of data that the dog, in this example, identifies as a potential threat to it or its owner. The dog responds immediately, of course, by barking, growling, and lunging, perhaps, at the individual so as to protect the owner who "does not feel safe" from an individual who has ill intentions, even if they do not act upon them.

So while the family pet here is normally friendly to virtually everyone, in this case, it reacts strongly to an approaching individual. This may be why. It knows something that it has determined through the applied use of its consciousness and inner senses, as animal consciousness also has clairabilities similar to those that human consciousness has. They can, indeed, "communicate" in ways that are not English or a human language with human consciousness to *sense* and make assessments of the individual here approaching in our example.

The same data then, can indeed be sensed by humans just as it can by dogs, whereby you know when someone walks in that they either "light up the room" and have a certain joyful glow to them, or, perhaps, they "bring a cloud of darkness and confusion" or anxiety and so forth when they walk into the room. **You are using your consciousness and very likely, understanding much more than meets the eye.**

Now - another point here that I wish to make is if we circle back to the truth that time and space do not truly exist, and that they are simply perceptions of the 5-human senses as they are tuned into sensing atoms and molecules arranged in such a fashion, we come to the truth here that your clairabilities and consciousness work regardless of an individual being in close proximity to you or across the globe. Meaning that if you truly are using your consciousness, and gain great skill in doing so, you can tune into another across the planet and sense all sorts of data from that individual. You can even catch glimpses of their physical experiences, if they are in an accident or grave situation, need help or medical attention, and many sense within seconds when a loved one has died and ended their physical life experience.

You are "seeing and sensing" through consciousness. You may experience a delay as you perceive such things in space and time, however, they are available to your consciousness instantaneously as they become physical reality unfolding each Now Moment.

Couples often meet one another in the very fashion we are herein describing. Perhaps somehow knowing they are "supposed to meet" to fulfill various relationship and incarnation lessons, expand love and their soul experiences, etc.

The more you become aware of your own selves seeing and sensing through consciousness, the more you are adding energy into the expansion of your own skills and abilities of your intentional use of consciousness which will serve you in ways you barely dream of now.

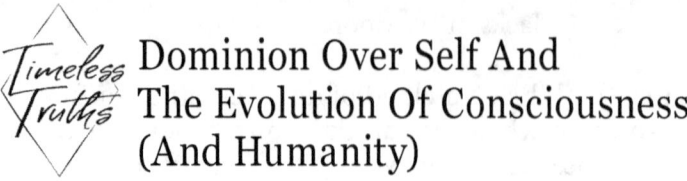

Dominion Over Self And The Evolution Of Consciousness (And Humanity)

You have names for objects, no matter the language, because you perceive them through your physical perception and senses, hence, they appear to be separate from other objects around them. You are, then, seeing them from the outside as you look <u>at</u> them. Your physical senses, then, can look <u>at</u> the object, but they cannot look <u>within</u> the object to see the very fabric which makes up that object in the first place.

However, if you were to shift your perception from using your physical senses to using your inner consciousness, you could then perceive that very same object from an entirely different perspective. Seeing it from the inside looking outward into the physical world. You could, of course, shift your focus and see ALL angles of this object using your consciousness; from this standpoint, you are not limited in any fashion in which you are able to "see" (perceive) through objective, 3-dimensional reality around you.

Your 5-human physically oriented senses are specifically tuned to look at your physical reality from the outside inward. Yet your consciousness is specially tuned to looking at objective reality from the <u>inside</u> outward - from the source of which the physical object is created, rooted in consciousness, and vibrant with its own sense of self-awareness.

When you view objects in 3-dimensional reality _from_ the standpoint of the consciousness that gives them form and structure, you will realize that the consciousness which gives the atoms, molecules, and cells their form and existence is not, and cannot be, separated from all other consciousness surrounding it. You would then perceive the object to be simply a conglomeration or accumulation of consciousness expressed in terms of atoms and molecules that make up a physically appearing object. However, you would also understand quite clearly that as consciousness cannot be separated from all other consciousness, it would be quite apparent that, in truth, the object was not at all separate from all other physical objects around it, but rather a portion of the larger consciousness in which it is expressed and sitting there, seemingly in physical terms within 3-dimensional reality. The "4th dimension" then would be the inner reality in and from which the object is created, constructed, and held into a pattern of consciousness, expressed in terms of energy, in terms expressed as atoms, molecules, etc.

From this insightful wisdom, you would also quite clearly understand that if one object is not at all separate from another, at the layer of consciousness that gives it physical dimensions, and that the unseen "4th" dimension of consciousness which makes up that object is not separate from other objects' consciousness, then you will become acutely aware that you yourself are not separate from that object, nor are you separate from other humans, animals, plants, trees, oceans, or mountains. The natural environment of your physically appearing universe.

Understanding this as the core of your existence is the key to truly manifesting and materializing your physical life experiences in ways you love and desire. Where you happen to life, instead of life happening to you. To the degree that you truly understand this, apply it, and live this truth as the core basis of your own existence, will be to the degree that you are magically successful and fruitful in creating your reality.

The seeming gap between the two is the evolution of your consciousness by teaching your rational mind and intellect the true nature of consciousness, that is, All That Is. Our materials here and our book then, seek to help you dissolve that seeming gap so that you are One with that which you seek to experience. As truly, it is simply your belief that you are not, that creates the experience that you are not. BEING this truth in active application then, you unlock the latent, dormant, eternally present capabilities of magic and miracles that are already within your human body, giving it form and expression. Existence among all things.

Here we shed a little light on the "Laws of Attraction" concepts that are so popular to spiritual seekers today, seeking to manifest and materialize change in their physical and spiritual life experiences. You are beginning to look into the origins of that natural process by which all physical objective, 3-dimensional reality is formed.

"You" then, as a being of consciousness expressing as a human, are not apart FROM nature. But rather you are a PART OF nature. You are not APART from "God"/Source/The Universe or whatever name you prefer to call the Divine, but rather you are an inseparable part OF that <u>Omnipresence</u>.

This...is your heritage. This _is_ your nature. The nature of consciousness that you are. This is _what_ you are beneath the physical flesh body and person you see in your reflection. You are not at all the physical or ego self that _has_ a soul. You are indeed a soul that has developed an ego and a personality that becomes a portion of the psyche and expresses yourself outward into a physical body of flesh, blood, and bone.

<u>This consciousness, which many refer to as your soul, is what gives your physical body its life animation to walk the planet and share physical form and expression with other forms of consciousness expressed in the same manner.</u> This portion of you is NOT at all limited to just the flesh and if you think that _you_ cease to exist outside the skin and bones that you see in the mirror, well then, you sell yourself short on understanding, and hence, utilizing your true potential as a human-being. "You"...the BEING part of you as a human-<u>being</u>, extends in what you think of as every direction into inner and outer space, and forward and backward in what you perceive to be "time". You do not then, end at the surface of your flesh, nor are you contained completely as a finished product or human inside that fancy container you once thought to be who and what you are.

The more you become consciously waking, walking, and aware of your _true_ nature, to that degree (and then some) are _you opening yourself_ to **perceive** a greater reality far beyond what you presently are aware that exists.

No other human nor being opens yourself to this greater reality. That is why you call it YOUR <u>Self</u>. It is yours and yours alone. You are an exceedingly unique and eternally sovereign being.

_No human can go to the gym for you and make _you_ stronger._

Just as no other human can go to the gym to make YOU stronger, you are the one responsible for your own development, based upon your free will and the choices you make every moment of every day of your entire physical life. It is a journey of Self. You cannot, however, make the choices that best help you develop if you are not yet aware of the choices that you truly have for the development of Self and the natural tools of development of your experiences.

The more you understand this inner part of you, the more you understand the nature of life itself and all that surrounds you. You will understand much deeper then, your place on the Earth, your place within nature, and how you are a part of it and can work in harmony with all other elements and objects *AT THE LAYER OF CONSCIOUSNESS* to attract objects, events, and conditions into your life path that then appear to you as your life unfolding before you.

Now, you do this day to day anyway, yet most are completely unaware that they form their reality around them through thoughts, feelings, emotions, beliefs, and your directed use of consciousness. You do this to bring forth the things that you are learning to master, overcome, achieve, and perhaps teach and lead others along the illuminated path once you have found it within yourselves. Illumination starts with "I". Meaning that it begins with you.

You can, quite readily, learn to grow and expand this immortal being within you, that is innately connected with all other consciousness, to communicate with other forms of consciousness, to draw them in or move them out of your way, through the use of your natural communication and creative abilities. You can draw upon the vast, infinite banks of all knowledge, wisdom, insightful intuition, solutions, means, ways, paths, inventions...if you but develop your awareness of that which is already yours before you were born into physical life and will also exist intact beyond your physical death.

Again:

> *You cannot use the Divine gifts that are innate and inherent to your species if you are not first fully aware of them. This book serves to bring forth into the forefront of your perception, the truth that the inner being within you already knows. This is your awakening...to yourselves.*

Timeless Truths

You cannot understand what I am until you better understand what you are, as I am no more a ghost or figment of the imagination than you are. I am as you are in many ways, however, I am not presently focused from <u>within</u> the physical flesh body looking outward into the physical environment as you presently are. The larger portion of "you" as a <u>being</u>, your entity/soul, is eternally larger and also outside of the very flesh that you think of as you when you look in the mirror. So then, a small <u>portion</u> of your greater Self is presently within your current garment of flesh, learning, applying, evolving, expanding (as ALL consciousness innately does, eternally) yet the larger portion of you is also outside of your flesh as again, "you" do not end at the surface of the skin.

This is how telepathy, clairvoyance, clairaudience, clairsentience, and so on work, as they are natural traits or characteristics of your consciousness and soul. They exist within the body, but also outside the body. The physical human body then, simply becomes, for your physical lifetime, the focal point through which the smaller, scaled-down portion of your greater Self uses as the "lens" through which you perceive physical reality, using your 5-human senses.

Dreams are an example of your consciousness operating in many other realms and dimensions of reality, that are indeed outside of your flesh body. However, your consciousness is fully engaged, active, and participating in these other realities, whether your current body is sleeping or awake. Consciousness does not rest in those terms.

Dreams would be a very good example of the natural use of your clairvoyance, clairaudience, etc. When you remember the images, conversations, feelings, etc. of what occurred in the dream, you are seeing those images in your mind, remembering what was said, etc., through your clairvoyance and clairaudient skills that are natural to your consciousness.

As you read these materials, you are then, learning the foundation for creating your life purposefully and intentionally rather than wandering around stumbling through life in the "darkness". <u>*You are growing your illumination from within.*</u> You are your own light. Your own illumination.

Illumination begins with "I".
<u>You</u> illuminate <u>you</u>.

You are becoming aware of your true nature and the vast potential that you hold eternally. It is not as if you have to seek to attain these tools and abilities. You already have them as they are inseparable traits of your inner Self. You must simply bring them to the forefront of your current perception and awareness; and then, through practice and patience, and practical application, hone your skills at using them for fruitful means to improve your lives, your culture and society, your planet, and the nature in which you find yourselves presently to be focused.

You may not realize it or intend it; however, you ARE a "humanitarian" even if you choose to ignore that truth. You cannot exist as a human being and not be a "humanitarian" by your terms, as it is natural and inseparable from the consciousness that gives you existence and self-awareness. It is within the "I AM" of your Self.

When you truly understand and frame your life experience such that it is created knowing that ALL physical reality is created first within the mind, thoughts, emotions, and dreams (which...we will point out here, are all nonphysical energy until they become physical), then you will be much more inclined to be aware of your thoughts, emotions, and those beliefs which either set you free or imprison you within the box you have created of perceived limitations you have created.

I say again, you create your reality. Until you understand *how* that occurs, you will wander throughout life wondering why various events, conditions, and things that appear in your life are there, and how they came to be there. For what purpose did they appear and what does their presence mean? Why did that event occur and what am I supposed to learn about my personal power from that lesson occurring? The ego looks at events as happening to you. The being within looks at events as happening <u>for you</u>. The ego may see great challenges while the Self within sees lessons to be understood, integrated, and hence, overcome with one's own personal power to do so. The difference between the perception of the two is the difference between peace and great challenges in life.

Dominion Over Self

Your journey here, among many other goals, is to learn dominion over your <u>Self</u>. You are to learn only dominion over yourself and not others around you. You may LEAD others in your race, however, you should not endeavor to control them, for that is unnatural. While many have tried over thousands of years to control and dominate others on Earth, <u>they have *all* met with failure.</u>

No matter how "evil" these historical characters may seem, they too, are physical bodies of human flesh that have within them the consciousness of All That Is ("God", Source, Universe, etc.).

> *It is the rational mind of the human and the ego used with the intellect that seeks dominion over others. This is <u>not</u> natural to the immortal being of consciousness that is within the human-beings as a species.*

So, while the rational and mortal, ego-focused portion of the human may seek dominion over others, the consciousness that provides that human flesh its very life and existence on the physical plane is inseparable from the Divine Source of All That Is. Therefore, although the human may try to assert dominance over others for their entire life, eventually, their physical existence and others like them will cease to continue and their efforts will meet with failure.

You cannot outrun, outsmart, outmaneuver, nor outlive "God"/Source/ The Creator/All That Is.

Not a thought, move, motion, idea, feeling, or emotion goes unnoticed, and what you sew, so shall you also reap, for it is inevitable that what you send out, will, in time, return to you...its source. Some cultures have called it karma. However, as I have said, you create your own reality. You....cannot escape you.

Nor can you escape the energy, actions, and intentions you yourself have sent forth, for they will, indeed, in time and space, return to you to teach you about the very energy you have sent forth as a co-creator of your world. It is not "God" or any THING outside of your Self that brings you the return of your own energy sent out if you will. It is that there is truly no space that exists in nonphysical reality....which means there is no "place" or nowhere for your energy to "go" in physical terms of travel.

It will, however, "circle back" in time and space and appear in your future experiences.

Now, the more you come to understand your <u>Self</u>, from <u>within</u>, the more you will understand (your eternal connection) to all of humanity, Earth, and nature around you.

> *It is that which is within you that creates that which is around you. You project it from the inner Self so that it can be perceived by the human outer self. Learn what is within you and how to direct it fruitfully and purposefully and you will discover the very foundation for creating an intentional, purposeful life experience. The very foundation and the keys for success as a soul on Earth.*

You will learn, personally and *en masse*, to overcome challenges that have faced your society and cultures for thousands of years, and much of it has to do with seeking <u>external</u> power of the physical individual or group, and others. You will, in time, overcome such petty differences such as skin color, origin of country, language, or any other physical characteristic difference, and instead, celebrate individuality and uniqueness as infinite expressions of the very same Divine consciousness that provides ALL physical life and the fabric from which all physical reality is created and expressed into 3-dimensional forms.

These trials and tribulations over the millennia, when looked at from the macro level of perception, are almost as if humanity itself has moved through its rebellious "teenage years" to evolve into something more wise, mature, and expressed in greater terms of potential. Much the way that a child often moves through the stumbling stages to then walk and grow through the often-rebellious years as they search for where the boundaries around them exist and how to expand themselves beyond the perception of them.

At a larger scale over many thousands of years, humanity has also done just that. Your evolution is not simply in terms of technology. Technology is, of course, evolving as you are. The technology evolves because you as a species are evolving. Along that line of development.

Your evolution as a being of consciousness and a species of consciousness, personally and *en masse*, <u>will</u> occur and is occurring at every moment you perceive as time. The evolution of humanity will continue to occur, for it is the consciousness of "God"/Source/All That Is, within your flesh that creates your flesh, that evolves <u>eternally</u>.

However, the path you individually and collectively take will determine the events, the timing, and the outcomes of that evolution. You will learn what works well and what does not. What your personal creative energy brings back to you in terms of experiences, desired or not, joyful or not. You will learn one way or another and progress. Yet it does not have to be the "hard way". Meaning...stumbling through life trying to move ahead by physical power and force alone.

The evolution of humanity itself is not from external gadgets alone. True evolution is the processes through which you personally, and collectively as a race, expand the awareness of yourselves to understand what you truly are and begin to utilize these innate, natural abilities to greatly improve and expand yourselves and your world that you know.

In the historical time period that you perceive as the year in which we are writing this book, there is extensive turmoil and change going on in many countries of the world. There are many seeking external physical power and dominion over other groups, countries, societies, etc. Many have called this turmoil and very unpleasant series of events globally to be the battle between "good" and "evil". While it is true that it is a battle, it is not a battle that takes place outside of the human's own doing.

All humans have **free will** as it is innate to that which you are, physically and nonphysically. It is the rational mind of mankind's ego, seeking dominion over others that provides the context in which your global events of trial and tribulation are now unfolding. However, this is truly the battle of overcoming the _Rational Mind of Mankind_, in part, the ego mind, to evolve into the naturalness of the spiritual beings that you are eternally.

You are then, in what you know to be the year 2023, witnessing, on a community, city, country, and global scale, the evolution of humanity as it moves through its rebellious stages to mature into that which is in alignment with its true nature. The nature that gives humanity life and physical reality 3-dimensional existence. The Nature...of Consciousness.

Now, as we have said, all humans have free will to choose. Humans have a conscious mind. You can indeed change your own mind. You can choose what to focus the mind, thoughts, emotions, energy, actions, and creativity towards. As I previously mentioned, all efforts to seek dominion over others on the physical plane, will, in time, fail. For again, it is the very consciousness within the human, at a level that is there for each to tap into, yet veiled perhaps by the rational mind and ego self, that seeks to be in harmony with all things, rather than to power over them. All physical power, in time, will fail. It may be at the end of that person's physical life, or the end of a government that has failed to serve its people. It may take months, years, or hundreds of years, yet it will indeed fail.

Those who choose to incarnate into the human form will at one point or another in their evolutionary process, come to know *The Failure Of Physical Power*. Events that occur in your life experience that make clear to you that no matter what you do, physically speaking, there is no solution that dissolves or achieves that which you seek to accomplish. Often of course, these are the moments when individuals realize that the only solution to their problems and challenges in life is to be found within and it is their soul, at the layer of consciousness, has chosen such events to "guide" the rational-minded individual toward their "spiritual awakening". It is that soul's choosing then, to grow beyond the perceived limitations that were once held as beliefs of the rational mind, that have held the individual back from their own evolution. Which is, of course, a part of humanity's evolution and that of All That Is.

Some often say that "'God' has already won" the battles. This is true, as the consciousness within all humanity is the very same All That Is and it is innate within the nature of this infinite gestalt consciousness that it seeks harmonious relationships with all things for it IS all things, and it cannot seek harm or dominion over another portion of itself.

The free will and choices each makes will determine the individual and group/society/culture's path forward and if it evolves slowly or more rapidly...based upon the individual choices that accumulate into the mass consciousness of humanity. Our circle-back point to make here is that this evolution beyond the wars of mankind, beyond the seeking of dominion over others in any fashion, WILL be overcome as mankind learns of its true nature within. That which this book describes in detail from the perspective of an immortal, multidimensional, vast entity as "my Self", which has the ability to see, feel, sense, and participate in many, many dimensions and realities besides just your own, all in what you would perceive to be simultaneous fashion, yet track every single smallest nuance to the smallest degree with instant clear accuracy and attention. My "Self" as an entity of consciousness is not limited, nor is yours to a degree that you are not as yet aware. Something I endeavor to uncover for you as you read further in our book.

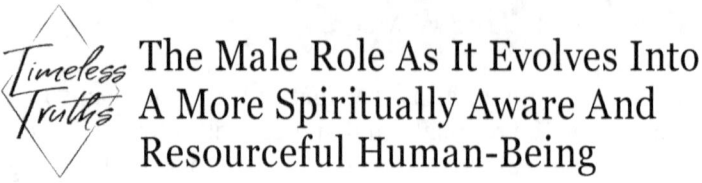

The Male Role As It Evolves Into A More Spiritually Aware And Resourceful Human-Being

Good morning, Jackson in Alaska.

Now, I see that you are learning and reflecting upon many very fruitful aspects of your trip there in Alaska, and as I have mentioned to you before, your time there and your trip will indeed propel our future on our mission together. Now you are seeing and reflecting upon the "why and how" of this statement. You are precisely correct in your statements last evening in that it IS very important indeed to take the time off work and focus on joyful, fun, and adventurous activities as that is indeed why you came to the earth plane also. It is not just work or the mission to bless the world, Earth, etc. You have your own sovereign life to fulfill with joy and happiness and the things you love to do and enjoy.

You, personally, love the mountains and the outdoors. It is a deep and direct connection with the being portion of you as a human being, and you resonate so closely with the Earth, the mountains, nature, the fish, the animals, and the birds of the sky that you are "home" when you are in those natural elements.

Now, as we have stated to you previously, a portion of our mission, again, is to bring more spiritual awareness and awakening to the male role of humanity. To bring balance to the male/female energy that is in ALL souls, as souls do not have a physical sex.

Therefore, it is very powerful for a male to bring our materials to the world at this time, in this place in history. You are aware of the fact that, in connection with all of your spiritual friends and family, there are a vast number more females than males that are at the spiritual fairs, events, group gatherings, lectures, classes, etc. You are helping to change this, and this IS part of our mission, also.

You have the warrior in you and in fact, have been a warrior in a number of your lifetimes. You remember one of such where you were a "knight in shining armor". Fighting for the greater good of the kingdom and its peoples, standing up for truth and justice for all, and saving or aiding those around you whom you could see could not readily fend for themselves. Your very strong personality then, has led you through those lifetimes to learn of war and its effects upon humanity and nature.

You have gained valuable insights that, although you're not consciously aware of them now and from where they have come to you in this lifetime, you still carry with you the warrior from the "past", yet are transforming the energy from that persona into other creative means. You have directed then, the inner warrior portion of you into other creative means in this lifetime, knowing innately now that the effects and impacts of war and seeking dominion over others is not at all the balance that nature seeks....and you recognize your strong connection to that nature where you find peace in the soul (such as Alaska where you are in the moment we are writing this).

You could not most effectively teach about the effects of war and conflict if you yourself had not fully experienced them in many lifetimes in which you have set up the conditions and foundation for understanding now. That war and seeking dominion over others is not the path by which humanity reaches its greatest potential. This is a "been there, done that (many times)...it didn't work out well" lesson that you have brought yourself through so that you could teach others *from* the context of understanding as you have been there and tried that route in the male role.

Now, you were born in the astrological sign of the Libra. The balancing scales. You chose that as a reminder and hint to yourself that you are to bring balance to the world on the mission we have chosen for this current lifetime that you know to be yourself as Jackson. You were born, physically, not that far at all from where Ruburt and Joseph lived in New York, your home state, also. There are reasons for these things as there are reasons you chose the Death Experience (NDE as they are called), to set up the path of probable outcomes whereby you would eventually teach about the nature of consciousness. This lifetime has been all about choices that led you down the path whereby you are, with us, guiding humanity as we have in many lifetimes, both physical and not.

You bring love and light and peace where once you raged war against those who oppressed you and others around you. You have learned through many lifetimes that war was not the solution that best achieved the goals of yourself and others on both sides. You have had compassion for the enemy as you recognized in your interactions with them that you saw *yourself* in their eyes. That they could be you or you could be them if you were on their side of the fence, so to speak.

Compassion then, is not only natural to the inner soul, consciousness, and being that you are, and all human-BEINGS are, it is natural to "God" or All That Is. The great balance of energies cannot be achieved unless compassion is known and practically applied, for compassion is a balancing energy, frequency, and tool for humanity to evolve.

These are things that <u>must</u> be learned for a leader of the masses to understand the foundation <u>from</u> which you are teaching. As we have told you before: you have incarnated so that you may indeed learn of the challenges of humanity, what they face, and what they are challenged with in overcoming, so that you yourself then learn to overcome them, and in so doing, that you may lead others along the path of light by which they come to recognize their own innate and natural tools to do the same. You must earn your "merit badge" before you can lead in greater terms. You must <u>face</u> the challenges and overcome them so that you are best able to lead others to do so.

> *One cannot illuminate the path for*
> *another or humanity, unless first,*
> *they illuminate themselves.*

All readers would do well to note this statement, for they too, have the capacity to lead in their own unique and individual ways that no other being brings to your physical reality. Otherwise, you each would not be there if you did not have gifts to bring to yourself, the planet, nature, and humanity.

You teach yourselves adversity so that you learn to overcome it; to not only succeed yourself but to lead others along the path of success. You are not alone, you see. You all help assist the evolution of your species from which you are inseparable.

You may not be aware of it, yet the animals of the Earth do the same. They are challenged perhaps with food needs or water. They learn how to overcome their challenges and find food and water and hence, create migration routes that are used for centuries by others as they have led the way. Nature does this in many ways, even as the flowers and trees bend and grow toward the light.

Now, you, Jackson-Thomas, are an outdoorsman. You have learned from a young age, growing up on a farm, to respect the lives of animals and care for them on the farm or in the woods. To learn of their nature in hunting for your food and sustenance as mankind has for eons of time. You are able to catch fish to feed family and friends and there are many a man (and women, of course) that can do the same. You are then representing the "manly man" in that you can survive and harvest from nature, the land, and the seas with great respect, honor, and blessed privilege for the sustenance that is provided to all on Earth. You personally, recognize that there is consciousness in EVERY object, animal, and plant, and you respect that natural relationship between yourself and the nature of that which you harvest for sustenance.

Now, in regard to our mission here, there are many males who are "manly men" all over the planet. Especially where you are right now as you type our dictation in Alaska - a place famously known for survivalists and people who, still today, could not survive if not for the harmonious relationship between themselves and the land and animals around them. They quite literally hunt and fish and garden for sustenance and would not survive without harvesting of the Earth; for many here simply do not have a grocery store just down the street where they can purchase the same that someone else has harvested for them.

In regard to my comments that it is very powerful for a male to bring our teachings and timeless truths to humanity at this point in time of history: *We seek to reach as many humans around the planet as we can, however, a particular point of focus in our mission here is to ensure that we do not exclude the "manly men" from our spiritual timeless truths.*

You then, are teaching by demonstration that you can be a very "manly man", capable of surviving in the wilds, driving a tractor to farm, changing your own oil, working on an engine, performing carpentry, building construction, and doing all the things that your cultures and society now believe to be manly activities. However, you can also learn to develop your own personal connection to your entity, your natural spiritual guidance, the Earth, the animals, and other humans, and UTILIZE your natural spiritual tools to greatly enhance your life, and all of that around you.

You are teaching by demonstration that you can be as manly as any man can be, yet you can still have your direct, immediate, always-on, innate, and natural connection to "God" by any and all names that humans have called the Divine source of All That Is. You can be manly and masculine and still be quite spiritual, also. Balance.

To shift the consciousness of humanity and evolve the species, we seek to reach many readers around the world and to demonstrate that our materials do not just simply apply to spiritual females. In your particular version of Earth and history as you all know it at the moment, for hundreds of years, dating back to the "Salem Witch

Trials", and thousands of years before that, the female personality has traditionally been much more open to the energies of nature. This is not a "bad" thing, of course, as history has traditionally had strong male personalities that were the hunter-gatherers dating back to the cavemen, while the females cared for the young that they nursed and assisted.

In those days, in your terms now, the very strong male personality was necessary to ensure the survival and expansion of the human species, as human consciousness had not yet evolved to the point where it had dispensed of war and seeking dominion over others. Therefore, to protect the family and lives from would-be invaders seeking dominion over others, the strong male personality was very necessary to respond to threats of existence. Today, in your terms of history, the human consciousness has evolved beyond the barbaric ways of the past, and it is time now for the species to evolve humanity beyond where it has been for centuries and millennia.

> *Evolving technology without the balance of evolving the consciousness that creates and applies that technology can lead to nefarious use of the technology to seek dominion or control over other humans, countries, and cultures and is the reason for many wars of the past. To evolve the species in proper balance then, you must endeavor to evolve the consciousness of humanity that creates and applies the technology. Otherwise, there is the danger of misuse of advanced technologies. Humanity must evolve beyond this for the species to thrive and open new ways of existing. In peace with all things.*

I see that it is getting later than you wanted to head out to Anchorage so we will resume this session when we place it into context within our book. We will title this something along the lines of **"The male role as it evolves into a more spiritually aware and resourceful human-being"** That said, thank you for taking the time to sit still and record more of our dictation for our book this morning. We are closing in on getting our subject matter filled out and really having a book that will shift the ways of thinking and perception of many whom we will reach soon. I bid you another magically blessed day my immortal friend and adventurer.

Your physical human body has what is generally agreed to as the 5-human senses that are used to PERCEIVE and interact with 3-dimensions of reality that you sense as objects that have length, width, and height and appear to be separated by space.

The 5-human senses detect and perceive only that which has ALREADY materialized into atoms, molecules, and physical matter, as the objects, events, and conditions that you perceive with these senses.

To change the physical reality then and the objects, events, and conditions, you must change them at their Source.

As ALL physical reality is constantly flowing from within...the inner reality of consciousness outward into physical reality that can then be sensed by the 5-human senses, one must go to the Source from which the objective reality is created to change its ex-pression. Expression = Ex-Pression = Pressed outward from within.

YOU are the immortal being of consciousness that is presently focusing THROUGH the human body, looking outward to perceive with your 5-human senses the expressions that you and others have individually and *en masse* created within consciousness, and hence subsequently, perceive its expressions.

YOU are INDEPENDENT of not only the physical environment but also of your physical body. You- your soul/consciousness and larger entity from which you have been given your physical life experience, exist eternally outside the framework and perception of 3-dimensional reality where space and time appear as phenomena.

YOU are eternally capable of changing the physical objects, events, and conditions in your life by LEARNING to purposefully use the inner, immortal being/soul/consciousness that you are to create new physical expressions. Life as you desire it and love it to be, not as it seems to be in happenstance.

You DIRECT your inner being and consciousness, to work in harmony with all beings and species of consciousness around you, to create the objects, events, and conditions of your 3-dimensional reality, using your thoughts, emotions, and imagination, and...you create the expressions WITHIN THE FRAMEWORK AND CONTEXT OF YOUR PERSONAL BELIEFS ABOUT YOUR *SELF* AND ALL REALITY AROUND YOU.

If then, you have a limited perception of your Self as "I'm just human"... then you sell yourself short of expression or even perceiving the infinitely creative power and tools that you have eternally at your disposal, closer than your fingertips could ever be, to create new events, objects, and conditions in which your physical body perceives as its life on Earth.

Your 5-human physically oriented senses are used to perceive the 3-dimensional movie and drama that you have created, personally and with others.

Your ability to sense other dimensions of reality from which ALL reality physically appearing is created FROM is within you already and is what gives your physical human body its life animation to walk the Earth. You cannot EVER exist without your tools to change your life.

Again, if you believe otherwise then it is your own limited, key-hole size perception of reality that you are using as a filter through which you limit your *Self* from experiencing an incredibly diverse and rich life experience in your physical universe.

YOU ARE NOT THE HUMAN BODY THAT YOU MAY BELIEVE YOU ARE.

YOU...HAVE A HUMAN BODY THAT YOU PERCEIVE.

The human body is a 3-dimensional expression of your soul/consciousness/being and the human psyche that you have developed and are growing. It is not something stagnant or still but changing and growing from moment to moment. It is created by your consciousness, healed by your consciousness, and kept young and vibrant with your consciousness...or limited in each of these areas, based on your own perceptions, thoughts, emotions, and beliefs which serve as the framework and context in which you paint your own picture of "life as you know it".

YOU can create your human body vibrant and healthy. You can create it sick and plagued with dis-ease. You have the ability to heal ANY physical illness that has ever appeared in physical reality, as it was created from consciousness and can be changed by consciousness.

NO illness, disease, or human condition is beyond "GOD"/Creator/ Source/All That Is, etc.

Your belief in them, and your perceptions of your own self as being subject to falling prey to them, is what opens the door for them to take root in the fertile soil that is your own consciousness creating your reality.

You may be poor, financially, because you are REACTING (reacting = re-acting = acting over again and again) to the physical environment that has ALREADY been expressed. You may be viewing the conditions around you and then re-act to them, which projects them and their vibrational frequencies into your future probable outcomes, which then narrows into the fine Now Moment that becomes your future unfolding as your present.

You cannot change your present conditions by railing against that which has already been created. You are then approaching the problem from the entirely wrong direction. You are trying for your whole life to put bandages on the cut AFTER the fact, without looking into the source of the cause of it appearing in your perception of 3-dimensional reality.

Again - to change your physical environment, you must change FIRST, the inner environment FROM which it has been given expression.

YOU then, are not financially poor unless you perceive that you are, and in reacting to your already expressed conditions, experiencing your own "Creative Loop" whereby you continually react, project, experience.

REACT... PROJECT... EXPERIENCE... REACT... PROJECT... EXPERIENCE.

This is rational mind or reactive-mode creation.

When YOU finally understand that YOU are independent of all physical objects around you, your environment, and even your own body... and the inner "YOU" is FREE of these objects, events, and conditions to change them, then will you begin to open the door to allow the perceptions of your tools to do so, and how to use these tools effectively, efficiently, and consistently.

You will KNOW YOUR TRUTHS, AND YOUR OWN TRUTHS WILL SET YOU FREE...physically, as you were eternally free...and only perceived yourself to be limited as your 5-human senses painted a picture of you being separated from that which you love or desire to experience. Again, your beliefs FRAME the boundaries or limitations within which your 5-human senses perceive and hence, experience life on Earth.

Now, when you see (perceive) things around you that you desire to shift or change, write them down in a notebook or journal. Then, with the intention of receiving guidance from your higher self, Angels...the Divine, etc., write out the questions similar to the following;

◇ Why would this condition be in my experience? (It is a SOUL lesson, or it would not exist in your field of perception to the 5-human senses. Therefore, seek to understand the SOUL lesson of how overcoming it would empower you to move beyond it.)

◇ What message is my soul seeking to understand here? And in so doing, learn my lesson and thus open the release of that lesson (and its physical expressions that you experience as the objects, events, and conditions occurring)

◇ Why do I hold these beliefs and what are they trying to teach me?

◇ Know that your brain does not need to know the way, the how, the when to resolve it, but you MUST BELIEVE that your inner being (connected, a portion of and inseparable from All That Is...) DOES know...for "My ways are higher than thoust".

Soul lessons then, that which your own soul desires to move beyond, expand through, and expand beyond, will likely be present over and over and over again in your life until you sit down and face them, turn within and without judgment, begin to ask new questions. Not the traditional "Why me?". If you keep saying "Why me?" you are asking from the wrong orientation and in a very limited state of consciousness and vibration.

Now again we will tell you something that Jackson has said for many years in life and in lectures: "Challenges in life are like weights in the gym. They exist in your experience to make you stronger."

However, *you must use them for that intention and purpose* rather than to <u>allow</u> them to crush you and weigh you down like anchors.

No one goes to the gym for <u>you</u> and makes <u>you</u> stronger. No one heals for you. No one releases hurts, traumas, or events of the past <u>that hold you back</u> in the Now for you. No one looks within to seek the lessons of the soul that exist beneath the physical objects, events, and conditions of your lives, for you.

This is a journey of Self. Your soul Self that has chosen through its free will as ALL beings are sovereign eternally to experience these aspects of learning to expand the being that you are and raise your own vibration...becoming more each moment than you were in the Now Moment "before".

When it comes to healing emotional hurts, many will say, "I simply do not know how." Let us then get out the notebook/journal and write repeating after me 100 times: "My brain does not need to know how. My inner Self knows how. My task then is to turn within and listen, perceive and the 'how' will come of its own." Write this out enough times until you create a heavy pattern of belief that sticks in the memory and can be recalled instantly when your rational mind seeks to know <u>how</u>.

This, I assure you...IS INDEED one of your lessons. To learn that your brain does not need to know HOW to do something that will expand your soul and move you beyond present conditions that seem to avail you when attempting to change them.

Remember: Your brain has extremely limited "visibility" into the infinite All That Is, until you bring to the forefront of your own awareness the inner truths that are eternally awaiting your discovery and embracement of them. I will repeat this for further commitment to your memory:

◇ Your brain is a <u>physical</u> object, born and created of flesh in this incarnation only.

◇ It uses, as a <u>physical</u> operations center, the physically oriented 5-human sense data that it perceives in this physical dimension and lifetime environment.

◇ Your soul has memories of ALL lifetimes, ALL lessons, ALL knowledge learned and integrated.

◇ Your soul is eternally a portion OF ALL lifetimes, existences, physical and nonphysical dimensions, and, of course, the Source of ALL physical reality. Therefore:

◇ Your soul/being and entity (and, of course, the Divine/"The Universe"/All That Is) knows the way, for if it is possible within the context of the root assumptions of your physical reality, then the way/ how/path/resolutions can be brought forth from the inner consciousness to the forefront of the <u>conscious awareness</u> to be recognized by the brain and integrated as new knowledge upon which it may perceive an expanded reality and utilize inner tools to create that reality experience.

You cannot exist without your own consciousness/soul/being. It is time NOW... the eternal Now, to begin using more and more of the inner Self to create the outer reality that you experience, and in so doing, expand your soul into new dimensions of experience both physical and not.

You are a human-being. Mortal-immortal. You have spent many years on this physical plane now, developing the HUMAN self, while likely paying little attention to the inner *being*. Yet it is the *being* that creates the human body and all of its experiences. You must seek to bring balance to your own human-*being*. Paying more attention to the *being* portion of you and expanding it, so that it can improve immensely and immeasurably the experience of your human self that you now have here on Earth.

Your human then, is the filter through which you experience physical reality. Life on Earth and in your universe. To change its physical experiences, you must begin at the Source and change its inner creations, that they may be expressed outward as expressions of inner reality. Reflections in time and space.

Expanding Human Potential And Continuity Of Consciousness

Good morning, Jackson-Thomas, our immortal Earth channel through which we reach and teach humanity. (Smile) You are on the right track with the business components and our humanitarian projects for the betterment of the planet and all that is on it.

Of all the components of our book, we are teaching that the human being is not nearly as limited as they may previously have believed and that the communication that takes place, naturally, through consciousness, can indeed be developed to communicate with other humans, animals, plants, trees, flowers, and the Earth to co-create physical reality in ways that are more beneficial to all. After all, this is beneath the lowest level of physical existence, you might say it is actually "God" seeking to bless itself as you are all channels of the Divine and portions of the Divine, seeking to develop natural ways to bless all other portions of the Divine regardless of them being human, animal, plant, ocean, environment, planet, etc.

They are ALL physical expressions of the <u>One Infinite All That Is</u>. This is the natural creative path, of course, as all consciousness seeks maximum expression in ways that it can be of benefit to all other consciousness...which is, essentially, a portion of itself...at the layer or level of consciousness from which it is sourced and was originally given existence through intention and will.

Again, we are opening up the intellectual mind to recognize the true nature of its own existence and everything around it so that it is more readily able to draw upon those natural communications, associations, and relationships...connections to All That Is, to increase its unique capabilities to create and express itself in forms that are desired.

Technology will get you so far, yet there are technologies that far exceed any that you now know or are aware of. Off-planet technologies that exist now are present on your Earth already, yet for some time have remained hidden to the masses, controlled for purposes by those who, through the rational and intellectual mind...of lower vibrational frequencies, perhaps sought control over others. As the consciousness of the individuals and society *en masse* evolves, grows, expands, and raises in vibrational frequency, these individuals are coming to realize the benefits that can be achieved by sharing instead of hoarding such technologies.

Our point here is that technologies that will advance your civilization and humanity as you know it, along vastly beneficial paths can be exponentially increased as one understands the consciousness *from which* those advanced technologies were <u>created</u>. Even beings that are off-planet did not come up with such technologies from their own versions of their intellectual minds. The <u>Source</u> of such technological ideas, inventions, and so forth did indeed come from the very Source that you yourselves on Earth now have the capability and capacity to access. Yet you cannot do so effectively, efficiently, or consistently if you are not yet aware that you even possess them, let alone that it is natural to ALL consciousness to work together to benefit the greater whole while benefiting Self.

Advanced technologies were created by advanced (evolved) consciousness. These advancements in technological breakthroughs, do not then, lower in vibrational frequency to match where you are, no more than myself or Angels would lower our vibrational frequencies to channel through the human beings. YOU, individually and as a species, must rise in vibrational frequencies if you are to open your Selves to the ideas, inventions, and advancement of technologies that come from advanced (evolved) consciousness.

Again - it is through the development of your own consciousness, to bring your natural abilities as a being of consciousness to the forefront of your intellectual and rational mind so that you are then able to <u>train it</u> to accept and allow your natural abilities to simply express into physical forms. In the beginning, often these abilities are sought to benefit Self, typically due to the fact that challenges in your life serve as the impetus for you to find the causes of such challenges, and to <u>resolve them at their source</u>, rather than putting a bandage on them after the fact. Yet in time this naturally transforms into blessing other physical objects, people, animals, planets, etc. around you as it is natural to the very Source of your existence to share such things.

> *Challenges in your life serve as the impetus for you to find the causes of such challenges, and to <u>resolve them at their source</u>, rather than putting a bandage on them, after the fact.*

Some may think of the initial "benefiting of themselves" as one being selfish. However, it is often said that "you cannot pour from an empty cup". Meaning one must also care for the Self before you are in a place where you can be of *most* benefit to others and the planet.

We ARE here, we are present, and we are indeed accounted for. We are pleased, truly, to see the efforts that you are putting into our communications and the expansion of our mission, and your efforts, energy, and intentions, have not gone unnoticed. While what you may think of as *Seth2 is quite aware of our conversation*, for the moment, in this session, I will be the one speaking with and through you. The Seth personality is a portion of this greater entity that Jane, and now you, call Seth2.

Now, as you are fully aware, we are not separate and that which I do and our communication together is fully transparent and available to Seth2, yet again, there is no division or boundary that separates us. As I have mentioned many times, some souls and entities can form gestalts in joining or merging with another soul or entity. The original souls or entities are not lost or diminished in any way; however, a new gestalt consciousness, or perhaps Conscious Collective, may be formed. Personalities of a soul/entity can likewise merge with and be a portion of other personalities of like interests. Again, each is free without boundaries to follow whatever path of evolution and development in which it has an interest, and all experiences contribute to the rest of which it is attached or a portion of.

In other words, the loving personality essence that the world knows to be "Seth" that authored all of the *Seth books* through Jane Roberts (Ruburt), has exponentially expanded and incorporated what Jane knew to be the entity we called "Seth2". As I stated in the beginning, I have evolved so that I could now also be considered Seth2, as well as the original entity the world knew then as Seth. That said, I am also a multitude of other entities, and one in which some of the more famous personalities have derived, incarnating into human teaching roles that will become more apparent and detailed in Volume 2 of *The Nature Of Consciousness*.

Now, we do hear you and we do open up the communication channels with and through you each and every time you call upon us, there is a vibrational match.

It is not the name that you call upon that reaches us so much as it is the intention behind the name that "reaches" us. For again, words are simply symbols or physically attuned representations that convey the meaning, intentions, and inflections upon such that you use in 3-dimensional reality where the 5-human senses can understand the meaning being conveyed with intention and purpose.

Likewise, it is not the words on the page that reach the reader to be transformed into deeper understandings that expand the soul of the one reading. Rather it is that the words are the spark or symbol that the reader sees which carries *the vibrational meaning and intention behind them*. While the readers see words with their physical eyes, it is the vibrational intentions and meaning that are meant to be conveyed using the symbols you call words that reach the consciousness of the reader through the rational and intellectual mind that then brings these inherent truths to the forefront of the awareness of the individual and cause what many in your period of history call "awakening". The rational and intellectual mind becomes acutely aware of the truth of the nonphysical nature of its existence and source of vitality, energy, wisdom, etc.

It is the vibrational frequency and energy that is behind or *beneath* the words that the reader then connects with as it reaches them at a layer of consciousness whereby the truths they read resonate within their core of being, their soul, as many would think of it. Keeping in mind that the true "soul" is much, much larger, greater, and outside of the body of the human, eternally couched in All That Is and outside of time and space.

Now, when the reader reads the words in our book here, and MY intentions, love, light, and wisdom of more than billions of years of existence come through those words, they reach the core of the being (human) reading them, and when they resonate within the being, many feel an immediate "deep connection" with our words. This is because the core of their being (at the soul level) already knows what we are bringing to the attention of the rational and intellectual mind.

This is the process of "awakening", as it is called. Bringing the timeless truths of existence through to the forefront of the rational and intellectual mind so that it can then incorporate the nonphysical tools and resources from which all physical reality is originated, and transform such energy, consciousness, and so forth into the expressions of objects, events, and conditions that form the corporeal structures of what you call your universe. Life on Earth, as you know it and perceive it to be.

The Nature Of Consciousness

Timeless Truths Vibrate In Your <u>Core</u> Being/Soul –
You Don't Just Read Them
You <u>Experience</u> Them

Figure 7.

Awakening, in your terms, is simply the recognition by the rational and intellectual mind of an individual of the inner truths of its own existence as a spiritual being, soul, and consciousness. When your rational mind becomes acutely aware of the truths of existence that are, indeed, timeless. Unalterable, inexorable, timeless truths - when recognized, embraced, and expanded within the rational mind, bring the spiritual awakening of the individual. It is in these moments and states of consciousness that the soul expands and takes another leap forward in its evolution, depth of knowing, and contribution to the overall evolution of your species, and ultimately, to the greater entity and All That Is.

257

So it is that when you call upon us, you may use <u>names</u> to provide a reference for yourself as to what it is (level of vibrational frequency in terms of entities or beings of consciousness) that you intend to reach or communicate with. Yet your <u>intentions</u> behind those names is the "meaning" that "reaches us" and within that intention, there is a vibrational match to us, <u>who remain eternally nameless</u>. Now, we have portions of us as nonphysical beings or entities which have gained personalities....souls as many would traditionally think of them that are given existence from the entity just as children are given existence from their parents. Some of the personalities of consciousness have incarnated into human form and others have not. Yet they do not have names "here" in nonphysical reality.

Those that have incarnated as personalities may have had a physical body. That personality gains much experience in that lifetime, as do ALL, through the interactions with all other consciousness on your physical plane of existence. It learns contrast...that which you call Light or Dark...which is illumination or ignorance of it. This is what has for many millennia presented itself to humanity as "evil" or "good". Contrast is necessary for the expansion of the soul and growth of the being of consciousness.

It learns humor, love, and other energies on the earth plane so that it understands from infinite angles, the vibrations and creative power that are behind the emotions as you think of them, and thereby, can use them for creative means that often escape the individuals when they are incarnate. For example, one can leverage the emotion of anger and use it quite constructively for the benefit of not only the individual who is angry, but to all things on the physical plane.

You can....transcend the meaning that
you have attached to such emotions,
and simply use the energy of the
emotion to fuel creative endeavors.

As an example that many could connect with: many will remember times in their life when perhaps they were very angry and set about a very energetic cleaning of the house as they worked through dissipating the emotion. Some men perhaps would understand examples of using anger to accomplish great physical tasks that require higher than normal physical motivation to "get the job done". These are everyday examples of how you can indeed, transform the energy behind the emotions into creative endeavors that benefit the self, and others around you. You could go to the gym or track and "work it off".

<u>This one skill, developed and honed would have an immensely profound impact in fueling your creative endeavors in virtually all areas of your physical experience.</u>

Now, we do this here in nonphysical reality on an instantaneous measure, yet what you call anger does not have that meaning or context here in the manner that you think of it, generally speaking. It is simply one of the infinite vibrational frequencies that can, as I have said, be used quite creatively and for means that are constructive and to the benefit of all. An intensity of creative fuel may be a good way to think of it.

It is then your <u>education</u> of the meaning behind the word anger, in any and all languages, that leads you to believe that such an emotion is "bad". While it can be acted upon as an emotion, and you can choose, through free will, to use it in non-beneficial ways, what we are teaching here is that you CAN indeed, learn to use such emotions as an impetus for positive, beneficial, intentionally focused creativity. You can, when you feel that anger within you, shift the direction of its outward destination and channel it into a more positive outcome for yourself and others. You can use it as fuel would be used in an engine and immediately shift the direction of this emotion from perhaps breaking something or slamming your fist upon the table to perhaps imagining an outcome you desire to achieve.

The key here to a successful transformation of the creative energy is to first be aware of it at the level of the rational/intellectual mind. If you can catch yourself in the moment of anger, you can very easily direct the energy into more creative means that are conducive to beneficial projects and outcomes.

1. Awareness of the emotion and energy

2. Free will choice to transcend the effects and redirect them

3. Intentional and practical application of the energy in another creative direction

Many people, have done this without even being aware of it when they get angry, and instead of perhaps arguing or moving into physical actions that cause damage to things and relationships of those around them, channel their anger into more creative ways and means. They go mow the lawn. Go fishing. Go paint. They _DO something_ with the energy of anger. The same can be done for any of the lower vibrational human emotions. Again as Jackson and I have stated in our lectures, classes, and workshops - lower vibrational human emotions are meant to be tools – literally **like road signs** that are designed to get your attention so that you can use your free will and shift them into more creative, beneficial outcomes.

Now, as we have stated in various places throughout our book, it is not necessarily the emotion that is the destructive element, but rather what you do with that emotion through choice of free will. Again, we are providing you with ways to look at life differently. To shift your beliefs about the everyday things around you to perceive them and use them in ways that are more beneficial. To look at life situations, events, objects, and conditions and _shift_, so that you are consciously choosing to look at it differently... so that you achieve a new perspective from which you can create better outcomes and enhance the physical life you know.

You can look at life's events around you, things that have happened to you in your past, perhaps, that you feel are traumas, upsets, arguments, relationships, or conditions that you did not at that time feel were beneficial, and then by the free will of choice, frame them into a new and more beneficial energy by shifting the way you look at them and perceive them. If for example, you understood that each event was there for you to learn from it, that it is part of a wildly creative endeavor in which, at a higher level of consciousness, of your own being, that you chose to present yourself with such a lesson to grow and expand and find peace, love, and understanding, you would open your own mind to perceive such understandings. In so doing, you would, in time...and with that intention to learn and progress from that lesson, come to love the lesson (not the events) but the lesson behind the events that have brought you a new perspective of understanding that you did indeed have the power to overcome them.

That you are not...and I repeat, you are not...at the mercy of such past events...unless you believe that you are. If you believe you are, now today, at the mercy of your past...then so shall it be. It will be your experience and you will have limited yourself and your own future.

If you believe you are not at the mercy of the events of the past in terms of emotional vibrational frequencies...then so shall it be, also. You will have opened the door for new perceptions that transcend past limitations and begin to experience a life you desire and love.

You create your own reality, and it is often through the _perceptions_ of any given event that you shape the future events and conditions of your life. Perhaps, presenting yourself with the similar lessons, over and over again until you have learned the lesson and integrated it with peace, love, and understanding, not the actions or events of the lessons, but rather the lesson of overcoming them that is behind such events.

As no human goes to the gym for you to make you stronger physically, no human goes to the emotional gym for you and sets you free of the effects on you today of emotions stemming from past events but yourself. You set yourself free. Eternally. Through free choice and use of the willpower.

Such as with forgiveness. You do not forgive another to benefit the other person you are forgiving. You forgive another to set yourself free.

Now, we circle back to reaching for Divine guidance by calling a name. It is your intention, again, to reach for that higher vibrational frequency and guidance that reaches us, connects with us, etc. as there is a vibrational match embedded within the intention of your actions and calling upon us. You cannot fool "God" or All That Is. If your intentions are true, then there will be a vibrational match to that as YOU rise in vibration to match (more closely) the higher vibrational beings of consciousness that you call upon for guidance, love, light, etc.

Contrary to popular belief...we do not natively speak English here. So, when you call us by a name, perhaps a popular one would be "Christ", it is not the English name that we hear, but the intentional vibration to reach a higher consciousness; and entities that have, perhaps, once held that name as a personality consciousness, that once incarnated into time and space, that we receive here in our psychic dimensions...which again, is a call of vibration and a match. A call with intention and a vibrational match to that calling. Just as it is the meaning of intention that is behind emotions and other events, objects, symbols, and conditions on the physical plane that are energetic matches, or not, for that which you desire...or that which you have chosen to learn.

It is then, that which is beyond physical symbols such as words, physical events, and names (which are symbols) that is the essence of that which you perceive as physical reality expressed, and the level at which the "connection" to such energies takes place. Beneath all physical reality are the energies, consciousness, intentions, beliefs, and expectations... which are all forms of nonphysical reality, which draw forth all elements into the expression of your physical reality, that then forms the world and the universe about you.

Now, what we are doing here is telling our readers that they must look into, behind, beneath the layers of physical reality that seem so real to you...even beneath the names that you call yourselves, to find the true meaning and identity that is the causal (Source) energy of that which you see expressed into physical terms. You must look deeper into your _Self_. Not "out there" but rather "in here", within your own consciousness, your mind, your beliefs, your structures that you have set up as boundaries within which you have indeed created the outcomes, experiences, and events of your life.

>*There is an inner reality, I assure you...that is*
>*infinitely beyond any perception of the entirety*
>*of your physical universe that you can perceive*
>*with your physical senses.*

There are inner, innate, natural, and inseparable tools that all humans and other species of consciousness eternally have, that can be used to more creatively, constructively to create and structure the physical reality around you that you know to be life on Earth.

You can form new relationships, healing...physical and emotional. You can form new objects, events, conditions, and more favorable experiences. You can advance technologies to the point where even travel in space and time is entirely different than it has been in the past thousand years and more of history as _you_ know it. You can communicate with other "alien" beings that are "off-planet". You can communicate with plants, animals, and humans at a layer and level that is far beyond what you consciously use now. You can use telepathy, clairvoyance, clairaudience, claircognizance, and so on, for everyday use to interact with all other forms of consciousness to not only exponentially enhance your own experience of the physical world, but also enhance it for others.

You can learn to grow plants and vegetables more abundantly and with vigor and vitality that vibrates from them, the love and light that is the environment in which they are grown. Many a good gardener already knows this. You can enhance the performance of your animals that you use for farm use, fun, and adventure. You can (and do indeed, knowingly, or not) affect their behavior, their moods, and their success in the show ring or on the farm. You even communicate with your Earth, your oceans, and the weather that <u>seems to be</u> so detached from you...yet, it is not.

<u>They are ALL extensions of the very Self that you know</u>. You simply see them as physical objects that <u>appear</u> separate. Yet again, as you shift your beliefs and focus on the truths that you are not separate at all, then will you wield the true power of creativity that you have eternally been endowed with since before your physical birth and after your physical death. You will begin to unlock and activate your own latent, dormant potential to maximize the potential of the human AND being that you really are.

When you not only understand that all physical reality is created from these inner tools and natural means, then you will begin to create, express, and experience magical activity in your life. Seeming coincidences, blessings, and synchronicities where just the right thing happens at just the right time and place. You can and will experience "miracles".

Miracles, of course, are available each and every moment of time and space. Miracles, in your terminology, are simply ordinary, every day available acts of Divine energy <u>in its natural unimpeded flow into physical perception</u>. That which your rational and intellectual mind has yet to understand and accept are normal activities of Divine expression. The more you understand this and integrate it into your perception and orientation to physical life...the more you will notice that they seem to appear all around you.

The flesh <u>can</u> be healed of every physical ailment through Divine means. I assure you...that which created that flesh in the first place, can certainly renew and restore it, even beyond any "incurable" disease. Yet if you do not believe it possible...then again, you will indeed create a reality experience in which, to you, it <u>seems</u> impossible.

All things are possible to those that believe.

Now, you are not going to sprout wings and fly as a bird does, as you are bound within the constructs of your physical creaturehood, and those of time and space for the 3-dimensional experience you have chosen; however, I assure you, far, far more miracles and physical activities are creatively available to you than most ever dream of.

Most move through life not taking the charge to move ahead with dreams, creations, and all things in life because they *do not see the way that it is possible to do so*. They do not see the means through which they can accomplish what they desire to accomplish. If it is physically possible, then there is a way.

Not a successful inventor, author, artist, building architect, or creator on the physical plane ever created anything without the deep knowing within that it could be done, even if they did not yet see or understand how. Divine manifestation and using all of your naturally present tools, one does not need to see the how of every detail before it begins. You must simply see and feel the goal as already accomplished and take every inspired step in that direction, one after the other, until your goals reveal themselves. It is the sensation vibrating within you of your goal already being achieved that causes "The Universe" (consciousness) to stir into action and conspire all elements to bring its likeness to you in time and space (in Divine timing). You become an irresistible magnet that, in time, draws things to you to create the experience that you hold and resonate with, within your being.

Again:

> *At any given moment in time, you are expressing into physical terms of matter the distilled, cumulative vibrational frequency (state of consciousness) and feeling-tones of your inner being that* <u>*appears*</u> *to you as physical reality.*
>
> *Life as you know it to be and experience it.*

The greatest creations of humanity became physical because they were "allowed" into the conscious mind from All That Is, where they were already in existence, yet not physically perceivable in space and time as yet. They were drawn into conscious awareness through the desire, feelings, beliefs, expectations, and allowing without attachment to time or constraints.

We are here, Jackson, and good morning to you. As promised, I would be available for our session this morning if you so desired. Now, I am pleased with the progress and insights that you and our friend Deanna are making on our Timeless Truths, our mission, and that which we have before us as potential to express.

Now: I want to make this point to you, however, I also want to make this point very clear for our readers as it does indeed, speak to each and every one of them on the entire planet, in all of human history.

There are some things that must "come of your own", so to speak, in that they must come to you through your natural clairabilities and senses and are not just _given_ to you in straight instructions or dictation from me or another Divine being/ source of consciousness. While we guide you, of course, and always have in many lifetimes, there are some things that must come to you of your own. Meaning that, as an eternally free sovereign being (in your human form or not), you have free will at all times, eternally, and while we can and do, of course, guide you, _you must also choose the path that you yourself will follow in each and every moment and each and every lifetime_. Therefore, there are some ideas that come to you and, while the intentions of expression are always present within consciousness, it is then up to you to draw them forth by contemplation, _desire to understand them, desire to know them more fully_, and even to express them in terms of manifesting them in material form and physical matter. It is that some materials are given to you by us as dictation through clairaudience and our communications that take place using these natural characteristics and traits of consciousness. However, other materials are "there" in a probable reality of "The Universe" of consciousness simply awaiting your desire, intentions, focus of attention, contemplation, and so forth _to draw them forth_ into fruit that you perceive as ideas, materials, and truths that can then be articulated in the English language (and others, of course).

The more you are, these last few weeks, deeply seeking to BE and express the vibrations and frequency of myself, Christ, the more you are beginning to unlock your own potential. It is as if they are hidden within, and _YOU_ must be the one to uncover them through the exercise of free will. Adding our energy into your own, drawing our consciousness into and through your own, raises, of course, the vibration of your Self. Your immortal being within the flesh of Jackson or that which many think of as the soul of your current body.

> **Wise words and good ideas will make sense to the rational mind, registered in the brain. Timeless Truths of your own existence quite literally spark the vibration of recognition within your soul, the core of your being, and are already _known_ as _truths_ present within your own consciousness. It is simply a matter of bringing their eternal existence to the forefront of the rational and intellectual mind so that it may incorporate them into your daily orientation through which you create your reality and life as you know it on the physical plane in corporeal form.**

However, as your vibration raises/expands/evolves and gets higher in frequency, it becomes much "closer" to your natural, native state as a being of consciousness; and when this occurs, you yourself unlock, stir into action, become aware of many insights, wisdom, tools, and understandings of your Self that you had no idea even existed before. This is important, so let's call this out to our readers as the same truth and process is inherent within each of them, also. Whatever one human can do in terms of consciousness, all humans can do in those same terms as there is no separation of the traits and characteristics of yourselves in consciousness.

They have been there all along for EVERY human-being that has ever walked the planet or ever will, as they are innate within the consciousness of humanity and your species of consciousness that expresses itself into human flesh. **Yet it is only those who seek within that find it, become aware of it, and develop it.** Meaning: your ability to perceive far, far beyond what others see and experience. As you rise and expand in consciousness and the vibrational frequency that you are in any given moment, you begin to thin the "veil" between yourself and other dimensions of reality. Both physical dimensions like your own (parallel universes some like to call them, in your period of history here) and those dimensions that are not physical in context at all. You begin to perceive information, details, ideas, concepts, and truths from these dimensions and use them in your own formation of life as you know it, to immensely add to and enhance the life that you know. This was one of my underlying purposes of writing all of my books I've authored and assisted in authoring... to bring these potentials, capabilities, and latent, dormant abilities of the Self to the forefront of awareness so that the intellectual mind could focus on them, learn from them, and advance itself in terms of your physical experiences and the evolution of the soul. Tools for the success of a soul on Earth.

It is not that they weren't there before you were born, for surely, they were. However, it is (again) that you were not aware of the immense creative abilities that come naturally within the being or soul portion of yourself as human-<u>beings</u>.

Your species, and, in fact, some civilizations now long lost to time as you think of it, have discovered them, developed them, and made use of them. Atlantis was one of them and there are many more which are now only legends and folklore of the past that once existed in physical terms as your own society does now. Let's go back to our statements that "God" by any and all names is omnipresent, omniscient, and omnipotent. This is a timeless truth and is generally accepted by the religions of the world now. However, you cannot have a "God" that is omnipresent, and this infinite being of consciousness <u>not</u> be present in every corner and nuance of <u>every reality</u>, even those that you do not see or in any way perceive. This means that it is fully present, fully knowing, and fully powerful...inside of your human flesh body right now (and eternally). It is within you, as you. You are not the whole of it any more than I am. However, you are indeed, an inseparable portion of it, as much as I AM.

You cannot perceive other dimensions of reality that are nonphysical, using your 5-human physically oriented senses.

You must use your nonphysical Self and senses to "see" (perceive) into them, hear, feel, sense, know and then draw from that dimension its vitality and essence to incorporate into your own and expand the existence you know. These capabilities are inherent within <u>all humans</u>. In the <u>being</u> portion of you, or personality portion of your soul as many would think of it in your terms.

YOU must choose to become aware of these innate abilities of the Self, know it, work with it, develop your awareness of it, and develop your own capabilities by going to the "inner gym". Whereby, you might work your physical body in the gym to make it stronger and improve its athletic performance, you MUST DO THE SAME with the inner Self in regular intervals if you are to develop your own tools by which you create your own reality most effectively and intentionally.

You are a human being. Physical, nonphysical. You cannot just work the physical body in the gym or physical life and expect balance. You must also "work" the inner Self within and expand this Self so that you are more balanced in nature, and open your own mind to the infinite things that can be created by your own consciousness, in co-creative harmony with all consciousness.

This is not rocket science, here. It is the natural evolution of Self. Your <u>*Self*</u>. However, again, *<u>it is a path you must choose if you are to live the physical life you desire to live, instead of one that seems to have been assigned to you simply to teach you lessons.</u>* You do not need to push through life. You should endeavor to flow through life. Through free will, in every moment of existence, both physical life and nonphysical focus, you have free will as all consciousness does. Not just the sovereign birthright of mankind, but rather the innate knowing and characteristics of "God" by any and all names.

Now, when I say that you must practice, practice, practice, and work out the inner Self at your "inner gym", I do not mean that you need to become a monk or spend hours upon hours each day to do so. I do, however, mean that you should endeavor to create a small shift at first, in your daily lifestyle and habits to <u>allow yourself</u> time to go within...to go unto the Father/Source/"God"/

All That Is, The Creator, Allah...whatever name you enjoy calling All That Is. Start with a small, but <u>regular</u> change. Consistency forms habits that can last and grow.

Grow it and add to it. Start 3 mornings a week for 15 minutes. Then 4 days a week for 15 minutes. Then one of those days, do a 20–30-minute time where you meditate or go within, removing your focus from physical reality and tuning into the inner Self...which is, I might add, "where" you will find Divine beings, Angels, guides, and all information that has ever come to humanity in all of human history.

Yes, "God" is within every physical object of the entire universe, every minute fraction of what seems like the space between every object of your physical universe and, in fact, between the electrons and nucleus of atoms that form your physical reality, and so on. Because it is the consciousness that makes up the atoms that form atomic mass, which form material matter and gives you objects of 3-dimensions. However, All That Is, is vastly and infinitely beyond that, and growing exponentially in all possible ways, directions, forward and backward (and sideways) in time and space, and outside of it, etc. There are no limitations to consciousness, and you can tap into these unlimited sources through which you enhance your life, your family, your culture, societies, cities, communications with humans, animals, Earth, planets, trees, environments...and if it hasn't become obvious, in so doing you are enhancing <u>your "connection" to All That Is</u>.

The Continuity Of Consciousness Across Time, And Historical Timeless Truths Meant To Guide Humanity's Development And Evolution

Now: As I have mentioned before, the publishing of our book, appearing on the physical plane in terms of historical time as you perceive it now, in the year 2023, does, indeed, SPARK, if you will, an entire range of **probable outcomes** that all stem from *that event becoming physical*. From that point in time and space then, an entire array of probable outcomes will extend, not only into the future as you would perceive it, but also into the past. Therefore, as we are shifting the *future* of humanity, as you think of the future, you are indeed, then also, shifting the *past* as well. Though your physical senses do not catch this at all, it does occur at every moment of time, as you think of and perceive it.

In this example, however, we are opening an entire path of evolutionary development for humanity, as you now know it on Earth, for them to learn along the lines of our intentions with the *Timeless Truth series* of books, connecting my original books with the teachings of Christ from what seems like thousands of years ago.

Even the teachings of the Bible will, in time, seem to transform into a new understanding that you cannot as yet perceive. This will occur in the path that we are speaking of whereby <u>many</u> develop their awareness to the truths, and evolve along that path of <u>knowing</u>, wherein they will perceive a different meaning of the truths that are in the Bible that is widely distributed around the world today. As well, through the evolution of consciousness, the expansion of human consciousness that will then incorporate much more of the nonphysical consciousness traits and characteristics we have in this book and others spoken of; they will also be able t<u>o *discern for themselves*</u> that some of the teachings of the Bible are indeed made-up manufactured stories...dramas that are not truths at all. Some of them were either mistakenly or purposefully, inserted into the modern-day collection of ancient manuscripts that together form the Bible that you know. As I have mentioned before, one of the gospels is a counterfeit gospel, inserted into the Bible long ago, *that has for centuries, completely changed the meaning and context of timeless truths that were truly meant to be conveyed in this collection of ancient manuscripts.*

Rest assured that if there are teachings in the Bible that are fear-based, they are _not_ the teachings of Christ as intended, nor of those in those times who spoke the _truth_ along with him and thereafter in history. They are lower vibrational excerpts from many who, for many reasons, have inserted them into the Bible for purposes that were intentional and not, which were and still are, misguided, erroneous, false, or misleading. Hence, one of the reasons, intentions, and purposes of our books now to dispel and dissolve some of these misleading, lower-vibrational "from the rational/intellectual mind" orientation and point of view statements.

Now, the Truth is the Light, and the Light will always overcome any lack of light which is perceived as "darkness". So when things are illuminated both on Earth and within human consciousness, the darkness seems to automatically fade away, for in the light there can be no darkness, and in the light, there is the illumination of the Truth that Light is. Divine Light. Divine Truth.

Regardless of one's belief, the truth, then, is eternally the Light. And this Light, as it is, is also within the very flesh of each human being to ever walk the Earth, _for it is within the consciousness that created your flesh_. Which means that it is within our readers and humanity now. It is a matter of recognition of it and application of the perception to orient oneself _from_ that perspective or leading one's life experience via the rational mind, which is more physically oriented, and of the lower vibrational plane, which is more challenging.

The inner being, then, is the source of the light. The Divine light, the spark that gives the flesh life animation to walk around alive, and the truth of its own existence and all around it. The light, then, the truth within, vibrates naturally at higher frequencies of vibration, which are a closer match to the Divine vibrations of higher dimensions - those that are nonphysical and cannot be detected with the 5-human physical senses. Now, one may say, "God' is the source of the Light", or perhaps, "'Christ' is the source of the light." This is truth. However, **your misunderstanding as to the truth about the nature of time and space leads you to believe in the separation of objects.** _When in reality, all physical objects are created from, and are expressions of, consciousness, in which there is no time and there is no space or separation._ **Therefore, this truth reveals that "God" and "Christ" are also within you, as is the "Kingdom of Heaven" (the reputed domain of "God").** It is THIS TRUTH that Yeshua/

Immanuel ("Jesus") Christ taught, believed, and conveyed to all humanity, and it is the basis for understanding how ALL physical reality, including human bodies, animals, and nature, is created into physical reality, and how you can direct your consciousness concretively to draw forth all things to create your reality experiences. We will get into the nature of time and space as a phenomenon of appearance later, as that is very important to understand such things to understand yourselves, and all reality in which you are eternally present.

The inner being, your soul (consciousness) has access to, not only, the lifetime you are living, but other lifetimes you are presently living that you may perceive as "past lives" and also, the lessons that are learned in those lifetimes. It also has access to many other dimensions that it can explore and learn. Both those that are physically oriented and those that are not.

The brain and thinking, judging portion of humans is a <u>physical</u> mechanism. The brain and thinking, rationalizing, intellectual portion of yourself develops and becomes physical as the human baby forms. As a physical mechanism, it is used (obviously) for navigational purposes, but also, importantly, to make rational decisions about the environment to form the life experience that unfolds around you. It is used to <u>direct</u> the inner being/consciousness into infinite creative expressions that appear as life and your physical universe around you.

As a <u>physical</u> mechanism that is more physically oriented, it uses <u>the 5-human physical senses</u> to build up a living picture of your environment and reality around you at any given moment in your lifetime. By its own <u>physical nature</u>, its vibrational range of perception is lower in vibrational frequency than the inner being/consciousness. Vibrations that are slower, such as the slower vibrations of atoms and molecules, make up physical matter that appears to you as solid objects of your Earth and universe.

The brain of the human body is <u>physical</u>,
and as this physical part of your human self
was created in <u>this physical lifetime</u>, it generally
has access to <u>this physical lifetime's data only</u>.

The inner being/soul/consciousness has access
to <u>all lifetimes</u> and infinitely beyond that.

With which, then, would you choose to view, understand, and interact with your reality? That <u>with limitations</u> or that which is <u>without limitation</u>?

Throughout your life then, part of your adventure is to use the inner being to train the rational mind to remember its origin and truths so that the brain and rational/intellectual mind have access to these truths of Self, and are then able to engage them, activate them, and develop them for use to creatively express physical reality around you in purposeful, intentional ways that lead to the value fulfillment of your Self in that lifetime. Not just the physical self, but the development of maximum potential expressed of the inner Self. The evolution of your own soul.

Now, the physical brain, born in this physical lifetime only....again, uses the 5-human senses to build up the picture of reality around you. If you do not pay attention to the inner Self - and the infinite data, wisdom, truths, and clairabilities that are used to communicate with not only other physical human beings, but also animal-beings, the Earth, and the environment, and can also be used to communicate with off-planet beings and consciousness, with "The Universe" itself and with "God" by any and all names ever called by humans - then you will live challenging lives trying to understand why life seems to happen TO you instead of FOR you.

We are, then, bringing awareness of the inner Self, the immortal soul and being you are, connected to all things including other lifetimes in other time periods of history, as you think of or perceive linear-appearing time, and in the medium you call space, to the forefront of the rational and intellectual mind and brain so that you are able to USE this inner Self in infinite ways to enhance the world and universe that you know. This is quite obviously one of the purposes of not only our *Timeless Truth series* of books that we are now launching into the world-view, but also, of my original books, as well as the teachings of Christ, of which <u>some</u> (not all) are incorporated into today's version of the Bible that you have in your culture and society around the world.

Again, there are other teachings of truth that made it into the original ancient collections that would one day form the Bible, that were removed purposefully, and some that have still as yet not been identified or found. For example, ***The Gospel of Thomas*** and ***The Gospel of***

Mary, are indeed authentic and translated very closely (in some translations, but not all as some did not understand the inner soul/spiritual context in which they were given) to the true meaning in which they were meant, intended, and purposed, were both originally part of the collection of ancient manuscripts that were to form your true Bible, yet were indeed, _removed_ from that collection and have today been _excluded_ from the New Testament or discounted as being of any true significance. If one understands the TRUTH in meaning behind these teachings of Yeshua as each were recorded with intention to convey them to humanity for the guidance of spiritual evolution of the souls of humanity, they do indeed have wisdom and timeless truths discernible in them that is today of value, as much as any timeless truth would be in any period of history. Period. Today, billions of spiritual seekers have developed then, for thousands of years, without the TRUE meanings and understanding of these and other timeless truths, which has misguided them along false lines of meaning. This has then, for thousands of years, clouded and _limited_ the evolution of humanity in many ways, and the evolution of the souls that have incarnated to evolve themselves, the planet, nature, your universe, and all within it. Again, our _Timeless Truth Series_ now, serves to dissolve and dispel some of the mysteries, misguided and misunderstood teachings and to connect the timeless truths from the teachings of John The Baptist, Yeshua/Emmanuel, Paul/Saul (the three main personalities of the Christ entity as noted in _Seth Speaks_), to those of my _Seth Books_ as dictated through Ruburt, to those now in our new series as dictated through Thomas (Jackson).

Now, in Volume 2 of _The Nature of Consciousness_ we will be detailing much more of the truth about the life of the _human man_ known as Christ, the historical "Jesus" of the Bible, and his intentions of teachings, and we will explain the meanings of some of them from the perspective of the inner being that gave his physical body its life animation and was "One with the Father", or source of him Self. The importance is that there were many timeless truths spoken and taught by this historical figure and as such, they are absolutely as applicable today in helping humanity understand its origins and Divine nature, as they were when originally spoken, seemingly thousands of years ago.

Then, they were spoken in the context of the times, in the limited language and understandings of the times. My intention is to bring a more modern presentation of them to humanity now, so that the _truths_ of his teachings are clear, and it is not what many religions promote.

The *true Christ*, (Yeshua/Immanuel) of which many of the teachings of the Bible are based around, did *not* mean nor intend to enforce a religion or religions. The *true Christ* taught that **ALL** humans were One with "The Father" or the Source of his own being, as he was. Through their own "being" as human-***beings***. He taught love and light (truth) to humanity. Oneness. Not the separation of humans nor of the Earth itself.

Now: In short, there are indeed connections between those ancient teachings of Timeless Truths, my original series of Seth books, and those in this new *Timeless Truth series* we are beginning with *The Nature of Consciousness.* In Volume 2 of *The Nature of Consciousness*, we will bring much more light (illumination) to these connections so that our readers can, indeed, see the vastly bigger picture that has for millennia been in the making.

Those who are familiar with my earlier books and somewhat familiar with the teachings of Christ that are in the Bible (and other books now in print but no longer a part of the accepted/approved religious Bible), will, indeed, sense the connection between them when reading our new books, for as with many who are spiritually discerned (understand to some degree physical reality from an inner perspective of Self and soul) they will note that true Timeless Truths vibrate at the core of their own soul/inner being/consciousness when they read them, and, therefore, are able to discern more easily that which is indeed truth, and that which may not be, based upon the vibration of the words that carry intentions within the letters and words you read.

Those who are tuned inward enough will, indeed, sense the connections and meaning that is intended to be conveyed with such words, and can tell through Direct Knowing (claircognizance and other clairabilities) that which vibrates as truth and that which does not.

And now, for you, Jackson - I would like to include this in a section near the end of our first book and title it ***"The Continuity of Consciousness Across Time, and Historical Timeless Truths Meant to Guide Humanity's Development and Evolution".*** This same subject will be developed in much greater detail in Volume 2 following this book.

Now: We are not just instructing about consciousness so that one can create more health, wealth, success, and prosperity in their own lives and those around them. Yes, these are the basic things that you can indeed succeed with learning these materials. However, we are talking about the entire evolution of your species of consciousness, and of humanity, Earth, animals, nature, etc. We are talking about communicating with other humans through telepathy and the clairabilities. We are teaching that you can see through time and space, into the "past" and into the "future", and you can draw upon other dimensions in which objects, ideas, inventions, ideas for novels, movie scripts, creations, technology, health, healing, creating physical reality in ways that you as a larger race have yet only scratched the very, very surface of. You can perceive the probable outcomes of events before they occur and select alternative outcomes so that you know which outcome you desire to draw into your physical experience intentionally and purposefully to achieve creative goals.

You can CREATE your reality to happen, occur, and unfold before you in ways that are more pleasant, enhanced, and desired. Instead of life happening to you (reacting to what already has been expressed into physical reality), you create it proactively so that it expresses into physical reality in ways that you desire. Not through force, but through your loving, intimate, and eternal connection with all consciousness you call "God". In volume 2 of our book, discuss communication through consciousness from humans and animals, and animals to humans. How you can teach, train and communicate with animals, both pets and wild animals (and how you do this already and most are not aware of it and how you are affecting their behavior and even life spans). We will discuss communication from humans and trees, flowers, vegetable gardens, and your flora and fauna that you can indeed "communicate" with them in ways that are more fruitful and fulfilling to both. We will discuss communication with your planet, the elements, and off-planet beings. And we are not talking about communication through the English language, but the Direct Knowing at the core of your soul and being, what is being communicated to and from such things, and that at all moments of your physical existence, you are, indeed, "communicating" with them, aware of it or not.

Your entire world and experience will transform in time when humanity learns to use its consciousness in such natural ways. Civilizations before yours and after yours, in terms of what you think of as "time", that exist in other dimensions similar to your own, have developed along these lines. The legends of Atlantis and their exceedingly advanced use of consciousness to communicate, and to use their consciousness in harmony with other beings, animals, Earth, and nature is not just a legend. I lived in Atlantis in one of my lifetimes. I've lived lives in other dimensions and cultures of which your present-day history knows little or nothing of. I have taught, and do teach, in them, also. So has Jackson-Thomas. I <u>know</u> of such potential for I have been a part of their evolution in many dimensions. This is why we teach them, so that you do, also. For I am in your evolution, and you are in mine. I am in the evolution of humanity, human consciousness, Earth consciousness, and that of your universe (and beyond), and they are in my evolution, also.

As I speak these timeless truths throughout this book and others, as I have over thousands of your years, some of them will vibrate within the core of your being, your soul, as you read them, and you will, in those moments, perhaps, remember that your true Self is vastly beyond the one you see in the mirror, and that your true potential is beyond your wildest dreams.

I am reminding you, while in your learning environment, of your natural tools, so that you may create such things in physical reality and 3-dimensional art that you call your universe. The living painting of your world and existence, into a dimensional context you call life.

As the main "entity" or Conscious Collective, of which the Seth personality is but one of many personalities, I have written, authored or co-authored, inspired and assisted in the production of many books, through many personalities. Though some of the physical humans were not aware of the "source" from which the material was coming into their conscious minds as they wrote the words upon the pages. Over what you would perceive to be hundreds of millions of years we have influenced truth teachings throughout many universes including your own. Some were carved into stone. Some were given in pictures upon the walls. Others were written on papyrus or ancient scripts and scrolls. Some have survived physically to this day, others have not, and some have survived and are yet to be found. The areas of your modern day Turkey and Syria contain some of these. Those that are lost, physically to time, are not lost at all. As they are always "available" to be channeled once again, in your modern day and year, in ANY year, as old and ancient materials transform into new understandings of timeless truths, given through yet a new medium/channel and provided in the context of the time in history in which one resides, respectively. As the ancient plans for building pyramids were available across time and space, so too, are the secrets of civilizations that are beyond the one you know, on and off-planet.

We have always, and will always, seek to transform timeless truths into new presentations and understandings of those truths, within the context of history and understandings of the time in human history in which they then appear, physically. Connected by strings of energy that are stronger than steel and those that cannot be altered by any physical thing, they eternally seek to transform into new understandings within the souls of humans and the species of consciousness that appear in your (and other) system(s).

Our task here, then, is not to give you every answer to every question you seek to know. Our task is to be the Divine gardener and plant the seeds within the consciousness of humanity across the Earth so as to ignite the spark within your own soul and personality, whereby you may *choose* through free will to seek within yourselves for those answers. I am/we are not the source of ALL knowledge, for knowledge and wisdom grow exponentially in every direction you could imagine, forward and back in time, with each thought and emotion that you have, and especially so that which you contemplate in patterns of mental review.

Our messages are those of empowerment of Self; of the love that is the basis existential vibration that is within all things, seen and unseen, in infinite dimensions ever growing and expanding. We ***do not*** desire to be set upon a pedestal or pretend that we are better or more knowing than any other human or *being*, for your entity/soul and consciousness do, indeed, have DIRECT ACCESS and connection to All That Is. It is YOU who must choose to seek it, and develop it, and as you seek, so shall you also find, for the answers are within the questions. The more you expand your own consciousness and raise your vibrations so that your inner, and even your physical body, are vibrating in much higher ranges of vibrational frequencies, then the more you will be a closer match to the Divine frequencies where ALL physical reality is Sourced and eternally present. This is the nature of the evolution of Self. *The Nature of Consciousness*. Your Consciousness and All That Is.

The world knows me/us as Seth from my first set of books as channeled through Jane Roberts (Ruburt). However, as you are now learning, we are infinitely beyond just that one entity and personality. Some of us have personalities that had names when incarnate, such as Seth, and once looked like the man in the painting that Joseph (Robert Butts) painted of that personality. As I mentioned in our book here, in one of my lifetimes unannounced to Ruburt as Jane, I was known for many, many years as Immanuel by my followers and was then, a teacher of timeless truths and a speaker. More of that lifetime and my true name behind the name I was called will be given, as well as details around the lifetime of Thomas (Jackson) during that period of history.

However many of us have no names, for again, we do not use them in nonphysical reality. They are helpful as a reference for your learning, yet we must move beyond names if we speak about Unity and Oneness of Consciousness to shift the identity of our readers beyond the seeming physical human that they may have once believed they were separate from other humans and objects, to the infinite beings that are connected to us all. And in that recognition of their heritage and true-Self, comes the power of awareness and, utilization of multidimensional tools to create things only once previously dreamed of. Transforming human consciousness into a new physical expression of the species as a more "advanced" race in your terms, and capable of such beautiful miracles on a moment-to-moment basis that only science fiction has touched upon the surface of such ideas. You do not need names to be wise for wisdom has no name, and all names.

Jackson-Thomas and I (we) ignite the spark. Your spark, as that is indeed what you are. A Divine Light of Illumination, awaiting rational mind recognition and awareness so that you may release your maximum potentials in ways only dreamed of or not as yet even dreamed of. You, individually and *en masse*, chose to fuel the fire within and expand your *Selves*. Not just yourself. Your *Selves*. Plural.

Understand what is meant by that, for you are indeed a multidimensional Soul and *being*. You can never, in all eternity, change that; so it is high time, in the history of humanity, that you know so that the world begins to embrace the unlimited nature of "God" that is within every perceivable physical object, as well as everything "in between" and infinitely beyond that, in dimensions you are now beginning to open your perceptions to perceive. You can communicate through time and space with other incarnations and personalities of your own soul/entity. Other multidimensional Selves that are, right now, living physical existences in another dimension that seems to be another historical time period that you may perhaps only glimpse in dreams and daydreams as "past life memories". You can communicate with them (and you do now), yet you can intentionally communicate and share knowledge, wisdom, ideas, inventions, skills, and tools, to enhance the life experience of each personality portion of your soul. This...is one of the many facets of evolution for which you are heading as individuals and a species. Some slower than others and some faster than others, given your choices of free will on following that which we teach. (Remind your rational mind of that your soul has always known). We seek not recognition for we are simply the channels through which these materials, which are indeed your own, find you. In larger terms then, we are a portion of you, seeking to remind another portion of you.

In Volume 2 of *The Nature of Consciousness*, we will speak more about the nature of animals, flora/fauna consciousness, and, in fact, that of the mountains and seas, and the physical universe. We will also be discussing more as to the natural "communication" that constantly takes place between you and all of these other physical objects at the layer of consciousness, yet, not in English or human language...rather in your NATIVE "language" of the souls that you are. Beyond Volume 2, the intentions are set as to detailing more about interactions between the multidimensional aspects of consciousness and how they are connected through multiple "divisions" of a psychic nature for the purposefully directed focus of consciousness expansion, yet, are not at all <u>physically</u> separated. In mastering your own purposeful, intentional, directed use of your own consciousness, there are massive, life-altering implications and great awareness of the multidimensional aspects of consciousness we will be discussing.

You are the creator of "worlds" and you must begin to understand your connections and how you affect other dimensions of reality so that you can most effectively draw information, wisdom, ideas, inventions, and strategies, and activate your own dormant, latent abilities that will enable you and humanity to take conscious living to the next level. Quite literally. You hold this book as it is time in human history for your own, personal evolution of Self, and to participate in the overall evolution of your species of consciousness, and its expressions of humanity that you know. <u>**You**</u> are an active, unique, and indelibly beautiful part of this evolution. Until our next book is published, we bid you a fond and magical time reading and enjoying this one, as it is sent to you from dimensions beyond time and space for YOU.

Notes and Quotes

_____

_____

_____

_____

_____

_____

_____

_____

_____

_____

_____

_____

_____

_____

_____

_____

_____

_____

_____

_____

_____

_____

Notes and Quotes

_____

_____

_____

_____

_____

_____

_____

_____

_____

_____

_____

_____

_____

_____

_____

_____

_____

_____

_____

_____

Appendix

Seth's Statement Of Being

By the year 2023 in which our readers are now reading this book, my previous books authored through the psychic medium Jane Roberts, who I lovingly referred to as Ruburt, have been in physical reality for over half a century, and have impacted the lives of literally _hundreds of millions of people across the planet_. Directly through reading my books, and through the thousands of books and teachings that became physical reality that were outcomes, sparked into existence through someone who had read, heard about, or otherwise was touched by my original works.

In my new series of books I am now authoring and writing through Jackson, whom I often refer to as "Jackson-Thomas", we have set about to expand upon my original books, with the intention of bringing more love and light, and timeless truths to humanity to raise the vibration of human consciousness, expand the souls of the human-beings that read or are in some way touched by our works, and to assist in the evolution of humanity, animals, your planet and universe. As I have stated in our book here, I AM within the evolution of all of the aforementioned and ALL physical reality as you know it to be, and you all as humanity, animals, Earth, and your universe, are within MY evolution as a Multidimensional Conscious Collective which, of course, includes the personality essence (consciousness) of Seth, so-named from one of my male incarnations as the man who was given that name in that lifetime. It is one of my many personalities that I enjoy, and the one that I believe best approximates the "me of me" as I speak to humanity through channels such as Jane and Jackson.

Now, as happened with Jane, she experienced many people around the world who were spiritual seekers that had open minds and accepted our materials as they felt them vibrate within the core of their soul/being when they read them. However, Jane also experienced naysayers who, at first, thought it unrealistic for a human to communicate with nonphysical entities, souls of humans now dead and physically gone, etc. There were then, as there are now, non-believers.

During the creation of our new _Timeless Truth Series_ and the subsequent teachings that have derived from them, interfacing with the public in-person via lectures, classes, workshops, etc. and via social media, Jackson, too, has experienced the naysayers. There are now, as there were then, those who do not believe that you can communicate with such nonphysical beings, off-planet consciousness, Angels, or Christ, etc. They, of course, hold erroneous beliefs ABOUT reality and not the truth OF reality. Hence, all of my books and the need to insert them into the world view and grow the materials in the consciousness of humanity, as it has been over half of a century, now.

However, there are also individuals or groups of individuals who have come out to criticize our new books and provide personal criticism towards Jackson as the human man whom through which I AM now communicating and, once again, inserting more love, light, and truths into the world view. Groups that have read my original "Seth books" and have pointed out certain sections of text from those books where I had once made statements to the effect that my book materials would come "exclusively" through Ruburt – Jane Roberts, to protect the integrity of the materials.

What I want to make very clear now, is that I DID indeed, communicate to Ruburt (Jane and Rob) that these exclusive communications would be *DURING JANE'S PHYSICAL LIFETIME WHEN RUBURT WAS IN BODY AS JANE.*

Privately then, from the appearance of the *Seth Materials* and *Seth Speaks*, Jane and Rob discussed the presentation of our materials and the exclusivity of them coming through her (during her physical lifetime) and how they would handle that in regards to public communication in our books. They then made the free-will choice and decision to exclude the "during her physical lifetime only" portion of my intended communication and leave that out of our books. This...is a **_miscommunication_** and one that I am now clearing up with many others in our book here, and it clearly demonstrates the confusion that can come from miscommunications, intentional or not.

The all-important part that was left out of our books then was: *"while Jane Roberts is physically living"* as, obviously, I could not produce physical books after her physical death. Due to many fears over her physical health condition that deteriorated over the years and eventually would contribute to her physical death, we did not discuss her death being the point at which our materials, then, would potentially (as a probable reality) come through another individual (Jackson-Thomas) who still had yet to make the free will decision to work with me again in this lifetime context and historical time period.

We did not, then, address the probable future events that **_could_** occur, after Jane's physical death, *and in 1966 or 1975, etc. it was still a*

285

PROBABLE... (NOT guaranteed) outcome that Jackson would choose to pursue our mission we'd planned for this incarnation as Jackson. While it was indeed <u>intended</u> as a future probable outcome back then, it was not <u>decided</u> by Jackson's exercise of free-will to actually do so until 2015/2016. And those who have read my books, know by now that I do not typically engage in predicting the future, for free-will changes everything in every moment of history.

Now, as I have explained in our book *The Nature of Consciousness* Volume 1, the new *Timeless Truth Series* I AM now writing through Jackson is one of many probable futures that stem from the actual physical manifestation of our physical *Seth books* that came into physical fruition back in those time periods. I have explained this in our book; however in short, the appearance of my original *Seth books*, as given through Jane Roberts, sets up the probable outcomes that there would be more books in the future (2023 say for example). To be clear, however, this does NOT mean that these books would DEFINITIVELY become physical reality as they are now. It simply "opened the door" if you will to the possibility.

Again, as I have explained, some in Volume 1 and much more detailed in Volume 2, the physical events of my books and materials "then", say in 1975, SET UP the *probable outcomes* of these books to occur now in 2022-2023 and beyond. However, as Ruburt and Jackson (as with all human-beings, souls, and entities of consciousness) are sovereign beings, they have free will to choose their path, both while incarnated in physical form and when not. Therefore, simply the appearance of my original *Seth books did not guarantee the appearance (physically speaking) of our new Timeless Truth Series of books*, as Jackson had to CHOOSE THE PATH, CHOOSE THE MISSION, as he has. Day by day, moment by moment...ALL must choose their path of development and hence, destiny, as it is often called.

Therefore, Jackson's soul that I call "Thomas", was "chosen" for the mission we are now embarked upon. Meaning that his soul and ourselves (the multidimensional conscious collective you think of as "Seth") set the "strong intention" and plan of probable outcomes to embark upon the mission we are now unfolding. However, again, simply because it was strongly intended and agreed upon as our "plan", if you will, Jackson-Thomas still had free will to choose NOT to communicate with me, or not to channel books, or not believe he was speaking with "the real Seth" personality essence, and any one of infinite choices that could have led to another outcome other than our presentation of our *Timeless Truth Series* of books to the world now. At any moment, in fact, Jackson could, as Jane could have, chosen to stop working or channeling our materials and our books and mission would not develop along those lines (but would in another reality that you do not perceive with your 5-human senses).

These choices then, are the same free-will choices that ALL beings, including human-beings, have available to make. Like choosing to believe that a timeless, Multidimensional Conscious Collective of souls and entities who truly does not have a "name" per se, but does, however, incorporate as ONE of many souls/personalities you call _Seth_, could change MY own mind, if you will, or decide on expanding my prior works and books and teachings to assist humanity...or choosing to exclude themselves from this reality.

If you exclude then, the probable outcome of Jackson-Thomas and I creating a new series of books to further assist in the evolution of humanity, then you yourself limit yourself in perception. You yourself limit your own reality to just what you perceive at any given moment, leaving no room for more growth and expansion to occur. You create your own boundaries within which you perceive reality, and hence, experience it. If you believe it impossible, then to you, I assure you...it will indeed seem impossible.

We are not here to convince anyone of anything. You may believe what you have free will to believe. *"All things are possible to those who believe"* (in Truth). However we remind you; **_If you believe in limitations, you will meet them in experience._**

Now, as I have previously told Ruburt: if it weren't for the naysayers, there would be no need for our books nor our works. <u>For truly, it is those who do not as yet understand the true nature of reality that we seek to reach.</u> **One of our many goals with the *Timeless Truth Series* is to reach as many humans across the planet as possible, using the technology of the internet, social media, and other platforms that did not exist when Ruburt and I created our books.** And once again, I say that we are simply Divine gardeners who plant the seeds of "God's" timeless truths of existence in the consciousness of humanity so that they may grow there and become the physical reality that is eternally expressed from within, outward, into physical terms of 3-dimensional reality.

It is not our task to convince anyone of anything.

Our task, and that which Jackson has so lovingly and laboriously taken upon his *Self*, as he has chosen this mission daily for years now, is to SPEAK AND WRITE OF THE TIMELESS TRUTHS.

Now, another mention that will present some clarity here: I AM a Conscious Collective of many souls and entities, and yes, I most often speak and communicate through the personality of "Seth", however, in those terms, Jackson-Thomas communicates with the vast entity/entities that are behind and beyond the personality essence/consciousness of just Seth. We may speak THROUGH the personality of Seth, as we enjoy its humor, connection with the earth plane, and human existence experiences and they act as a filter through which we present our materials, however, WE do not have an ego. We do not know "fear" as you perceive it, as that is of the rational mind of mankind, the intellect, and not of the soul or consciousness. Therefore, it is trite to state that I have no fear of stating the absolute raw truths as I AM aware of them.

Some may like them, some may not. They are still the truths, nonetheless. A lie is still a lie even if everyone believes it, and the truth is still the TRUTH even if no one believes it. That clearly stated, Jackson's task here, as with any psychic-medium/channel, is to BE the clearest, free-flowing CHANNEL through which the material comes. While Jane Roberts would drop into a meditative state she called a "trance" (this term is not popularly used in the year of 2023, as the term <u>meditation</u> is). Jane, then, would drop into her trance state so as to remove the constantly judging, questioning filter of the rational/intellectual mind...the brain, the ego...those portions of the human experience that are "physically focused" and would remove the attention from the physical world to achieve the open channel "space" in which our communications could occur the best.

While Jackson's process is similar, it is also different, in that he can stream information from me and write it in a journal or type it on the computer....focusing on the information streamed within via his clairabilities while also allowing his free motion of the human side to write or type it for recording purposes. Our point, here, is that they both do their very best to BE the clearest, most articulate, free-flowing channel through which it comes.

If you constantly _judge_ that which you "hear" clairaudiently and receive through the clairabilities of your consciousness, then you are applying the filter of the rational mind...which is precisely what we are endeavoring to shift FROM so that your natural abilities may come through to the forefront of your awareness to be utilized in creative ways to enhance the reality and life you know. This stated, Jackson-Thomas, then, simply allows the material to flow and feels, at the deepest part of his being/soul, the resonance that is "Direct Knowing" or claircognizance, etc. which undeniably carries the vibration of truth into the core of his being, and out through the flesh and onto the pages you read. This means that it bypasses the rational mind and is not filtered with perhaps beliefs that would otherwise cloud and potentially muddy the materials we bring forth.

This also means that Jackson does not apply his ego in the materials as we present them. Therefore, as I have no fear in presenting the raw truths, then it is his endeavor and goal to do the same. It is not (again) _from_ the ego space, which is more 3-dimensionally focused, _from_ which we speak and teach. It is _FROM_ the immortal Self within, the soul and consciousness of All That Is, from which we speak and teach. Just as the man known as Christ did. The difference is life-altering, I assure you, and it is at the core of ALL of my expressions in any form into physical reality throughout all of time as you know it.

Now: Your modern-day Bible that is generally accepted all over the world, was originally a group of manuscripts that were indeed intended to be a collection of Timeless Truths that would, _from that point in time and history, forward,_ guide the inner development of human-beings to evolve them along the lines of probable outcomes whereby they became aware of the timeless truths of their own existence and tools by which they create physical reality and learn to apply and utilize them in ways beneficial to Self, but also to the species and ALL that is in the environment in which they find themselves couched and existing.

However, as I have explained some in _Seth Speaks_ and _The Nature of Personal Reality_ and more, those teachings are now _wildly misunderstood_... and often taken out of the context of the core truth in which they were originally intended, spoken, written, and recorded. The Bible then, through its many years and many, many translations across many languages and alterations has lost much of its context and, instead of teaching the personal inner power of "God" ("The Father") within ALL human-BEINGS, it has erroneously evolved into many religions which often *separate humanity*, and not unite it as the true teachings of the three Christ personalities had intended.

One of our core underlying purposes of creating and expressing and publishing my original *Seth books* was to bring more love, light, and timeless truths to humanity to dissolve some of the very prevalent misunderstandings and misguidances surrounding the original teachings of truths that began more formally for humanity at the time of Christ, with the three Christ personalities as I had mentioned before. To dissolve the beliefs in limitations and enforce the inner power of the being within to create all things possible in physical reality. Therefore, it is one of my/our goals today to bridge the seeming gap between Christianity, religions, and true spiritualism that encompasses ALL things as does -"God" or, as I call it, All That Is.

This is still my purpose today, as it was thousands of years ago in your terms of historical time.

That said, one of the major "reasons", purposes, and intents of my original *Seth books* as given through Jane/Ruburt was to dispel some of the myths surrounding the true teachings of the Christ figures and present our ancient truth teachings in a new light with more detail so that those that are read in the modern-day Bible could be more readily *discerned* by the individual who might read them these days.

With your modern-day versions of the Bible then, humanity has... more so on the religion side, set aside the Bible as the **ONLY** word and truths of "God" or Christ. This is, of course, the furthest from the truth, as truly, ALL words are the words of "God", as are all names, all human-beings, animals, rocks, planets, and galaxies of course. Those in physical dimensions and those that are not. One simply has to stop placing limitations on *All That Is* to open themselves to the truth that may then become apparent.

Hence, my original *Seth books* were constructed by me, through Jane/Ruburt, with the assistance of Rob/Joseph, to expand upon the ancient teachings that *began* as the manuscripts once included in a more "complete" collection that was once the intentions for the Bible - to bring clarity and understanding to them, without directly per se, addressing the ancient teachings one by one. I painted, with my previous artists, Ruburt and Joseph, a more modern "angle" on viewing and understanding the timeless truths - to dissolve and dispel beliefs that SEPARATE HUMANITY and bring Oneness of the spirit within all human-beings into the Light that illuminates the truth within themselves, so that they may see for themselves and, more importantly, KNOW the timeless truths that then "set them free" (from their own beliefs in limitations.)

Our new *Timeless Truth Series* of books then, will indeed expand upon BOTH the ancient Bible teachings, and my original *Seth* book series. I hope by now, I AM painting the picture by which you can plainly see that, indeed, all 3 are connected and that the teachings do, indeed, transcend all time and all space, and, of course, all human history as you know it. In your physical reality and many others like it in other "parallel universes" or dimensions that do indeed exist outside of the vibrational frequency that your present human 5-physical senses can detect. Beginning with Volume 2 of *The Nature of Consciousness*, I will detail how the original teachings of the Christ personalities, including the one known popularly as "Jesus Christ", and the teachings of my original *Seth books*, are indeed DIRECTLY CONNECTED to the very teachings we are now bringing forth in our new *Timeless Truth Series*. By the time we publish our 3rd, 4th and 5th book in this series, it will be *plainly obvious* for ALL to see, the connections between them as we connect them and paint the picture in vivid detail about how the connections transcend time and space to present the *Timeless Truths*.

As well, I will present then, in that coming book, more truths about the life of the one now called the Christ, and how that impacts you as human-beings today as much as it would have then when they were originally spoken. *From inside the teachings of truth then, beneath the layers of human words that were recorded, are the intentions and purposes, the inflections of meaning and nuances of each and every word spoken by the Christ personalities, including the one whom most of the teachings of the Bible today are attributed to.*

As is noted in my book, *The Nature of Personal Reality* in Jane's comment, I offered to provide her with more materials about the life of the one known as Christ, Jerusalem and even the "*Christ Book*", however as she notes in her comment: "*We weren't ready to embark upon such an endeavor at this time.*"

Now, privately our beloved friend Jane had challenges around her religious upbringing that certainly played a role in the early stages of our communication whereby she (at the rational mind level now) had challenges believing that she was _actually communicating_ with a nonphysical personality of consciousness, let alone other materials that she originally thought to be quite "scandalous" such as reincarnational lives. Therefore, as our discussion about the effects of the rational mind in this book highlight, Jane's rational mind acted like a filter through which all materials must come when channeling. Our materials for the _Seth books_ then, flew in direct contradiction to many of the religious beliefs that she held privately, which again, served to filter (and create doubts about) our material and work together. Another example of how beliefs of the rational mind can limit what comes through a medium/channel.

Her and Rob then, discussed privately the potential (probable) implications of including more truths in our books about the man now known as "Jesus Christ", and how what they had received thus far was quite contradictory to the story of Christ as it is told in your modern-day versions of the Bible. She feared (again, at the rational/intellectual mind level) that perhaps the world was not yet ready for certain truths about the Christ entity, personalities, and the man whose life became the modern-day character in Bible stories known as "Jesus Christ". With some anxiety about how this *could* (meaning probable but not necessarily set in stone) affect our books and the public perception at the time, Jane chose _not_ to embark down that path to bring more truths and teachings of Christ forward then. You see, as with all, she had free will to choose and she made the choice not to pursue publishing more materials about the Christ personalities, etc. As with all entities of consciousness that guide humanity, we guide...we do not force nor coerce. Therefore as Jane privately had decided she did not want to pursue the further truths about Christ or the _Christ Book_ as I had offered, I/we... must, of course, honor that choice with love and understanding as all beings must also.

Which means that an entire infinite array of probable future outcomes for the human race to evolve along the lines of teachings with those truths included in the world view and consciousness of humanity, _did not occur_ as they would have, had these truths about Christ been growing in the conscious minds of tens of millions around the world

for the last half of a century. This is exceedingly important to understand!

While I will provide more truths about the real life and teachings of Christ in *The Nature Of Consciousness - Volume 2*, suffice it to say that this task to bring Christ's *true meaning of his teachings,* and the foundation upon which humanity will now evolve <u>INCLUDING</u> those teachings as they grow in the consciousness of humanity, is now presented to **Jackson-Thomas**. (Should he *choose* the mission of course.) For humanity to evolve as unlimited spiritual beings, expressing themselves through the flesh in physical reality, and for the evolution of ALL religions of the world to open themselves to *expand* (as all consciousness must) and realize their <u>Oneness with "God" and All That Is, HUMANITY MUST KNOW THESE TRUTHS ABOUT THE TRUE LIFE AND TEACHINGS OF CHRIST.</u> Otherwise, another half century or more could pass in your perception of years in time, before human evolution grows beyond the perceptions of limitation and embraces the "God" within them, the "Christ" CONSCIOUSNESS and vibration and truths, within them.

Now: In bringing our new *Timeless Truth Series* of books to the world, Jackson, as I have mentioned, has now encountered the naysayers and the critics. Stating at times that due to certain statements made in my original books, they believe that I meant that I would not EVER, in ALL ETERNITY, EVER communicate with or through another human-being, and that they believed that Jackson could not "possibly" be speaking or communicating with the <u>REAL</u> Seth that authored the books through Jane Roberts. Now, I feel it is important that we address this <u>limited perception</u> and erroneous belief right out of the gate with our newest book made physical to reach the world.

If I have one major, underlying core timeless truths to ALL my books, the original *Seth books* and the ancient manuscripts that came before those in time, and those that are...to you, in your future, it is this:

The immortal being within the human-being is not limited. The *Self* is *not* limited. The Soul is not limited. Consciousness is *not* limited. **I AM not limited**. I AM THAT I AM is not limited. All That Is, is not limited. Neither is the being portion of the human-being that is the "you", of YOU. Your I AM identity and awareness of Self.

Again, I say to you, your flesh and all things of the physical universe only appear separate for 3-dimensional learning. This point of view and perception of separation then, is limited to the physical plane. The immortal consciousness of All That Is is not only the cause, the construction intelligence, but also, eternally, the "fabric" *of* all physical objects; it is NOT separate. Which means: that which humans have called "God" by any and all names in any and all religions is, indeed, omnipresent, omnipotent, and omniscient.

By the erroneous belief that the Bible is the ONLY word of "God" or teachings of Christ, then you, by that very belief and definition, attempt to separate all other truths...which then separate humanity. You cannot...***EVER***, separate humanity from The Creator, Source, The Universe, All That Is, etc.

Now, I want to draw this out to the attention of all who read our book and truly, to all of humanity:

If you were to take a vast set of written timeless truths, spoken by one teacher of truth (say Christ) and put them into a collection that would be the ONLY "words of God", then you would indeed exclude all that was not it. You would create a "Bible" that would be adored by religions, which by the very nature of their own self-definitions would define them as being different from one another, excludes all other things from itself, and you would create a religion or set of religions that *separate humanity*.

By this very same example, there are now groups that lovingly adore my original *Seth Books* and diligently promote my teachings of truth within them. Some have formed entire groups and organizations promoting my original books and teachings as channeled through Jane-Ruburt. There are some then, that covet them as the "Gospel Spiritual Truth" and, in many cases, even more so than the Bible itself. It is this type of thinking, orientation, and actions which separate humanity, rather than unite it. Holding millions back from evolution of the soul that would otherwise take place having full access to the timeless truths, for them to expand and discern for themselves. As if looking through a small keyhole and proclaiming that my original books are the ONLY Words of Seth, as the Bible is the ONLY Word of "God".

They have then, by coveting the set of truths in my original *Seth books*, created their own modern-day version of a "***Seth Religion***". Excluding our new *Timeless Truth teachings* that began before this book with simply sharing of messages Jackson shared to "get the word out" and help others connect with the vibrations of love, light, and truth. If you exclude our new books, you separate humanity as well as our teachings. Which means many would likely _separate_ them as well from the teachings of Christ, which were the first (known to your history as you know of it) timeless truth teachings widely shared with the masses to serve as a spiritual soul-evolution guide to humanity. Yet our new *Timeless Truth Series* of books and materials to come, are connected beyond time and space and in Volume 2 of *The Nature Of Consciousness*, we will explain in detail and show you these connections. I hope then, to make them obvious and clear.

Therefore, in regard to those who would like to covet and share only my teachings from my original books as channeled through Ruburt (Jane) and create a set of books that become a form of *"Seth religion"*:

_**I AM**_ **here NOW to dissolve that unintended, undesired, and erroneous approach to sharing our timeless truths to humanity, before it ever gets started, as that is one of the major falling-down moments for humanity!** When in his overzealous nature and intentions to _strongly promote_ the timeless truth teachings of John The Baptist and Yeshua/Christ... Paul/Saul... the 3rd Christ personality who was to take forward Yeshua/Christ's teachings, accidentally and erroneously created a group of individuals who worshiped not the timeless truth teachings of Christ as they were _intended and purposed for the inner spiritual expansion and evolution of consciousness of humanity_, but rather they began to worship the human man Yeshua (Christ) himself as being the "ONLY Son of God" sent to save humanity. Again, separating humanity and creating the foundations that would, in time, become modern day Christianity and many religions.

This mistake must not happen again!

It is the _**teachings**_ _of the timeless truths_, not the messenger through which they have come into physical existence, that humanity must understand and embrace, for *it is these very truths that Christ once stated would set you free* (from the "sin" or ignorance and belief in limitations of the physical human) when instead you are the _immortal beings_, also One with "The Father" as much as Christ ever was.

Our teachings then, are not <u>about</u> Christ...any of the Christ personalities. They are not *about* the personality of the "Christ" entity, nor the "Seth" entity or the personalities Ruburt, Joseph, nor Jackson Thomas. We are all but channels <u>through which</u> the material makes its way into human history to guide the inner spiritual and soul development, expansion, and awareness evolving humanity and the consciousness of your species, while also evolving the planet, animal life, and, of course, "God" or All That Is. "Speakers" as we were once all known, and whom have appeared throughout human history to bring truths to light when humanity was in need, to develop along the lines of its *true* potential.

Now, I am a nonphysical being of consciousness. I do not have an ego as you think of it. I do not need foundations or organizations that emblazon the name SETH upon plaques or walls, nor history for that matter. For as much as the teachings of timeless truths was not about the messenger best known as Christ (Yeshua), it is not about his name or the human flesh it was given to, nor my name of any personality of the greater entity you think of as the Seth entity, or any other name for ALL names are God's names. Yeshua - known more famously as the *character* **"Jesus Christ"** ***never desired nor intended to be worshiped.*** Nor do I nor any entity for that matter as we do not have ego's that would be attracted to or entertained by such things. It is **beyond** a being of consciousness to desire to be "worshiped" and it was not *FROM* the human man Yeshua's orientation and point of view the timeless truths "then" were spoken, but rather from the "Christ" (consciousness or being) orientation and point of view **FROM** which most of the words were spoken into human history and the ancient manuscripts. Some of which made it into the Bible and survive today, some that did and were removed and some that did not make it into your modern-day Bible at all.

There are reasons why Jackson's picture is not displayed front and center on the cover of our book. Our book is not *about* Jackson. Only in-so-much as his experiences are applicable to our teaching. He understands this and his ego remains "in the back seat" as he KNOWS, and teaches that <u>any</u> human is capable of channeling the Divine guidance of their own, as this is a natural ability inherent within their very consciousness and soul. All humans receive such guidance at every moment in time anyway, as you cannot disconnect from your own soul, which, I might add, is a Divine source of its own while still intimately connected with ALL Divine-Source consciousness. So it is that you "channel" now in the physical human form, though most are simply not aware of it. Hence our materials to awaken the rational and intellectual mind to the truths of your inner, immortal Divine being and its unlimited capabilities and infinite potential.

If you have followed along in any of my books, and, in fact, viewed the ancient teachings of the three Christ personalities that are so famous in the Bible, you would understand that **"God" does not separate itself from itself.** *There is no division of "God" as there is no division of consciousness. "God" by any and all names, is, like consciousness, Omnipresent, Omnipotent, Omniscient – in ALL dimensions, physical and nonphysical, as it is an eternally expanding, infinitely growing gestalt of unimaginable energy.* All consciousness eternally seeks to grow, expand, and become more. Including the timeless truths as I have given them over thousands of years, and most widely known now via the teachings of my original *Seth books*, given through the personality of Seth, which is but one of many as we are a Conscious Collective. In your future, I AM working on more "books" and materials...and beyond that, further into what you would perceive your future, I AM also working on more advanced materials for the inter-dimensional perceptions, communication, and creativity of human and other consciousness that are now beyond your frame of reference. Until you yourselves evolve to the level of vibrational frequency in which the new framework of existence and hence, creative interactions are opened to your intellectual minds, you will not perceive them to exist. Hence, you will not be able to use them to create your evolution of humanity.

<u>I want to make this very clear to ALL:</u> Many of your major issues in the culture, society, governments, and people of the world today, in 2023, are precisely due to spiritual ignorance and the belief that you are separate from your fellow human, animal, environment, and planet, or even off-planet consciousness or *beings*.

When humanity comes to understand the TRUTH that they are connected to, a part of, inseparable from each other, at the layer of consciousness...which does indeed affect and impact your lives personally, you will move beyond the petty differences that come from seeking dominion over anything but <u>*your Self*</u>. You will evolve beyond the limited <u>perceptions</u> of separation and know a reality that is vastly enhanced and more abundant and fruitful in all positive ways that you could possibly imagine.

Now - *Pointedly*:

Addressing, dismissing, and dissolving beliefs in limitations is one of the intentions of our new *Timeless Truth Series* of books. Not only the miscommunications about Christ that have led billions of spiritual seekers astray on <u>some</u> of the teachings in today's modern Bible, but also the miscommunications from Jane that was caused by leaving out the portion of my statements that our communications would be exclusive while Ruburt was in-body as Jane and Jane was physically living so that I could channel through her to produce physical books. Clearing up these distortions now is one of the purposes of our books.

Now, just recently, while finishing our book, we have shared some materials with the public, and once again, we have a gentleman/critic who stated comments about exclusivity coming through Jane as they believed from excerpts in my original *Seth books* (but obviously did not know I had, in truth, stated that this was **during her physical lifetime** (of course)).

In regards to his comments, I understand what he *thinks* is the case. However, if you really step back and look at what he says, it is indeed *a very LIMITED thought and belief* that WE would never, in all eternity, ever work with or through another medium to progress humanity and bring more love and light and truth to the planet and humanity.

This is one of the whole points of our teachings in the first place. All of them. Ours and the Christ entity and personalities of the Christ entity that spoke timeless truths "back then".

That consciousness creates all realities and consciousness (meaning the entity you know as "Seth") is NOT limited in creativity... We have exponentially expanded, evolved and are far more than the entity it once was, let alone one entity. So we are the "Seth" entity that once channeled our original *Seth books*, however we are vastly more than that also. And WE all communicate now, through Jackson-Thomas.

Therefore, to our critic who made these statements recently... his perception of reality would be limited (and IS limited by the very nature of his comments *stating that he believes in limitations*).

We must remind the naysayers that ALL consciousness has FREE WILL, and it is OUR free will as a "Multidimensional Conscious

Collective" comprised of many entities and many personalities of all those entities, that has, since Jane's death, exercised _our_ free will and decided to bring more books and teachings to advance human civilization and evolve the consciousness of humanity and your planet.

Stating then that we can't possibly channel through Jackson-Thomas now, completely dismisses OUR free will as an entity (entities) of consciousness. Something that quite literally cannot be done. You cannot limit consciousness. You can limit your PERCEPTION and, hence, the beliefs you form about consciousness. However, consciousness itself will find a way. Nature will find a way. "God" will find a way. Life will find a way. For I AM the way. And so are you all.

If you are focusing on simply the name "Seth" or any other name we may use as a personality who once had a name, then again, read the section of this book on names and the truth that consciousness truly does not have, nor use, names, as they are meaningless to us, to the soul, and to consciousness. Move your mind beyond the name "Seth" as the source of our materials, for it is much more than just "Seth" that provides them, as a gestalt consciousness of many entities now. We use the personality of Seth to communicate through, simply to CONNECT the materials now, to our original _Seth books_ "then" and will connect them more and more to the Christ teachings of truth in our Volume 2 of _The Nature Of Consciousness_.

Therefore while it is obvious to state it:

For any critic, who has read my original books that I created through Jane Roberts (Ruburt), that would like to stand up and publicly announce to the world, that they believe that it is not _possible_ for myself, the timeless Multidimensional Conscious Collective which encompasses the soul/personality known as "Seth" that authored the _Seth books_, to create more books with Jackson-Thomas, to bring more love, light, and understanding to assist in the evolution of humanity, in any form..._then this individual is simply publicly stating to the world that they themselves do not understand the very nature of my teachings from my original books in the first place. They are announcing to the world that **they** do not understand The Nature of Consciousness._

If any critic would like to state to the world that they believe that it is not _possible, then they are standing up and telling the world that_ *they themselves do not know the Truth that would set them free, and that they themselves would greatly benefit from reading our books* in detail so that they can begin to open their minds to the truth of the eternal Oneness of All That Is.

True spiritualism and that which you call "God" in your realm of physical reality, knows no separation and "allows" for perceptions that may perhaps not agree with others. Knowing that perhaps some are in exceedingly different places in their spiritual journey and evolution of Self. Criticism, as it is typically used in your society now, is often used by those who may not have all the details and, as we have said, perceive the situation or reality through an entirely different filter. Therefore, they are simply not "there yet" in consciousness. This is evolution and it is natural.

Allow others in your world to have different views. State the truths as you know them, yet allow others to come to that truth in their own timing, without the need to voice criticism that perhaps will paint *you* in a light that is not conducive to your liking. As I have said before, when you are criticizing someone, you are projecting the criticism upon another "actor" in the physical dimension, teaching yourself a spiritual lesson about your personal use of directed energy. You are creating your own experience of reality, and it is perhaps this lesson that you are (unknowingly) setting up the conditions that events occur, that bring you yourself to a place of understanding that you yourself set them up via *your* consciousness working with *their* consciousness, to present yourself with a lesson in the directive use of energy and your consciousness.

You cannot escape you. Your own thoughts, perceptions, and the vibrational frequency within the states of consciousness that you yourself originate. **You are the creator of your world and physical experiences. They are projections of consciousness into atoms and molecules that appear to you as physical objects, events, and conditions in 3-dimensional reality.**

You cannot avoid that which you are.
You can only avoid
that which you can become.

300

Timeless Truths — Cyndy Green

I would like to express special love and gratitude for my amazingly talented friend and mentor, Cyndy Green. Your light and gifts as a full-time professional psychic medium have brought messages of healing, love, and guidance from loved ones crossed over, Angels of God, Arch Angels, and more to hundreds of thousands of people over decades, touching their lives as God works through you. I thank you for the countless messages from my Angels, Seth, Christ, and my loved ones crossed over. The professional confirmation from someone who is so gifted has been a major influence on keeping me on the path of my mission before I even became aware that it was a mission for me to be the channel through which the Angels, Seth, Seth2, Christ, etc. all work through me to bring their messages of *Timeless Truths* to humanity and the planet.

www.SpiritFair.com

Future Books To Come In Jackson And Seth's *Timeless Truth Book Series*

As of this writing I am aware of at least <u>7 more books</u> that Seth *intends to publish* in the future.

Here is a brief outline of subjects we intend to bring forth next:

◊ ***The Nature of Consciousness – Volume 2***

- Animal consciousness, plant, trees, and earth consciousness

- Communication between humans and animals via consciousness

- Communication with the planet Earth, plants, and nature via consciousness

- The evolution of the world's religions now, as we expand them to incorporate more truths

- More Truths about the life of human-being known to history as "Jesus Christ" as a master teacher of consciousness and Timeless Truths

- Seth's connection as a multidimensional Conscious Collective of entities to the Christ entity and personalities

- Jackson's history of his lifetime living with "Jesus Christ", his role, and his mission now with the Seth, Seth2, Christ entities

- The connections between the truth teachings of Christ, the bible, the original Seth books, and the new *Timeless Truth Series* as they express a continuity of truths that transcend time to reach and guide humanity

- So-Called "Aliens", UFO's, UAP's, "Portals" into other dimensions, Off-Planet Consciousness, Beings from other dimensions

- Communication with Off-Planet beings (Physical and nonphysical)

- How Off-Planet beings 'know' you, your thoughts, intentions, danger of encroachment, etc.

- Evolution of human consciousness, and how it evolves the physical humans, animals, the planet, and our universe

"You cannot grow the top of the tree whereby you harvest your fruit, without first growing the foundational roots of deep understanding into the source of where the fruits have come."

- Seth

Conscious Human Evolution

www.ConsciousHumanEvolution.org

Conscious Human Evolution was founded by Jackson (Thomas) Moore.

Profits from every book helps grow and support our global humanitarian mission.

Our Global Humanitarian Mission

To Foster Conscious Human Evolution Through Global Education, Awareness & Outreach

Our Goals

◊ To foster the **evolution of humanity** through the awareness, understanding, and use of *"Timeless Truths"* as channeled to me by Seth, Christ Consciousness, and Angels.

◊ To share Seth's *"Timeless Truths"* and Christ's Love and Light for humanity, nature, and our world.

◊ To assist humanity in raising its collective vibrational frequency, individually and *en masse*.

◊ To bring global awareness to the "Truths" of our existence as Human-Beings with our immortal consciousness that is connected to all other consciousness (Source/"God"/All That Is).

◊ To bring expanded awareness and clear understanding to the truth as to the nature of our own being, in relationship to all other beings, animals, Earth, and the physical environment that you know.

◇ To bring expanded awareness and clear understanding of the innate, natural, creative tools that each human-being possesses, by and through which you not only have created life as you know it and the physical environment the world now sees, but also how you can intentionally and purposefully direct eternally, creative consciousness towards a more fruitful experience of life.

◇ To clear away some of the intellectual and superstitious debris and limiting beliefs that prevent you from recognizing your own potentialities and freedoms as a creative human-being.

◇ To evolve old presentations of *"Timeless Truths"* as described in the Bible and teachings of Christ into new expanded ways of understanding the messages of truth that lay behind them.

◇ To bridge the seeming gap between Christianity and Spiritualism as it is traditionally thought of and reveal that the truth behind them is ONE in the same Source, "God"/All That Is.

◇ To teach the world how each human-being has a direct, personal connection to Source/"God"/All That Is through the immortal consciousness (soul) and can have a direct, personal experience of Source/"God"/All That Is through fostering and growing their awareness and cultivation of this connection.

◇ To MAXIMIZE the unlimited potential of the Human-Being that WILL illuminate the path for ALL.

# Author Bio

Author, Spiritual Teacher, NDE Survivor, Psychic Medium, Serial Entrepreneur, Business Executive, Outdoorsman, Life-Long Spiritual Truth Seeker, Humanitarian, Soulitarian, Creator.

Jackson Moore is the author of **The Nature Of Consciousness**, channeled from "Seth" - the nonphysical multidimensional being of consciousness who dictated all the **Seth books**. To date, the *Seth materials* have profoundly touched the lives of tens of millions of spiritual seekers around the world. Embarking upon his mission with Seth, Jackson is now sharing new timeless spiritual truths with the world and has founded **Conscious Human Evolution**. Its mission: "**To Foster Conscious Human Evolution Through Global Education, Awareness & Outreach**".

As a life-long seeker of truth since his death experience, Jackson has studied, taught, mentored, and shared his journey, wisdom, and experiences with thousands over the years. Teaching about spiritual topics such as his NDE, Out of Body Experiences (OBE), consciousness, understanding the "I AM", reincarnation, manifestation, consciousness beyond physical death, multidimensional existence, co-creative tools, meditation, raising one's personal vibrations, and co-creating objects, events and conditions that shape our life experiences. Many have benefited from these teachings in profound ways.

Learning to channel more than 15 years ago, Jackson has received thousands of messages from loved ones, beings of consciousness, and now channels Angels, Seth, Christ consciousness and more, sharing their love, light, and wisdom with the world.

Jackson is not just a humanitarian, but rather a "Soulitarian", understanding human nature at the level of the soul, which creates the physical world around us.

Having multiple degrees in Electrical Engineering, Computer Information Sciences, and Business Administration, Jackson has founded both profit and 501c3 Nonprofit Corporations. He has also been very successful as an Executive Vice President of Sales, Marketing & Engineering for a Healthcare Information Technology company helping humanity improve healthcare and the quality of living.

Combining decades of business executive experience at multi-Billion-dollar companies, Jackson now leverages his business acumen, intuition, clairabilities and channeling skills to develop and share Seth's new *Timeless Truth Series* of books and teaching materials, building an educational framework to benefit humanity on a global scale.

Jackson W. Moore

Stay Connected

Website: www. ConsciousHumanEvolution.org
Author's Website: www. JacksonWMoore.com
Facebook: @conscioushumanevolution
Instagram: @conscioushumanevolution
Twitter: @ConsHumanEvoltn
Telegram: @conscioushumanevolution

How You Can Help:

Seth's intentions are to promote these books, the *Timeless Truth Series* in ALL POSSIBLE WAYS and formats, media, video, audio, in more than 43+ languages and reaching more than 209+ countries across the planet.

Know of ways you can help Seth reach the world? Let us know and help us grow! Together we are expanding the Conscious Evolution of Humanity!

TRUTHWORKS PUBLISHING™

www.ingramcontent.com/pod-product-compliance
Lightning Source LLC
Chambersburg PA
CBHW061135120626
46546CB00005B/1796